FIRE IN THE SKY

FIRE IN THE SKY

Flying in Defence of Israel

Brigadier General Amos Amir

Translated by
Ruvik Danieli

Pen & Sword
AVIATION

First published in Great Britain in 2005 by
Pen & Sword Aviation
an imprint of
Pen & Sword Books Ltd
47 Church Street
Barnsley
South Yorkshire
S70 2AS

Copyright © Amos Amir, 2005

Translated from Hebrew by Ruvik Danieli

ISBN 1 84415 156 5

First published in Hebrew © 2000, Ministry of Defence, Israel

Typeset in Palatino by
Phoenix Typesetting, Auldgirth, Dumfriesshire

Printed and bound in England by
CPI UK

Pen & Sword Books Ltd incorporates the imprints of Pen & Sword Aviation,
Pen & Sword Maritime, Pen & Sword Military, Wharncliffe Local History, Pen
& Sword Select, Pen & Sword Military Classics and Leo Cooper.

For a complete list of Pen & Sword titles please contact
PEN & SWORD BOOKS LIMITED
47 Church Street, Barnsley, South Yorkshire, S70 2AS, England
E-mail: enquiries@pen-and-sword.co.uk
Website: www.pen-and-sword.co.uk

Ezer Weizman

On the author and the book:
"Fire in the Sky"

Gen. (Ret.) Amos Amir's autobiographic roman tells the story of the man, the warrior and the commander as well as it tells the story of the struggling, newly-born, Israeli Airforce.

The IAF was born with the new, independent State of Israel, and has come to its maturity only years later when it proved its ability not only to support the fighting forces but to play a decisive, leading role in the young nation's wars. From the Six-Days-War, 1967, and onward, the IAF turned to be an extremely important component of the overall Israeli defence power. These years, from the Sinai War, 1956, through the Six-Days-War, and until the Yom Kippur War, 1973, and the Lebanon War, 1982, were the years of Amir's flying, fighting and commanding career.

Indeed, it was while reading this book that I so clearly realised how intense were the lives, and how determined and active were Amir and his fellow fighter-flyers in those magnificant days.

Amir tells his own, individual story in a talented, vivid and fluent language. He succeeds in pulling the reader, every reader, to his narrow cockpit from the early stages of his flying school to later air combats and reconnaissance missions, and on telling of his dramatic experiences as a senior commanding officer in the field and in the main nerves-system of the IAF.

No less interesting than those flying stories are his youth stories, pleasantly woven into the book, telling about the growth of an Israeli child in those early dramatic days of our country. Especially lovely I have found that episode when the young 12-years-old kid met Prime Minister Ben Gurion face-to-face in the kater's private home, realising the greatness of the moment.

I have found 'Fire in the Sky' one of the best books to be written on aviation, and I wholeheartedly recommend this book to all readers, women and men, old and young, civilians, military and ex-military individuals and, of course, to all aviators.

Ezer Weizman

Contents

Preface

The ten viewfinder diamonds sank lower and lower from the intensity of the centrifugal force as I rapidly turned and dived at a speed of 480 knots (889 kph). At a slowing and controlled rate, the 'peeper', that murderous point of light in the centre of the viewfinder diamonds, zeroed in on the MiG's cockpit canopy.

My mouth was dry and my breath turned raspy. The voices of the outside world pouring from the earphones seemed to fade in the background. I stabilised the turn, an immense force of 6 Gs pinning my body to the pilot's seat and draining the blood from my brain to my feet. My view of the MiG in the sights became a bit hazy, but I didn't lose it. There were only 250 metres (274 yards) between us. Ten years of practice were paying off now. The peeper's motion came into alignment with the motion of the MiG's canopy. With the back of my right finger I uncovered the cannon trigger, black and cold to the touch, and squeezed it. A long round of shells shot out from the Mirage's two cannon. The results were immediate and spectacular. A ferocious fireball burst out from the centre of the MiG and engulfed it completely. I banked the aircraft slightly to the right, outside the circle of the turn. But with my eyes I continued to follow the plane as it fell downwards and to the left, towards the brown-green-grey chequered squares of the Nile delta district.

My mouth parched and dry, and panting erratically, I felt my brain and body return all at once to the site of battle, as the first flush of victory surged through my nerves and bones.

CHAPTER ONE

Tel Aviv Skies, 1943

I was riding atop my father Aryeh's shoulders, and both of us were gazing west out to sea from the promenade beside Tel Aviv's shore. I was a child of eight, of rotund though not corpulent build, with golden curls and blue-green eyes. I was well-tempered and quick on the uptake, making friends easily wherever I went. Furthermore, I was my parents' pride and joy.

It was during the Second World War: at the time of the clashes between the Allies and the Germans in the North African desert, and the Italian air strikes on Tel Aviv. Air-raid sirens would occasionally shatter the stillness during the nights.The lights of the city and the houses were darkened. Car headlights were painted black, leaving only a narrow strip of illumination for the purpose of orientation and identification. The civilian guard supervisors paced down the city streets, blowing their insistent whistles and shouting loudly, 'Turn off the light! Up there on the second floor, turn off the light!', to the delight of all the neighbourhood children.

I have fond memories of the nights during that period. When my parents grew tired of trudging back and forth to the narrow and cluttered basement that served as our shelter, the whole family set up camp together in the hall, underneath the massive dining table that stood in the middle of the room. There, between Mother and Father, curled up in a thick blanket, I felt as secure as I could possibly be.

Every week, early on Saturday evening, Father would sit down at the big black desk in his room, in shorts and a vest to analyse the war's progress. He would spread out large maps of

Europe and North Africa, marking the movements of the various forces with big arrows.

'This is as far as Marshal Zhukov's forces have got. And this is the line that General Teherniakovski has retreated to. This is where we can expect the stupendous clash to take place between Rommel's German armour and British Field Marshal Montgomery's divisions. And here, in Brittany, is where the Second Front will open, most likely', he would mutter, partly to himself and partly perhaps to me, with immense gravity, as if the outcome of the battles depended on him.

I would usually climb atop a stool to see my father's maps and hear his explanations, which were like the word of God to me. Nachum Gutman, the eminent painter and a family friend of ours, was a frequent visitor to the house. I loved Nachum dearly: he was an ingenuous, warm and wonderful man, who was like an uncle and a grown-up companion to me. With a beret perpetually perched upon his head, Nachum would lay down his paintbrush in his house next door to ours, come inside and sit down beside my father, and try – usually in frustration – to make some sense of the strategic situation in the world.

'Aryeh, Aryeh. Tell me, what is going to be?' he would ask, like someone lost in the wilderness.

'Amos, in these matters I trust your father implicitly,' he would turn and confide in little me, when he grew tired of Father's explanations.

From the radio came the voice of Efraim Goldstein (who would one day change his name to Di-Zahav) singing the *Mavdil*, the Hebrew prayer which marks the end of the Sabbath, and concluding with a warbling rendition of *Shavua Tov* ('Good Week'). After Nachum had gone home, during dinner we would listen to Voice of Jerusalem radio, to the political review of commentator Moshe Medzini, of whom my father was always bitingly critical, but to whom he never stopped listening. My mother Anda and I were his dutiful, and certainly sympathetic, audience.

My father and I had a custom of going to visit Grandmother Matilda every Friday afternoon. We would troop down Rashi Street and pass by the Orion theatre. From there, opposite the bustling Atara café, we would continue down Allenby Street from the corner of Geula Street to the promenade beside the beach.

On our way we would sometimes stop in Mugrabi Square, at the foot of the clock, and Father, feeling gracious, would buy me a hot dog with mustard from the burly gentleman who was always there. He stood upright behind the shiny copper tub, drawing out a bun from the bin on the right, picking out a hot dog with the copper tongs from the bin in the middle, and spreading golden mustard from the bin on the left on top of it. The burly gentleman spoke feeble Hebrew with a pronounced German accent. He always wore a long white cloak and a white cook's hat. It was said by those in the know around town that the gentleman had been a great opera singer in Austria, before immigrating to Israel and occupying his central position in Mugrabi Square. Often in my bed at night, before falling asleep, I would try to imagine the 'hot dog gentleman' singing on the opera stage. Time and again, the image always made me laugh.

In the reddening western sky the sound of aircraft engines was suddenly heard. Two clumps of dark spots were seen in the sky, flying from south to north along the shoreline. My eyes were glued to the spots, which slowly approached the promenade and resolved themselves into two formations of six aircraft each, fighter planes following in each other's tracks, each sextet perfectly arranged in phased order to the right and backwards.

'Hurricanes,' hissed my father Aryeh, who was, as far as I was concerned, the leading authority in matters military, and a corporal (no less!) in His British Majesty's Army here at home. We both followed the aircraft, which were advancing northwards. Suddenly – just as I had once seen in the Carmel newsreels in the movie theatre – the leading aircraft raised its nose, picked up a little altitude, and began turning and diving to the left and downwards, in the direction of the setting sun. One after another, each at the same speed, the other aircraft followed the leader: first one sextet, and then the other immediately afterwards. To me, at that time and in that place, those twelve aircraft, disappearing to the south between the red sky and blue sea, were a rare and magical sight. I tried to think about the small men inside those big machines, their enormous engines thundering so loudly, but in my mind I was unable to make the connection between such puny people and such huge machines.

This marvellous spectacle remained engraved in my memory for years.

CHAPTER TWO

Fire – Cairo-West Skies, 5 June 1967

A t 4 am the telephone rang in our home in the pilots' neighbourhood. I picked up the receiver even before the first ring had died.

'Flight briefing at five o'clock,' said the voice on the other end of the line.

'Affirmative, roger,' I confirmed the notification in a clear voice, as if it were taken for granted. There was no need for additional explanations. The order had been given, and the nerve-racking wait was finally over. We were going to attack Egypt in order to remove the suffocating noose it had placed around our country's neck. There were no doubts or vacillations. Everything was crystal-clear.

For the past three weeks we in the Mirage squadron had been 'scraping the rust,' so to speak. The pilots had been assiduously reviewing their targets; practising the prospective attack formations time after time in training flights; and going over the possible scenarios and responses, mishaps and emergency routines, procedures for rescue and being captured by the enemy; and every other vital detail – going over them almost *ad nauseam*.

Before leaving the house, I caught sight of the date in the calendar: 5 June 1967. I bent over and kissed Rachel, who drowsily bid me, 'Good luck!', in an understanding and courageous manner. I passed my fingertips over the cheeks of our two boys, and stepped out into the chill of the night.

Yes, I could feel the fear: a compressed, hidden, camouflaged fear, stuck somewhere between my gut and my entrails; fear at the threat of the unknown; fear of setting out and not coming back.

We take our places in the briefing room, the senior squadron leaders – myself among them – in front, and the rest of the pilots behind us. Lapidot, the squadron commander, conducts the briefing in a confident tone of voice. On the blackboard, written clearly in white chalk, are the formation rosters, targets, time-tables and codes, with the title in prominent letters above them: Operation *Moked* (Focus). This is war.

'5 June 1967, one day before the great defeat of Egypt and its satellites. My hand is trembling! Let someone else write!' wrote Lieutenant Yair Neuman, who was sitting in one of the back rows of the room during the briefing for Operation *Moked*, the objective of which was to destroy the Egyptian air force in its own airfields. The next day, 6 June, Yair Neuman would be killed during a sortie over Egypt. The handwritten note, which was meant to be the beginning of a war diary, was found in his clothes after he fell.

With a single, swift motion I shut the canopy of my Mirage's cockpit, glancing at the mechanic, who clambered down and took the ladder aside. Twirling my finger, I signalled my intention to start the engine. The mechanic gave me the thumbs-up, and I pressed the ignition switch. A loud outrush of compressed air was heard, and the powerful jet engine immediately began to turn. At just the right moment came the dull sound of the internal combustion catching fire. The shrill of the jet rapidly grew louder as the engine went into action independently. The ground crew armourer swiftly slipped under the plane's belly, drew out the security pins from the bombs and cannon, and held them up at a distance for me to see and confirm.

With a last glance at the mechanic standing at the exit, his arm raised to indicate that I had the green light for departure, I began rolling up the rampway out of the hangar. Once again I locked eyes momentarily with the mechanic, who deviated from his routine, impassive procedure and gave me a special 'Good luck!' sign, both his arms upraised with fists clenched.

In the unusual silence over the headphones – not a word was spoken and there was none of the electronic noise of communications equipment and radar – the aircraft, which were heavier than usual because of their full fuel tanks and the complement of arms on their wings, were taxiing along all the approaches to the runway. I slipped into my assigned parking spot and saw my numbers two, three and four fall into place next to me. Although we hadn't been practising in specific designated formations, I was personally very well acquainted with Maoz, Yitzhak and Yochai and had utter confidence in them.

My initial feelings of fear and concern in the face of the unknown gave way to an absolute concentration on the flawless performance which would be required of me. There was room no more for feelings, only for astute or practised action, dedicated in its entirety to the accomplishment of the mission.

I gazed at the formations of aircraft whose take-off times came before mine. One after another they opened up their engines and began their take-off runs. From each engine in turn came the thud of the afterburner kicking in, and an orange flame burst from the gigantic exhaust pipe for the wink of an eye and disappeared. One after another their images grew hazy in the distance, and – quite out of the ordinary – they were not seen to climb after gathering speed but, staying at a low altitude, vanished on their way westward out to sea.

A glance at the clock showed that it was three minutes to take-off: an Aldis lamp, operated by a special supervisory unit in order to avoid using radio, sent a beam of green light in my direction. I pushed the throttle forward, and in response the aircraft began to move onto the runway. Looking right, I saw the faces of Maoz, Yochai and Yitzhak turned towards me, ready and waiting. It was time for take-off. The clock's second-hand touched twelve. I took my foot off the brake, gave the engine full throttle, and with another twist of my fingers to the left to turn on the afterburner, the aircraft shot forward with that familiar burst of power.

At high cruising speed, the aircraft gathered into a widely dispersed arrowhead formation, with about 300 metres (328 yards) between each one. They flew at very low altitude; the waves passed by underneath in close aspect and vanished to the rear. Number three wagged his wings slightly to draw my attention to a formation of Vautours from Ramat-David Airbase, which were also almost lapping the water and flying from right to left on a course that was converging with ours. Without climbing, the two formations literally passed through each other, not a word being uttered. Only the wagging of the two leaders' wings indicated that everything was under control. The formation of Vautours passed and disappeared to the left into the morning mist over the sea. This silent encounter left us with a sublime feeling of enormous unity in the overall effort.

It was 7.48: exactly three minutes past 'h-hour'. Over the earphones we began to hear the voices of pilots from formations that were in the thick of the fight. The clear sounds of battle: the war had begun. I turned the nose of the plane in a south-westerly direction and waited to come up over land. We were flying at a faster speed now, and all at once the blue background of the sea turned into a pattern of grey-green-brown chequered squares from horizon to horizon, the flat expanses of the Nile delta in northern Egypt. Ahead, three peculiar installations that looked like gigantic houses rapidly drew nearer – a bewildering and completely unexpected sight. Another twenty seconds of swift progress and the peculiar apparitions became recognisable. My formation flew over the Suez Canal and the 'gigantic houses' turned out to be the superstructures, tall and visible from afar, of the cargo-ships sailing through the canal.

A quick glance at the stopwatch in front of my eyes told me that the sight-seeing tour of the Middle East was over. 'Red, pull!' I announced over the radio, and pulled up the plane's nose at a steep angle. All at once the horizon around me receded, and an incredible sight came into view: in the middle of the farflung, dusty-yellow desert landscape emerged a huge airfield, with black smoke casting a dark shadow over the entire area. My eyes picked out the pattern of runways that I had memorised visually through countless practice runs in the past. With a quick look I ascertained that the planes of the formation were with me and that the sky was clear of enemy aircraft. With a practised hand I rolled the aircraft downwards toward the centre of the runways, to make my bombing run. From the corner of my eye, on my left,

I discerned the flashes of flak, apparently from ground anti-aircraft guns, and put any thought of them out of my mind.

Everything that went before and everything that came after was dwarfed at this critical moment, in view of the supreme need to hit the target accurately with the two bombs. In my diving run to the target I flew through a cloud of smoke that momentarily darkened the cockpit. In the light on the other side the 'peeper,' the centrepoint of the gunsight, was close to the centre of the runway. I glanced at the altimeter, stabilised the 'peeper' over the target, and squeezed the bomb release switch, putting all my heart and soul into it. The escape manoeuvre to the left at high speed dragged heavily on all my limbs with a G-force five times their natural weight. Behind me, in perfect order, I saw my numbers two, three and four diving after me, and their bombs striking and blasting the centre of the runway.

These are the tensest moments of the mission. Soaring away from the airfield to turn and approach again for the next run, the leader must ensure that the entire formation stays together, and that no MiG has managed to slip in among them and latch on to somebody's tail; and he has to glance over the cockpit instruments for any sign of malfunction. Most of all, he must carefully reconnoitre the airfield area and pick out targets, aircraft, which must be destroyed in the next run. It takes only a few words for the information concerning the identified targets to be disseminated among the formation members. As planned, the rest of the formation climbed to a higher altitude and returned in a relatively steep run to fire their cannon at the planes parked in the slipways, while I straightened out my aircraft to make a low, horizontal run along one of the runways.

An additional two bombs had been hung from the wingtips: these were special munitions, the latest development from the Rafael Armament Development Authority, designed to crack runways from a low altitude. The bomb release was squeezed again, and on the way out – while gathering the formation together for departure – I took advantage of the low overpass above the centre of the airfield to spot several gigantic Egyptian Tu-16 bombers, the bane of Israel until not long ago, parked intact in lots that hadn't been dealt with yet. After a split-second's indecision, I ordered the formation to assemble for a third run, noting the location of the targets I'd discovered. The dilemma, swiftly resolved, pitted the risk of being hit by enemy fire during this extra interval and the limited fuel supply (even more critical because of the long way home), against the chance of destroying these additional aircraft and thus forestalling the need to return. This implacable logic was augmented by my 'hunter's instinct', that subtle element which turns an ordinary human being into a warrior, hunter and fighter pilot. No, here and now we would not relent. We would pursue our enemy until he fell in defeat. We performed another circuit and another three Egyptian bombers burst into flames behind us.

At a speed of 550 knots (1019 kph) and flying at low altitude, the four Mirages left Cairo-West Airfield, wreathed in flames and smoke. Without a doubt their mission, like those of the two formations before them, had been executed to perfection.

A glance at the instrument panel inside the cockpit told me that trouble was brewing. The fuel gauge indicated that the fuel supply was significantly lower than planned. I decided to climb immediately to higher altitude and seek flight conditions that would save on fuel, despite the danger that we might be dis-covered and become involved in needless dogfights with the enemy. The formation assembled into a horizontal line at distances apart from each other conducive to our mutual defence. The horizon rapidly opened up again, affording a view of all northern Egypt. Columns of smoke were rising from various scattered sites, prominent testimony to the destruction of other Egyptian airfields and their aircraft.

For a reason that was still unclear to me, my aircraft's fuel situation continued to deteriorate, with a significant discrepancy in my fuel supply compared with the formation's other three planes. When we reached a fuel-efficient cruising altitude of 35,000 feet (10,668 metres), I eased down on engine power and allowed my speed to stabilise under optimal conditions. A simple calculation showed that I had, in fact, no chance of bringing the aircraft safely back to base in Hazor. Above the Sinai coast, near the eastern edge of Sabkhet el Bardawil, the gauge showed there were only 300 litres (66 gallons) of fuel left.

'Red three, pay attention!' I said over the radio, 'I've got enough fuel to fly another seven minutes. You take the formation and continue leading it back to base, to land as planned. I'll glide east as far as possible and make it on my own.' Number three confirmed my announcement.

Approximately over El Arish the plane's engine went dead. A sudden and worrying silence enveloped the cockpit, although most of the aircraft's vital systems continued to operate owing to the turning of the engine turbine as the air rushed through it at my cruising speed of 300 knots (550 kph). To maintain this speed, I dipped the plane's nose beneath the horizon. The altimeter needle began to turn anti-clockwise at a steady rate, indicating an alarming loss of altitude.

I notified the controllers of my predicament and my plan, and turned the aircraft's nose to the right, where I imagined the Hazerim Airfield to be. My greatest concern was whether I'd be able to glide beyond the borders of Sinai and eject over territory held by our own forces. This problem appeared to be behind me a few minutes later when I passed over the Nizzana district at an altitude of 20,000 feet (6,100 metres). I asked for and was given the coordinates for Hazerim by the controller, and switched the radio channel to the Hazerim tower frequency. Luckily I was very familiar with Hazerim, having served until recently as a flight instructor there. At an altitude of 7000 feet (2134 metres) I caught sight of the grey complex, in the middle of which I knew lay the runway.

I fingered the handle of the ejection seat, knowing full well that I would almost certainly be needing it. I notified the tower that I wouldn't be able to perform the regular circuit and land from the east, and that only a direct approach from the west was feasible; I asked them to keep the runway clear of all other aircraft for me. This was confirmed.

At this stage the runway became clearer, and I began to believe that I might actually land at Hazerim. With a soft touch I pulled the stick and lowered my speed to 240 knots (444 kph). The runway in front of me grew wider in the window, and at 1000 feet (305 metres) I made my decision to lower the landing gear, knowing it was irreversible. The landing gear dropped into place more slowly than usual because of the low hydraulic pressure, but locked into position to my great relief, as indicated by the three green lights. With no power and with the landing gear deployed, the aircraft descended more rapidly. At 200 feet (61 metres) it passed over the beginning of the runway. I exploited my slightly excessive speed to soften the touchdown, the wheels settling securely on the runway. I let the plane's nose drop to the runway and pulled the switch to open the braking parachute. An extraordinary silence descended on the cockpit, reminding me that the aircraft's engine wasn't running. I released the parachute and the plane rolled slowly and silently into the lot at the end of the runway, coming to a stop. It was only now that I had time to feel the small tremor in my hand, the rasping dryness in my throat, and my overwhelming relief.

Two fire engines and an ambulance were the first to arrive and circle the aircraft. Following them came a team of mechanics, all prepared to give my aircraft an initial inspection and tow it to the hangar. I released the seatbelts, put the security pins in place, and extricated myself from the cockpit. I clambered down and took a look at the plane from the outside, and froze in shock.

'Damn Rafael, and damn the squadron armourers!' I muttered to myself. From the tips of the aircraft's wings, still attached and appearing to smile, hung those two special, newfangled bombs, which had been meant to crack the Egyptian runways. The mystery was solved. Those two bombs – two hefty chunks of metal and explosives, which for some reason had failed to detach from the wings – had been the cause of my unexpected shortage of fuel and of my daring adventure, which luckily ended well this time.

A pickup truck came to collect me and drove me to the Fuga squadron. In the offices of the squadron – which ordinarily served as the advanced training squadron for the Air Force flying academy – sat a large group of pilots, most of them reservists, either before or after sorties. The light and relatively ponderous Fuga jets had joined the war effort. They were being used to provide air support to ground troops and to attack enemy positions and forces on the move in the Gaza Strip and the Rafah corridor. The jets' vulnerability to anti-aircraft fire made their missions all the more dangerous and cost the squadron many casualties.

When I arrived at the squadron it was still fairly early, and the first stage of Operation *Moked* hadn't ended yet. The Fuga pilots gathered around me and peppered me with questions about the attack deep in Egypt. I excitedly shared with them the sights I'd seen of burning airfields and the voices and reports I'd heard over the radio. Everything appeared to indicate that the tactical surprise, which the Air Force had initiated that morning, was complete and astounding. In the air you could already sense the heady smell of success and overwhelming victory.

Lanky Aryeh Ben-Or (Orbach) came up to me in the squadron's operations room. Aryeh was an excellent Mirage pilot, a courageous fighter and a man of principle, solid opinions and exceptional leadership qualities. He had been 'plucked out' of the prestigious Mirage squadron and posted to command the 'inferior' Fuga squadron, a task he carried out with notable dedication and enthusiasm. We embraced and clapped each other on the shoulder, and I told him everything I'd seen and heard in the past two hours. Wide-eyed, he listened to me with unconcealed enthusiasm and then went back about his business. His longing for the Mirage, his old 'workhorse', was quite candid and natural. It was now his duty to lead his men into battle in warplanes that were less suited to exposure to enemy fire. I knew he'd do the job better than anyone else. He was a real tiger.

Five days later, in the penultimate day of battle, just a few hours before the war ended, Aryeh Orbach was killed by anti-aircraft fire as he flew over the Golan Heights.

'Amos, maintenance informs us that your plane is ready to go,' the excited conversation was interrupted by the squadron's operations officer.

Late in the afternoon I landed my aircraft back at base in Hazor.

CHAPTER THREE

Tel Aviv, 1947

Father said that the curfew would end, this evening. The neighbourhood around Rashi Street in Tel Aviv was free of traffic. From the gigantic sycamore tree in the hushed yard drifted the sound of cooing pigeons. All was as quiet as the Sabbath.

The delightful scent rising from the pages of the book I borrowed from the local library pleasantly stang my nostrils. I lay sprawled on the sofa, my chin in my hand, and plunged into the book. Dozens of my childhood heroes stared at me from the covers of the numerous books which lay, in congenial disorder, on the shelf opposite me. As a child I was a bookworm, an indefatigable reader, capable of rereading the books I loved countless times. Karl May's Vineto the Indian, Franz Mulner's Buka and Namechek, Erich Kastner's Emil and his detectives, Jules Verne's Captain Nemo and the first men on the moon, Gutmann's Lubengulu and Beatrice, Janos Korchak's King Matthew, and General Panpilov and his fighters – these and untold others were the heroes of my youth, the bold adventurers of my dreams and shapers of my personal development.

I got up from the sofa, went outside, leaned against the railing of the large balcony, and peeked through the thicket of potted cacti at the intersection below the house. The street was empty, there was none of the ordinary traffic. The familiar cry of the Arab who sold oranges from the back of his donkey-drawn wagon – 'Maranzen, maranzen!' – would not be heard today. Neither the 'Ma'avir' buses nor the kerosene carts were passing by in the street. The city had fallen silent.

Two 'poppies' – British paratroopers in their uniforms and red berets, with tommy-guns slung from their shoulders – paced leisurely down the street, looking rather bored. A military jeep sped down Ahad-Ha'Am Street, the roar of its engine fading in its wake as it disappeared north in the direction of the Habima theatre.

It wasn't the first time the city had been clapped under a curfew. There had been several of them already, and the rules of the game were becoming clearer and clearer. To be truthful, my neighbourhood pals and I thoroughly enjoyed these curfews. First, we were freed from the onus of school, which was very nice. Second, we liked the 'hide-and-seek' games with the British 'poppy' patrols. We quickly learned the routes and schedules of the troop movements and began moving through the yards and streets, almost without restriction. We loved the tension and the fear, as well as the need to 'contend' with an adversary whom everyone loved to hate and make fun of. Blood, injuries and death were distant and unreal to us. It all seemed like a big and fascinating scouts' game.

From the neighbours' radio came the sound of the famous whistle, the line 'We have not yet lost hope' from 'Hatikva,' the national anthem. Within minutes radios in the entire neighbourhood had been switched on, and the whistle was heard again and again, at short intervals, from almost every home. After two minutes of silence, the voice of the female announcer of the 'Hagana' underground broadcasting station came on the air. There had been reports of violent searches for arms in Jewish settlements, and of clashes and arrests throughout the country. This was how I soaked up the voices, the responses at home, the echoes of my parents' conversations with their friends, and the tension that was everywhere.

On the second day of the curfew, in late afternoon, the situation took an interesting turn. Father called me into his room. He was sitting in shorts pants and a vest at the black desk, the centre of which was covered in green felt and polished glass, between which photos of the family lay trapped.

'Amos, I have a mission for you,' he said. I was all ears.

'Do you remember that lovely house on Rothschild Boulevard, almost opposite the "Shderot" movie theatre, where Yitzhak Sadeh lives?'

'Yes, of course. We were there a few weeks ago.'

'I want you to deliver an important letter to that house. It's a secret message, and you'll have to make your way there through the yards and avoid running into the British soldiers who are patrolling the streets. Can you do it?' he said.

'Sure thing,' I replied.

I felt filled with pride. Thus, all at once, without any warning, I had been entrusted with a 'covert mission' that made me part of a secret network, on which the fate and independence of the Jewish nation depended. Through my mind ran various scenarios concerning the contents and immense importance of the letter. I had long known that my parents were members of the 'Hagana' organisation, but this knowledge had never yet been associated with concrete action of any kind.

'Will I get to know more secrets in the future? I sure hope so . . .' I thought to myself.

With bated breath I took the sealed envelope in my hands. I stashed it beneath my shirt, went out into the street, and walked up to Rothschild Boulevard. Once, at the corner of Balfour Street, I saw a military jeep driving away down the street. I could feel the envelope beneath my shirt touching my skin, seemingly scorching hot. I scooted from one yard to the next at a run. When I delivered the envelope to the lady on the second floor, it felt as though a great responsibility had been lifted from my shoulders. Mission accomplished!

That night, when I went to bed, I tried to trace in my mind the series of further missions with which I would be entrusted. The more I thought, the harder and more dangerous they became, until I . . . fell asleep.

It is 29 November; I'm twelve-and-a-half years old. The entire family and Uncle Marek's family have congregated around the gigantic radio in Father's room. I have taken up a strategic position near the orange-lit station finder, staying on my guard for Aunt Rocha, who might – at the slightest moment of in-attention on my part – hit me from the flank with a ringing and unexpected kiss.

Father takes high-handed control of the radio, its volume and frequency settings. Electronic beeps rise and fall at intervals, interfering with the reception. He is holding a ruled page carefully torn out of my arithmetic exercise book, for the sake of posterity. Two sharpened pencils are ready to record the impending vote.

Now the broadcast shifts to New York, to the General Assembly of the United Nations, where the vote on the Palestine Partition Plan is about to be held. I understand what is going on, I feel unconditionally involved. Sometimes I was angry with my parents for having me so late, and thus forestalling any active participation of mine in the civilian and military struggle against the British and the Arabs. My mother hadn't been home with us for several months. She was gone for a year, in the service of the Jewish Agency and UNRWA, working at refugee camps in Central Europe. Her absence had strengthened the bond between me and Father.

'Argentina . . . Yes! Czechoslovakia . . . Yes! . . . Saudi Arabia . . . No! The United Kingdom? . . . Abstention!' – the delegates' voices are heard one after another, replying to the Secretary's call. The Secretary General's high, slightly froggish voice repeats each declaration accompanied by typical electronic background noise. Carefully, making no mistakes, Father writes down the votes in three columns. Three parallel vertical lines, followed by two diagonals – completing a quintet, and so on. We are all holding our breath. Uncle Marek bites his fingernails and is immediately 'punished' for it by none other, of course, than Aunt Rocha.

'The Soviet Union . . . Yes!' The declaration is greeted by a roar from all of us. 'The United States of America . . . Yes!' A two-thirds majority has already been reached, but Father will not relent and punctiliously keeps count of the votes. Only when the work is done does he allow himself to rejoice, and everyone rejoices with him. Father's outburst of jubilation is for me the supreme and final proof of the importance of this moment. Everyone falls into everyone else's arms, and I endure, relatively calmly, a gigantic, ringing kiss on the cheek from Aunt Rocha – something I would not normally willingly entertain. I go up to Father and take the paper from him. Instinct tells me that this note is of historic significance, and I hide it away in a safe place, next to my diary, where it will stay secure for many a year.

*   *   *

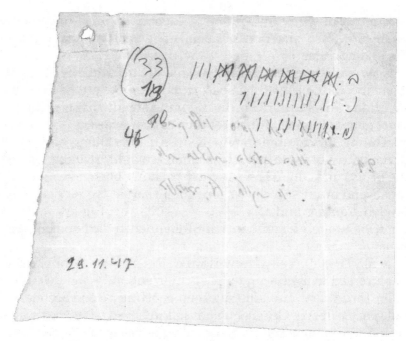

The page from my arithmatic book with the
United Nations' votes marked by my father.

Approaching midnight, crowds gather in Mugrabi Square and in
Magen David Square. The joy is real and all-embracing. Hand in
hand, shoulder to shoulder, rings of dancers form and twirl
around in the traditional *horah*. Complete strangers, the thin and
the fat, the pretty and the ugly, the old and the young – un-
reservedly, without compunction, all together.

The next morning I went out as usual, briefcase in hand, to the
school up the street near Meyer Park. A row of pickups, trucks
and buses was parked beside the curb. Around them people were
being organised into groups under the supervision of attendants
with special ID armbands. My classmates and I stood at the top
of the stairs in the school entrance and watched what was going
on. 'These guys are enlisting in the Hagana,' the rumour passed
by word of mouth among the kids. Yesterday's sweeping joy
gave way to a feeling of concern – not fear – and a sense of the
importance of the occasion.

I would only rarely see Danny, my Uncle Carl and Aunt Lucia's son. They lived in Jerusalem, in a small attic apartment in the Rehavya neighbourhood. I loved visiting them, especially because of the huge birdcage that stood in the middle of the guest room and took up half the space and the two large lizards that swam in a big aquarium on the window sill. Uncle Carl, a lecturer in zoology at the Hebrew University, would tell me interesting things about animals, insects and birds, and Aunt Lucia, who was an artist and sculptor, would give me clay to knead and make figures with to my heart's content. There, at my Uncle and Aunt's home in Jerusalem, I first discovered and avidly read *Alice in Wonderland*.

I remembered Danny as a well mannered, soft-spoken and especially quiet youth. At home I was told that 'Danny is a student'. I didn't really know what a student was, but I was too embarrassed to ask.

On 15 January, 1948, in the evening, Mother came home pale and greatly upset. 'Our Danny has fallen,' she said to Father and me in a trembling voice, and tears filled her eyes. 'There has been a terrible disaster. Thirty-five lads, university students from Jerusalem, fell in battle today on their way to the Etsion Block. None was left alive. Their bodies will be repatriated tomorrow apparently,' she explained to us in a shaken voice.

'Here lie our bodies, in a long line . . . We, the bleeding Hill Company . . .' so poet Haim Guri would write one day about that wonderful group, 'the band of 35'. The group had set out to reinforce the Jewish settlements of the Etsion Block, but ran into hundreds of Arab insurgents and bravely battled them until the last of the fighters, their ammunition exhausted, finally fell, stones clenched in their fists.

That night, as I went to bed, I felt – more powerfully this time – to what an extent the conflict taking place before my eyes involved my own family, and myself as well.

CHAPTER FOUR

Fire – Ras Sudar Skies,
7 June 1967

Pinto and Neuman were killed on the second day of battle, and David Baruch was killed at night on the third day. In the euphoria of our stunning triumph, the everlasting fact of war came home to rest: there is always a price to be paid.

On the fourth day of battle, before dawn, some especially important intelligence reached the operations room. A squadron or two from Algeria had arrived as reinforcements, and their aircraft were deployed at two airfields near Cairo. Before noon the squadron received the order for the requisite mission: to attack the Algerian force deployed at Cairo-West Airfield with a team of fighter jets from the Mirage squadrons. I was assigned to lead the formation, a quartet. Now, as opposed to the sorties during the first day, 'Mr Fear' kicked in with a vengeance.

The intelligence we had received was paltry in substance, we no longer enjoyed the element of surprise, and the knowledge that success has its cost in blood had been bluntly brought home. The flight briefing was serious and to the point. The question regarding the necessity for the mission hovered over the room, but was removed from the agenda even before it arose, as a matter of course. Yochai was once again assigned to be my number two, Uri number three, and Baruch 'Buff' – a classmate of mine from flight training academy and a close personal friend – number four. We went through the familiar process of learning the targets, maps and other flight elements, partly as a team and also separately. Two grizzled reservists took us to the aircraft in their pickup trucks, which had also been conscripted.

During the few minutes of the drive the images of Rachel and the boys went through my mind, and a feeling of warm, tender longing filled my heart. What were they doing? What was Rachel thinking? What were Noam and Ram doing? And Mother, how was she? I was well aware that this time the mission was harder than any that came before, but it would be performed in full, exactly as required, in letter and in spirit.

The formation assembled at the edge of the runway. Everyone arrived and glanced up at the leader to confirm their readiness. I straightened out my aircraft on the left side of the runway, the others phased behind me and to the right. A quick engine check, a quick visual check of the readings on the numerous dials inside the cockpit, and it was time for the take-off run, straight ahead. With a gentle pull of the stick, the nose rose, and the aircraft – heavier and carrying a greater load than usual – disengaged from the runway. This time we would be flying at high altitude to save fuel.

Our route passed over central Sinai, under the watchful eyes of the flight controllers of the southern control unit. Their job was to track the formation, warn us of enemy aircraft and receive and relay reports from Central Command at the 'Pit' (Air Force head-quarters in Tel Aviv). Passing through the Sinai skies at this height, one could view the entire breadth of the ground war theatre. Very prominent on the ground were the motor traffic routes running the length and breadth of the desert. They were especially prominent on this day because of the abundance of burnt vehicles and tanks along and beside the roads, columns of black smoke still rising from the 'fresher' kills. The number of 'fresh' kills rose, the farther west we flew. About 70 km (43 miles) away from the Suez Canal I eased up on engine power and began to descend to a lower altitude, the formation following me. The main part of the mission was about to begin. Tension surged, and the adrenaline racing through my body evinced itself in an accelerated heart rate and heightened clarity of mind. In my mind I pictured the planned attack in every detail.

'Red formation, this is Carmel, do you read me?' came the controller's voice over the radio.

'Read you loud and clear, carry on,' I replied.

'Red formation, receive change of mission. I repeat, receive change of mission.'

'I read you, carry on.'

'Red formation, stop your descent, assume a course azimuth two four zero. I'm taking you to intercept an enemy formation in the Ras Sudar area. Do you copy, Red?'

'This is Red. Roger, I copy, keep us posted.' This was good news for us, relieving us of the glum feeling of flying a dangerous mission of rather dubious necessity. My comrades and I were fighter pilots to the very core. We would perform every other type of mission, especially attacks on ground targets, because they had to be performed; but to meet the enemy face to face, battle it out in a dogfight and shoot him down – for us there could be no higher ambition.

In this regard my frustration was multiplied by the fact that in 1964, at the time of our clashes with the Syrians over the Jordan River diversion project, with Yochai as my number two, I had chased after a pair of Syrian MiG-21s all the way to the outskirts of Damascus. This was the first aerial encounter ever between a Soviet MiG and a French Mirage. I fired an air-to-air missile at one of the aircraft. The missile was a first-generation Shafrir and the first of its kind manufactured in Israel by Rafael, but it fell like a stone to the ground, missing the target, of course. I kept up the chase, closed the distance, and fired my cannon at the Syrian, hitting the fuel tank hanging from the MiG's belly. After confirming the hit I disengaged and turned west, on the controller's orders, towards the Sea of Galilee. To my amazement, when I looked back, expecting to see the MiG falling in flames, I discovered that he had apparently managed to get rid of the damaged tank, and could now be seen escaping to his base. There was no way to rectify the failure now.

A few days after this incident, Air Force intelligence confirmed what had happened. I carried this frustration with me for three years, consumed with doubt whether I should ever get a chance to set the record straight. And I also took note then of an important lesson, namely: a hit and a kill are not the same thing! A fighter pilot sticks to his quarry and doesn't relent until he destroys him – *no less, and not before!*

* * *

The formation banked left, as per instructions, and assumed attack formation, two pairs phased backwards. I ordered the release of our bombs somewhere over the hills of western Sinai, in open territory.

'Red formation from Command, there's a target for you, flying south to north, same altitude, distance: eighteen miles.'

'Roger, I copy,' I confirmed.

'Red, drop detachable fuel tanks. Pepper go! [switch on afterburners]' I ordered the formation. A jolt of the aircraft indicated to me that the tanks had detached. I saw the large fuel tanks dropping from the belly of my number two's aircraft, rotating and spinning crazily, then falling away behind us.

The jet, its belly free of any impedimentary cargo, lurched forward wildly, under full engine power with the afterburner on.

'Switches on!' I ordered the formation members, doing the same myself. I fingered the cannon trigger, cold to the touch, as if to make sure it really did exist. I strained my eyes, looking in the direction from which the enemy planes could be expected to arrive. Owing to the lower altitude and the growing distance, communications with the control unit had been cut. It was clear to me that from now on we were on our own.

The dark hills of western Sinai were left behind; ahead lay the bright plain of Ras Sudar, and beyond it, in the background, the stunning azure-blue of the Gulf of Suez. For me and my comrades, this landscape's only importance was to serve as the background against which we would discover the formation of MiGs that was supposed to be in the vicinity.

'Bogies (enemy aircraft) flying low at ten o'clock, follow me!' I snapped over the radio. My eyes had caught sight of two MiGS in relatively tight formation. I raised the nose of my aircraft to turn back and roll onto their tails from above, from south to north. As I was performing this manoeuvre. I noticed the second pair of MiGs.

'Three, there's another pair flying low at eleven o'clock. See them?' I asked.

'Eye contact, I'm taking them,' replied Uri confidently. Uri and 'Buff' widened their turn and spilled away left towards the second pair of MiGs. I now focused all my attention on the quarry in front of me. I noticed that I was closing the gap between us too quickly and lowered speed accordingly. The two MiGs stayed close together, about 100 metres (110 yards) apart, growing larger and larger in my front window as the range diminished. I could now identify them as MiG-19s, few of which we had ever encountered before.

'I'm taking the one on the right,' I notified number two, without taking my eyes off the MiGs. I knew for a fact that Yochai was there, covering my tail.

Over the radio I heard exchanges between numbers three and four, who by the sound of it seemed to be in control of the situation, which didn't divert my own attention from the target.

'This is two, I copy. You're clear, one,' Yochai answered immediately.

At a range of approximately 1500 metres (1640 yards), the Egyptian pilots apparently noticed that they were in real trouble. It was a little too late. The two MiGs broke away left and slightly upwards, but not enough. I rose slightly above the circumference of the circle and immediately closed tight again, to the inside. Out of the corner of my eye I saw the MiG on the left roll over on its belly and fall steeply, towards the Gulf. I had no time to deal with it, for I was concentrating on the MiG on the right, my specified target. I estimated the distance to him at about 300 metres (328 yards) and waited another instant.

The MiG's entire wingspan now filled the gun-sight. The 'peeper' (focal point of the sights) settled on the back of the aircraft, just behind the cockpit. I unsheathed and squeezed the cannon trigger. A relatively long burst of fire, like music to my ears, shot towards the MiG. I was surprised how swiftly it produced an effect. While my finger was still squeezing the trigger, an immense flame burst from the left side of the plane and engulfed it completely in a flash. I tilted my wings slightly outside the turn and made a pass above the burning MiG. I thought I saw the seat ejecting from the cockpit, but I had no chance to confirm this. Now I tried to find the second MiG, but in vain. The blue background of the Gulf waters made its discovery more difficult.

It was now necessary to regroup with numbers three and four. Over the radio came a jubilant cowboy whoop, straight out of the Wild West.

'Ya-hoo, ya-hoo, I shot him down!' There was only one pilot capable of squealing like that – 'Buff', of course.

'Buff' was an inimitable, impulsive character and an excellent pilot. He held the world record for the lowest flight ever made, having once managed to dip the tip of his Harvard's propeller in the Dead Sea, the lowest spot on earth, and returning safely to base with bent propeller blades. I was almost as happy for him as I was for myself.

Without further incident, I quickly found the other two Mirages south of us, and the formation reassembled to fly home.

On the long eventless flight back, after the blood in my arteries returned to its normal rate of flow, I thought about my impending conversation with Rachel. She had been such a close confidante to my long-held desire for such an achievement, as well as the frustrations preceding it on the way.

I also thought about how happy I would have been to report the outcome of the battle to my father. His heart had given out on him only three months before – my beloved father, that stern, seemingly cold man, who followed my life with such great understanding and left us at the most inappropriate hour . . .

When I saw the runways of Hazor Airbase in front of us, I gave numbers two and three the go-ahead to land. I told number four, 'Buff', to fly in an open lateral line behind me, and I called the squadron to notify them of the results and our approach. We both, one after another, made a very low pass above the squadron building, concluding the pass with a steep nose-climb and overhead victory roll, as has been customary among the fellowship of fighter pilots around the world since the First World War.

CHAPTER FIVE

Growing Up, 1948

Saturday morning. From the neighbours' apartment come the voices of the Lev family, singing the Sabbath hymns. The voices, so familiar to me, mingle in my ears with the cooing of the pigeons and the sound of the piano being played by Therry, the pretty girl from across the street, who is practising scales with infinite patience.

I open my eyes and the memory of Noa's face from yesterday evening comes to mind. Beneath the lamppost on the street corner, near the youth movement clubhouse, the gang gathered together after the Friday evening itinerary. Two harmonicas were whipped out, and we all danced with a reckless abandon that only young people like ourselves are capable of.

After we tired a little, we split up into couples to dance. Everyone knew that when it was time for the Circassian dance, as though by a mysterious guiding force, Amos and Noa would come together. As expected, I took my appointed place at exactly the right time, and just when the first strains were heard from Amnon's wonderful harmonica, our hands met as if by accident and our bodies began to move through the steps of the familiar dance.

Excitement coursed through my veins when I recognised the familiar fragrance, the touch of the immaculately ironed white blouse around her swelling breast, which stirred my imagination, and the meeting of her waist with my robust hands. Everything was so familiar, so dizzying, so convivial. Everybody around us was dancing, we were all such good friends; but around us, I felt, there was a bubble that set us apart. We were hovering inside that magical space, the two of us, as if there were nobody but us in the world.

The youth movement signature whistle and sounds of laughter burst through the window and penetrate the room from the street. Ami, Uzi and Uri are here already, boisterously awaiting me. 'Rise and shine, woodchuck!' their voices urge me.

'Leave me alone, let me sleep. I don't feel like going out to sea today,' I complain, even as I surrender without a fight. I slip out of bed, reconciled to my harsh fate. I grab a slice of bread with something on it, comb my fingers through my curly hair, and go out into the summer's day to meet the group waiting for me on the steps outside.

At the *Hapoel* boathouse in the Yarkon estuary, the boats are already prepared to embark. In my group there are seven boys, two girls, and a counsellor. The damp of the sand and the salt air nip my nostrils from a distance. From out of storage we take the masts, large sails, oars and other necessary equipment. In bathing suits, with a rag or shirt tossed over our shoulders, we all clamber onto the boat called *Berl* and set the oarlocks and oars in place. Amihai the counsellor is at the rudder, six of us man the oars, and the boat sets sail in a wide turn towards the Reading power station and the open sea.

At the mouth of the Yarkon River, beneath the surface, following a route known only to the cognoscenti, lies the twisting deep-water channel that provides the only outlet to the sea for the heavy boats. Any deviation from this route and the belly of the boat is sure to wallow and settle in the soft sandbar on either side of the channel. And then we're stuck.

'Into the water!' orders Amihai. We all leap into the water and put our shoulders against the side of the boat to lift and free it from the sandbar. I have a perverse liking for this drill. I like the feel of the coarse damp sand against my feet, the smell of moss and algae, the light sea breeze blowing in my face and the cold current, which at short intervals is suddenly displaced by the outflow of hot water from the adjacent power station.

'Heave, ho! Heave, ho!' cries Amihai, setting a rhythm for our efforts. The two girls, Ruti and Ilana, also climb off the boat and grab hold of the gunwale, to 'lend' a helping hand of sorts . . .

From the river's northern bank, in the direction of the power station, the boat's progress is being followed by the indifferent gaze of an elderly Arab who is sitting cross-legged on the tip of a camel's hump, his mount the first in a row of four camels carrying huge bales of sand on their backs.

Our brown, young bodies stretch tautly. The boat groans and finally surrenders to our concerted effort. Our eyes glittering, feeling triumphant, one after another we leap over the gunwale back into the boat. We put our hands to the oars, and once again the helmsman's voice rings out, setting a pace for our strokes.

The difficult part is still ahead of us. There's a high sea this morning, and row after row of towering, outspread waves greets us on our way out to open water. Amihai's eyes strain in search of the way through, following the cadence of the onrushing waves. He regulates our direction and rate in order to arrive at the most difficult point of the passage at a quiet interval – during the relatively short break between one surging wave and the next. The oarsmen are alert and familiar with the imminent manoeuvre. The helmsman keeps the boat's prow turned into the oncoming waves, its forward motion slow and steady for the time being. The bow pitches up and down at a steeper angle, increasingly alarming each time.

'Now!' cries Amihai. Full speed ahead. 'Pull . . . and pull . . . and pull . . .' Moving together in unison, with all our might, our bodies bend forward as we dip our oars in the water, then lean backward with straining muscles, pulling hard. The boat leaps forward despite its weight. Though the last billow of waves has indeed subsided, the next one in line is already nearly upon us. Amihai's eyes betray his obvious concern lest we be caught by the large, shattering waves before making it out into the open. The group of boys continues its focused effort.

The crests of the first waves of the approaching billow rock the boat, but now the worst is behind us already. The next surge of waves rushes towards the shore, jolting us about, but the waves are crashing behind us and are out of harm's way. Now we can go back to paddling at a more moderate pace. Our youthful eyes glitter with a sweet thrill as the foaming, shore-bound waves slip

away behind us, and the open sea welcomes us into the monotonous arms of its gentle swell.

It's time to raise sail. As one man, we grab hold of the mast and
raise it in place in the middle of the boat. Next the mizzenmast
goes up, and three sails rise and snap into the wind with what
sound like small detonations. Now the sails stretch taut, gathering the entire force of the wind.

'Lower the gaff mizzen to three-quarters!' Amihai orders.

The large wooden boat, which has until now been horren-
dously clumsy, is now transformed into a swift, responsive and
powerful vessel. White foam sprays from both sides of the bow;
tilting on its side, the sailboat travels south towards the beaches
of Tel Aviv.

Three or four dolphins join the expedition, tagging along
behind the boat, their sleek dark bodies performing incredible
manoeuvres to demonstrate their supremacy in the water. This
was a sight that captivated my eyes and heart each time anew.
My heart soars in response to these wonderful animals. I envy
them, simple as that, for their freedom of movement through
their natural environment, without any visible limitation.

The gigantic, rusting iron hulk of the *Altalena* can be seen
approaching. The boat circles the sunken ship and comes within
a few dozen metres of it. Our group of sailors does not, and did
not, have any sympathy for those who sailed upon it and their
motives. Our education at home and in the youth movement
embedded in us a clearcut sympathy for the Hagana, the
Palmach and the leftist camp, and an utter abomination of the
Right and the activities of the Etsel and Lehi undergrounds.
However, the picture that meets our eyes is sad and gloomy. The
surface of the water is smooth on the quiet, northern side of
the huge wreck. There are no traces of the fire and smoke that
were here only a few months ago.

The westerly wind has refilled the white sails and the boat,
tilting on its left side almost to the waterline, speeds south. Here
and there bob the heads of the braver swimmers who have
dared to come out into the deep, waving hello to us. A *hasake* – a
variety of flatboat used by the local lifeguards resembling an
oversized surfboard – elegantly rides the waves not far from
them. A tanned, muscular young man with a wide-brimmed

straw hat on his head is standing sturdily astride the aft-deck, dipping his long paddle in the water to the right and left. A young woman wearing a skimpy bathing suit is lying on her back in front of him, in an attitude that fires my imagination and that of the other boys in the group. The boat moves forward with a gentle rocking motion, splitting its way through the waves, while the rest of the world moves backward at exactly the same speed.

The rudder is occasionally entrusted into the hands of one of us. I wait my turn with well disguised impatience. When I finally hold the wheel in my hand, I am truly delighted. I feel how the great wooden body obeys me, responding to the touch and pressure of my hand. I love the sea, the wind, the boat and Noa. I also love my group of friends. I always feel comfortable with them, and confident of our mutual ability to execute, in the most harmonious manner, the most intricate plans of action. This feeling of belonging to a group is, and will be all my life, of great importance to me.

We sail south to the hills of Palmachim, then reverse direction and sail north to the cliffs of Netanya. We reverse direction again and return to a spot opposite Reading power station. The sails are lowered, the mast comes down, and the boat returns, powered by our oars again, to the smooth, green waters of the Yarkon estuary. I feel that strange sensation, which I feel each time we return to shore, of stepping on solid land with my two feet while my mind and body continue to rock with the waves in a pleasant state of dizziness for quite some time.

Our group walks south along Dizengoff Street, scattering separately to our homes. In the evening, I hope, we will meet again at the clubhouse. I long agonisingly to see and hear Noa, and perhaps even to touch her, as though by accident.

I pace up the street to my home at the top of the hill. Opposite me, the Ziskind Bakery's breadwagon is coming down the street, its two brakes shrieking against the wooden rims. The horse is also rearing back and drumming his hooves on the empty roadway. Yosko the coachman is sitting on the wooden bench, more asleep than awake, his ever-present grey cap slanted diagonally on his head, stroking the exhausted horse's backside with his whip. As the wagon passes, the smell of hot fresh bread fills

my nostrils and awakens pangs of hunger. Darkness has begun
to descend on the city.

As I walk, I am intoxicated by the sense of my body's growing
power. It is as if the sun and the smell of the sea have been
absorbed by my maturing body and are swelling its muscles. I
am a broad-shouldered fourteen-year-old of average height: the
rounded plumpness of childhood has disappeared, giving way
to a strong, almost perfect, torso. My golden childhood curls
have given way to a brown-black, wavy forelock. I lengthen my
stride and the soles of my feet drum against the sidewalk – I am
dancing, far more than I am walking. In this manner I pass the
faded green wooden kiosk at the corner of Melchett Street and
approach the empty lot, scene of my childhood games. I feel like
a prince in his court there. Who can stop me?

I leap up the stairs home three at a time.

Mother greeted me cheerfully at the door. Mother was a
very special lady, an artist to the core, open and companionable, imaginative and adventurous. She wasn't a
'housewife' and never ascribed too much importance to the
management of the household, but nevertheless succeeded
in maintaining a warm home for all its residents. She
would often sail off into the fruitful realms of her imagination, which to many seemed an appealing sort of
absent-mindedness. The story made the rounds in the
family that once, as she stood before the gas-burner with
the intention of lighting it, holding a slice of bread in one
hand and a burning match in the other, she badly burned
her lips when what she put in her mouth was . . . the
burning match.

She had completed her mission in Europe not long ago.
Upon her return to Israel, she sprang a surprise on Father,
myself and the other family members: at Lydda Airport
Mother approached us, carrying in her arms a baby girl
wrapped in a colourful wool blanket.

'This is my daughter – your sister, Amos,' she said, with
a merry twinkle in her eye. On our way home the matter
was cleared up. While at the refugee camp in Germany, she
had listed the baby as her natural daughter in all her

documents, and thus had managed to smuggle the girl into the country even though she didn't have a 'certificate' – a British entry permit, of which only a limited number were issued. The next day, the baby was passed on to her relatives in Israel.

Within a day or two, the house opened its doors again to the dozens of friends, artists, poets and writers, who were attracted like moths to my mother's enticing flame.

Father sat ensconced in his room. He was pedantic, cautious, wise and introverted. He was a handsome man with a pair of piercing blue eyes, punctilious and knowledgeable, as befitted a student of the Viennese school of the early twentieth century. Whereas Mother would tear through the house like a storm, bringing with her friends and acquaintances, animals abandoned in the street, and rare plants she'd found in the corner of a secluded yard, Father would go back and forth to his job as an agronomist in the fields, or at the experimental station in Rehovot, quietly, regularly, and with exemplary punctuality. He had his small, close circle of intimate friends; she had her 'flocks' of companions from this place and that, from all backgrounds and everywhere. Two people, two very different worlds. They clashed not infrequently, but a great love also linked these two.

I grew up and matured between, and out of, the three focal points of my childhood years. From Father I came by my logic, strength, ambition, conservatism and a measure of severity, as well as my honesty and leadership ability. From Mother I received the warmth, sentimentality, imagination, creativity, and adventurousness. And my environment gave me Eretz Israel (the land of Israel), its natural beauties and landscapes, the ideals of the youth movement and the camaraderie.

When Mother called, we sat down the three of us at the massive table in the simply furnished hallway. My older sister Tsippor had already left the house and moved to a moshav in the Jezreel Valley, and would visit us only seldom.

As I ate my omelette, which was made from egg powder

rationed out in return for government food coupons, and the salad served at table, I listened to my parents' desultory conversation. Father was speaking about how the young Agriculture Ministry was being set up, the Minister and his staff having moved into the former German colony, *Sharona*, recently vacated by British Mandate officials. Its new name was to be '*Hakirya*'. In turn, Mother reported on the progress in her work of memorialising those killed in the War of Independence, who would be commemorated in a large volume entitled *Gviley Esh* (Scorched Parchment Rolls). I was very interested in what they had to say and tried not to miss a word.

'Amos,' said Mother, 'I'll be stepping in to Ben-Gurion for a few minutes tonight to present a new book to him. It's an opportunity for you to meet him. What do you say?'

'I'm prepared to come along,' I replied.

An hour later the two of us entered the narrow path beyond the hedge, which led to the door of David and Paula Ben-Gurion's modest home on Keren Kayemet Boulevard in Tel Aviv. My heart was beating rapidly in excitement, which I did my best to disguise.

Paula opened the door and led us inside.

'Ben-Gurion is slightly ill; he has a cold. He's lying in his room, but he's willing to see you. Don't stay long,' she admonished us. Paula's concern and devotion to her husband were the stuff of legend, and her assent to our visit was testimony to a large measure of goodwill.

On a sofa in the corner of the room lay Ben-Gurion, a wool blanket tossed over his legs, perusing a book with his head propped on one arm. On the cabinet beside him stood half a glass of tea, the same as one would likely find in the sickroom of any ordinary mortal with the flu . . .

'Come in, Anda, come in,' said Ben-Gurion in his familiar, clipped voice. 'And who is your young comrade?'

'This is Amos, my son. I wanted him to meet you,' said Mother.

With trembling knees I approached the sofa and shook his warm, pleasant hand. I sat down in a chair in the corner of the room and waited patiently while Mother spoke with

Ben-Gurion. I had absolutely no interest in the subject of their conversation. I simply sat there and looked around the simple room, soaking up the experience of a face-to-face encounter with Israel's greatest leader since Moses and King David, son of Jesse.

CHAPTER SIX

Fire – Wadi Al-Hafir Skies, 8 June 1967

I read the mission order and gathered the formation – Giora number two, and Uri number three – and the squadron's intelligence officer in the briefing room.

South of the town of Suez, at the mouth of a large wadi leading to the Cairo district and the heart of Egypt, stood a battery of SA-2 surface-to-air missiles, sealing off the entire area to the Israeli Air Force. This battery had to be destroyed, and we had been entrusted with the mission. The decision had been made not to use routine tactics for an attack of this type. The formation would be lighter, consisting of only three aircraft rather than the usual quartet, and for armament we would be using the two 30 mm cannon built into the aircraft rather than heavy bombs of relatively doubtful accuracy, whose weight and shape considerably reduced our planes' manoeuvrability. Despite the greater risk of being hit by anti-aircraft cannon and machine-gun fire from within the battery enclosure, owing to passing low and very close to the battery, the pilots flying the mission were happy with the chosen method of attack.

Many of my comrades, myself included, preferred the light cannon to the heavy bombs, which turned us from 'fighters' into 'bombers'. Using the cannon to deal with a target, any target, at short, almost intimate range, gave one a greater sense of 'fair play' – something like the gunslingers' duel in *High Noon*, down the main street of a Wild West town. In the familiar dilemma between the light cavalryman and the armoured chariot bristling with heavy weapons, I have always favoured the former.

Take-off and the flight over the Sinai peninsula to the Gulf of

Suez were by now almost a matter of routine. Again we saw burning vehicles and tanks along the roadways. After passing over the hills of western Sinai I took the formation down to low altitude to avoid premature detection by Egyptian air control radar or the radar of the target missile battery itself. At a speed of 1000 kph (715 knots), the bright sandy hills leading to the Gulf pass by beneath me.

Our aircraft are rocketing forward when the yellow background of the dunes change all at once into the dark blue of the Gulf waters.

'Red formation, break away, break away!' comes a loud cry over the radio.

No time for questions, no time for explanations! I bank left steeply and pull the stick hard. I feel my body grow heavier and the blood drain from my head. My vision turns foggy, but I don't lose control. I let up on the turn after 180 degrees, the plane's nose pointed east back in the direction of Sinai. Now I look for, and immediately find, my numbers two and three. My eyes almost pop out of my head as I seek the enemy, aircraft or missile, on our tails. Nothing! Absolutely nothing!

'Number two, three, are you okay? Report.' 'Two okay,' 'Three, okay,' come back their reports.

Who had called us? What was the true meaning of the call? Was there another 'Red' formation in the area? If so, why hadn't it been heard before, and why wasn't it heard now? Maybe the call came from an Israeli intelligence aircraft, which had detected a missile launch and intervened to save us. Or could it have been intervention on the part of an Egyptian or Russian espionage element? But if so, how could they know the name of the formation and its critical location? My mind runs feverishly with questions for which I can find no satisfactory answer.

The formation returns to the vicinity of the western Sinai hills. I check my aircraft's fuel gauge, and ask numbers two and three to report on their fuel situation. A quick calculation shows that we are in good shape, and I congratulate the mission planners for not having chosen the heavier and less fuel-efficient mode.

'Whoever the mysterious caller may have been, it is no reason to abort or change the mission,' I say to myself.

'Stop and retreat, or regroup, press forward and attack again?' Since the dawn of warfare, this question in all its significance has repeatedly faced warriors on the battlefield. A bare-chested hunter with a dagger in his hand versus his animal prey; an infantryman with rifle and bayonet versus a red-eyed foe; a tank company commander with half his company lost versus an outpost spitting fire; or a jet fighter pilot versus searing anti-aircraft fire.

A core of steel is structured deep inside one's character, wrapped in a sheath of education and practised dedication to the goal. There is also a layer of absolute commitment to comrades, platoon, team and squadron. Since time immemorial, these qualities have combined to push back self-evident, natural and primal fear – damn the torpedoes, full speed ahead!

'Red, turn left and back on course!' I order, focusing all my attention now on returning precisely to our route of attack on a new timetable I have determined. Again we descend to low altitude, pass over the sand dunes and the blue waters of the Gulf. This time all is quiet, except for the adrenaline pumping through my veins, in preparation for the battle about to break out.

The waters of the Gulf are left behind and the formation now soars over the hills on the Egyptian side. From memory I extract the picture of the intersection between wadi and highway, over which we will be passing in another twenty seconds. My practised eyes try to pick out terrain features that I studied back at the squadron. Another ten seconds go by. There it is! The intersection is directly below me. Change of direction left, exactly ten degrees; two minutes' flight on this new azimuth. The target should appear to my left and slightly ahead. There it is! I discover the dark spots protruding from the embanked fortifications, and a glance around reveals the missiles themselves, standing in their dugouts.

'Target left, prepare to pull, check switches!' I notify the formation. I continue straight ahead, 2 km (1.2 miles) west of the target, and raise the nose of my plane to make a horseshoe-turn back.

Now the battery lies spread in its classic format, straight ahead of us: the fire-control centre in the middle, the missile-dugouts and accessory equipment in a ring around it, and anti-aircraft gun positions scattered all over the area. My own target is the fire-control centre, the heart of the missile battery. Numbers two and three are targeting missile dugouts on either side of me. We will have only one flypast, very risky, and there is no room for error. My eyes are trained on the fire-control centre and the radar antenna turning on top of it. Flashes of anti-aircraft cannon and machine-gun fire impinge upon the edge of my vision from several directions, arousing anger rather than fear.

'May the best man win,' flashes through my head. The 'peeper' is on the fire-control centre; the range is rapidly decreasing. I squeeze the cannon trigger at a range of 1000 metres (1100 yards), and this time I don't let go. The thunder of the automatic, rapid-fire guns immediately sounds in my ears. Dust rises from slightly in front of the target, and then all the shells smash into the command post. At a range of 200 metres (220 yards), just about 'spitting' distance, I stop shooting. The command post approaches below me, every detail visible. Like a picture out of a surreal film, I see metal parts and entire bodies flying up into the air right in front of my eyes. At a very low altitude, my aircraft passes only metres above the now razed and gutted post, wreathed in dust, smoke and fire.

I feel several light blows to the plane, which immediately pass without any perceivable ill effect. I check the engine readings and other systems – no sign of any malfunction – and put the matter to rest. A glance right and left finds numbers two and three in their places, spread off to the sides just as in training, to allow for efficient mutual defence.

'With fellows like these, it's a pleasure to do business,' I say to myself.

Our aircraft once again pass through the skies of Sinai, this time on their way home. In the small mirror in front of my face, I can see my eyes and forehead, peeping out between my helmet visor on top and the green oxygen mask over my nose and mouth. My lips twisted wryly in a smile of satisfaction, I exchange winks with the odd, familiar character, who is looking back at me from the mirror.

The aircraft slowly rolls into the fortified hangar, under the watchful eye of the signals mechanic and the pilot's control. I switch off the engine, put the security pins in their grooves, remove the helmet from my sweating head, and unhitch the parachute straps and seatbelt to which I was harnessed. I notice a bunch of mechanics excitedly gathering around and examining the plane's belly and left side.

I climb down the ladder, hand the helmet and rescue belt to the mechanic, and join the crowd. The usually smooth and handsome metal surface of the plane is now disfigured by five or six holes, two of them as big as a football. I'd been hit by anti-aircraft shells. 'They almost managed to screw me this time,' I mutter to myself. Those 'light blows' I'd felt when the plane passed over the target hadn't been so innocent after all. I'd come within a hair's breadth of an ignominious end to the mission. The debriefing at the squadron is conducted expeditiously; the war is still raging, and all the men scatter to their various affairs, especially concerned not to lose favour with the duty officer and be left on the ground instead of flying more missions.

Postscript: I will never be able to come up with an authoritative and reliable answer to the intriguing question of who was the mysterious voice who ordered 'Red' formation to break away. It shall remain a riddle.

CHAPTER SEVEN

Mount Tabor, 1952

I met Dan at the Tel Aviv central bus station, beside the Afula bus platform. I was fifteen-and-a-half, and Dan had just turned sixteen. The surprising decision – to leave the prestigious city high school and transfer to the 'Kaduri' agricultural school at the foot of Mount Tabor – was, surprisingly enough, my initiative. A spirit of adventure combined with the youth movement ideal of *hagshama* – fulfilment of the Zionist pioneer dream and way of life – and the charm of Father's profession, agronomy, the distance from home, as well as the slightly mysterious reputation of the Kaduri agricultural school, influenced my decision. Dan, my old and close friend, was easily tempted, and enthusiastically joined me.

The Afula 'central' bus station was small and dusty. Actually, it was nothing more than a narrow platform and parking space for two or three buses. Two heavily loaded GMC trucks were parked in the plaza in front of the station, their drivers gone, apparently, to grab something to eat. In the far corner of the plaza stood a cart hitched to two horses with bags of straw hanging from their heads, twitching their tails from time to time to get rid of the pestering flies. One kiosk, a haberdashery and a barbershop with three empty chairs and a drowsing barber completed the picture of the station plaza. No, this certainly didn't look like the busy centre of a big city . . .

We both got off at the station, each of us carrying a suitcase and bag. An hour later we were on another bus – slow, creaking, and unsightly – sitting in the springy back seat, on our way to Kfar Tavor, and from there to Kaduri. After a forty-five-minute drive, the bus stopped beside the huge eucalyptus trees and stone-paved road which led up to the school. We got off. The bus drove off, leaving behind a cloud of black smoke as it continued on its way to Sejera and Tiberias. Both our hearts were pounding in excitement as we trudged slowly up the road.

Dinner, in the dining hall in the large stone building, began punctually at seven o'clock. The second-formers occupied the left side of the dining hall, sitting crowded shoulder-to-shoulder, making merry and acting like they owned the place. When we, the first-formers, arrived in small groups, walking a little hesitantly as if we didn't know the way, the second-formers burst into song, bellowing loudly and in unison:

> First-former, you're just a bag of wind
> First-former, we'll take you for a spin
> First-former, watch out for your ass
> First-former, each time you make a pass

As they sang, they banged their fists on the tables in time to the song. This certainly added to the general overbearing impression they made on the new first-formers. The singing went on for another quarter of an hour, until one of the teachers, a Kaduri alumnus himself, came in. He asked for quiet, said a few words that nobody listened to, read out the last names of the students, who answered with a 'Yes' or a 'Present', and wished everyone a hearty appetite. The first-formers didn't seem to have much of an appetite at all . . .

For months before our arrival, stories had been circulating among us, the soon-to-be students of the first form, about the reception accorded to first-formers at Kaduri. Friends and friends of friends handed down legendary tales about the institution, telling us about the nights of the 'blues' – the heavy bedcovers that were employed to whip the newcomers on their first night. To tell the truth, the 'blues' had been replaced in the meantime and turned into the 'browns', but the name remained unchanged. For everything at Kaduri was governed by hallowed 'tradition'. We had also been told about the 'swearing-in' ceremony at which first-formers were admitted to the 'monastery' – for in those times only boys attended Kaduri, in a two-year study programme with only a first and second form, equivalent to the eleventh and twelfth grades in city high schools. And so there were two monasteries there: one atop the summit of Mount Tabor, and another, ours, at the foot of the mountain.

Dan and I were assigned to a room with Gideon and Gad, who were city boys like ourselves and members of the Mahanot Olim youth movement. The four of us immediately established a rapport and an easy companionship grew among us, which would only intensify and continue to weld us together during our two years of study at the school.

After dinner, before dispersing to our rooms to go to sleep, all the first-formers gathered in one of the rooms. There was tension in the air in anticipation of the 'surprises' that the night held in store. There was general agreement among the students that we would not 'be led like lambs to the slaughter', and that it was necessary 'to meet force with force'. The stronger members of our company were quickly identified, most of them muscular, work-hardened moshav boys, and it was decided that we would stand together in the face of the imminent 'threats'. Approaching midnight, a procession of rollicking second-formers arrived at the dormitory of the first form.

'First-formers, up on your feet!' the cry went around the rooms.

We all assembled in a long file and went down to the 'Cattle Deep', a rundown stone building at the bottom of the hill, which had once served as a place to bathe and wash the herd of cattle. There, in the dark, under the light of torches and the supervision of the second-formers, the ceremony was conducted, our 'swearing-in' to the 'monastery' of the Kaduri school and the institution's 'tradition of honour', the exact meaning of which was known only to the few . . .

When we all returned to the dormitories, the first-formers were given strange and peculiar nicknames, themselves the fruit of longstanding school tradition, such as 'Bellybutton', 'Joker' and the like.

At this stage tempers began to flare, and here and there blows were struck. The second-formers enjoyed the 'home court' advantage, superior social cohesion, and the clearcut physical ascendancy of seventeen-year-olds over sixteen-year-olds. We the first-formers, however, displayed a fighting spirit and a surprising level of cohesion, the product of shared jeopardy. At the end of the night it was decided that each class would appoint a fighter, and combat between the two representatives would decide the issue. Outside, in the open, the fifty students of the two classes assembled in a wide ring. With bare torsos, the two contenders met in the middle of the ring and the cockfight began, loudly cheered on by the onlookers. Amikam, a rangy and particularly robust moshav boy, represented the first form and restored some of our damaged honour. Two years later Amikam Richlin, a man among men, would be killed in combat on a mission with an elite IDF (Israel Defence Forces) unit.

However, before the fight could be decided, one of the school teachers emerged from the darkness and put an end to the night's activities. At three o'clock in the morning the last lights went out in both classes' dormitories. The students of 'Kaduri' had begun their school year.

Days and months went by. Our still boyish bodies grew tall and straight, our skin tanned, our muscles swelled, and the boys were quickly turning into men. Mount Tabor, Mescha (Kfar Tavor), Arab al Shibli, Bet Keshet, Sejera, Kfar Kama, the Turan Hills all became the immediate environment of our lives: the Galilean Land of Israel, rooted and vital, simple and captivating.

Each week the 'doctor' from Mescha, a large, fleshy man, would arrive on his routine visit to the school. He rode a big donkey, his legs dangling on either side, his brown, weather-beaten doctor's bag hanging strapped to his chest. The sight of this country doctor brought smiles to the faces of all the students, but it also struck a bit of fear in us. To tell the truth, we usually tried to avoid submitting to his ministrations.

On Saturday evenings, if we hadn't gone home, we would gather together after dinner and set out on foot to see a 'movie' in Kfar Tavor. At the corner of the road into the village, we passed 'the shop' – Pinchas' shop, 'Pini Tsibrochen', a prominent institution well known to every child in the settlement and in the district.

Two houses further on we would enter the backyard of a typical Mescha peasant dwelling. There, inside what was probably an old barn, benches were set out. The man who owned the place charged us a few cents a ticket. A creaking movie projector stood on a raised platform in the back with a translation machine beside it. When the movie began, the audience became an active participant in it. Cries of 'Look out behind you!' rang out to warn the hero of the bad guy waiting to ambush him. Others would be yelling, 'Translation, move it forward!', at the man running the translation machine, who could never synchronise the text with what the actors in the movie were saying. A couple of hours later the whole merry band, joking and laughing at the top of their voices, would make its way back to the school. Thus we bonded with the place and with each other, and we loved every minute of it.

Mutzi, Oded 'Shoshik' and Tanchum 'Murabba' came up the path of poplar trees, which led from the silo tower and the milking station to the stone main building of the agricultural school. Tanned from the sun in the fields, their hair ruffled and chests bared, they strode up the path. Bits of corn leaves and husks were glued to their hair and the sweat upon their bodies, which was drying quickly in the strengthening southern wind. The sun had dropped and was slipping past the slope of Mount Tabor. One after another, the rows of Galilean stone bricks that comprised the large building's upper storey came into view.

The voices of their classmates came drifting up from the plaza in front of the building. The pitch of the ascent abated, and a familiar sight greeted them. The students of the second form were lying, squatting and sprawling in a pile on the grass in the middle of the plaza. The students of the first form, our class, those of us who had finished our chores, were sitting in convivial disorder on the stone steps of the entrance to the building. This deployment, which began on the odd occasion when the first hot days came in the beginning of March, turned into the evening routine with the arrival of the hot *hamsin* days of April and May, and it was clear to everyone that it would continue to be the routine while the summer lasted.

From the narrow road encircling the hill on which the school stood came the rattle of the 'Massey-Harris', the red-brown wheeled tractor, towing an empty platform with bits of fresh straw scattered on it, indicating where it had come from. Sitting in the driver's seat, Dan expertly drove the tractor around the plaza and switched off the engine in the lot at the side of the road.

He leapt from the tractor just as Gadi, Arnon and I jumped off the platform, and all four of us joined the band of first-formers idling on the steps. Out through the school's main entrance came the second-formers Ehud, Zorik and Dror, joining the pile of their classmates on the grass. A pleasant breeze wafted down from Mount Tabor, and a heady, intoxicating atmosphere typical of the lower Galilee transfused our laughter and joking remarks.

> The Mustang shot from north to south like a storm. It passed over the roof of the stone building at the top of the wooded hill and only a few metres above the plaza. The pass was so low that the wind it raised behind it blew leaves off the poplar trees in front of the building. The fighter plane raised its nose with an ear-splitting shriek of its engine, turning in a steep dive, and almost disappeared momentarily, coming back again to pass above the group standing in stupefaction, mouths agape. As it turned towards the familiar, rounded summit of Mount Tabor, it wagged its wings right and left in farewell and disappeared where the Tabor monastery, aircraft and sun fused into a single blinding spot.

'Yak!' 'It's Yak!' the students excitedly cried. Some of them, myself included, jumped to our feet and ran to find better vantage points to view this spectacle, which sparked our imaginations.

Yacov 'Yak' Nevo was a graduate of the agricultural school, and the rumour of his attendance and success at the Air Force flight training academy course passed by word of mouth among the students. In suspense I watched the exhibition, which reminded me of an incident from childhood by the Tel Aviv shore. Again I found myself thrilled by the spectacular sight and thinking about the tiny man in the flying machine, and my heart leapt.

I could not have known then that 'Yak', and two other second-form students – Ehud and Zorik – who were among those lolling on the grass, would soon join me in the air. However, all three of them would be killed as pilots.

CHAPTER EIGHT

Fire – Aswan Skies,
14 August 1968

U ri, the squadron's reconnaissance officer, and I took off the grey overalls we'd worn for the routine training flight that had just ended. We put on our light khaki parade uniforms, and went down the stairs of the squadron building to the parking lot. Leaning against the balcony railing, Asher, my senior deputy, and Anat, the squadron's operations officer, followed us with their eyes.

It was by now a familiar process. The squadron commander and his recce officer would be summoned personally before Head of Operations at Air Force headquarters, for a 'briefing' – no explanations or clarifications, no hints, just a date and an hour. Something serious was afoot, that was for sure. I asked Uri to drive the pickup truck, and sat down next to him with a brief-case of papers that Anat had prepared for me to peruse on the way. The pickup drove off, leaving behind a cloud of thin smoke and the smell of incompletely burnt fuel. Anat and Asher went back about their business.

Asher Snir, experienced and competent, stepped over to the other side of the building and walked up to Alon the 'Chef,' the squadron's technical officer. 'What's the situation with the 98 and the 99?' he asked. 'Chef' didn't need any explanations. He went over to the aircraft roster-board and glanced down at the bottom of the list.

Those two aircraft, 98 and 99, were the darlings of the squadron. They were the most advanced spyplanes in the Israeli Air Force, the only ones of their kind. They were serviced by a select team of mechanics, and their maintenance regimen was especially exacting.

The entire team, without exception, was aware of the grave responsibility that they carried on their shoulders. These aircraft spent hundreds of hours each year flying behind enemy lines, inordinately more than any other Air Force aircraft, and the missions they performed were of the utmost operational importance. Furthermore, the cameras that they carried in their elongated, rather peculiar noses were expensive equipment, the most sophisticated of its kind in the world. It goes without saying that access to these planes, and likewise to the facilities and the laboratories adjacent to them, was restricted to authorised personnel only.

'The two planes are serviceable, but the "Adir" camera, one of the two used to perform low-altitude photography, is having its periodical checkup, which will take another week,' replied 'Chef' Alon.

'In my estimation,' said Asher, 'you haven't got more than seventy-two hours to finish the job.'

'No problem, we'll make do. Let me know just as soon as the picture clears.'

Asher smiled. He had never, but never, got a 'no' from 'Chef' Alon when an operation was on the line – if there was any way to solve the problem at hand, no matter how slim the possibility, he would find it.

After Asher left the technical officer's office, 'Chef' Alon flipped the switch on the intercom.

'Aryeh, can you hear me?' he asked.

'Yes, "Chef", what's the matter?'

'Cancel all leave for the photo-technicians team, and prepare to begin a special mission checkup of 98 and 99, starting this evening.'

'Roger, "Chef", will do,' answered Aryeh, signing off.

Yacov, Air Force head of operations, received us in his office and invited a senior intelligence officer to join the discussion. Maps were spread out on the large briefing table. I felt my heart skip a beat when I saw which ones were lying on the table this time. Prominent in the centre of the map was a thick dark line that almost split the map in half down the middle: the southern Nile Valley. A tight ring in red pencil circled the target – the Aswan High Dam.

Uri and I were well aware that our spyplanes did not have the capability of flying that far without making a stopover to reach such a distant target. The approach would require flying at low altitude, necessarily entailing a high level of fuel consumption. I traced the flight course marked on the map, and the solution struck my eyes: Ofir Airfield in Sharm el Sheikh.

Three months after the battles of the Six-Day-War subsided, Defence Minister Moshe Dayan visited the Sharm el Sheikh area. During the visit he toured the area, held discussions with the local commanders in regard to development plans, formulated his position on a number of issues and made several decisions, as is customary on such occasions.

As evening began to fall and the tour was coming to an end, the Minister and his entourage – which included Air Force head of operations – arrived at the small, dusty airfield north of the bay to fly back north to Israel. As they waited to board their light cargo-plane, the conversation turned to the issue of requisite air defence for the area. The Air Force officers who were there pointed out the difficulty of the mission, owing to the geographical remoteness of Sharm el Sheikh from Air Force bases in Israel's south.

'In fact,' they said, 'under the existing conditions we find it impossible to credibly carry out our mission.'

'What do you need to be able to carry it out?' asked the Minister.

'We need a regulation landing runway of two-and-a-half kilometres' length and elementary facilities beside it,' replied Yacov.

'So build an airfield!' Dayan offhandedly pronounced, as though he'd had the answer prepared beforehand. A hush fell upon the small shack at this far-seeing, unexpected reply. But the Air Force didn't lose any time. A year and three months after Dayan's visit to Sharm el Sheikh, the black asphalt landing strip was paved in its entirety, and the new facility had a name as well: Ofir Airfield.

'A small technical team from the squadron will deploy at Ofir Airfield the night before the mission, and be prepared to receive, fuel and outfit the planes for the mission, to send them out, and to receive them again on their return, on the way north,' Yacov explained.

'The flight course to the target will be taking you over the eastern desert at very low altitude. At a speed of 750 kph (446 knots), it should take you forty-five minutes each way. You'll be photographing the target from east to west at 500 feet (152 metres) above the ground,' he went on to elaborate.

The atmosphere at the briefing was intimate and informal. Analysis of the mission revealed four critical aspects during the course of its execution. The first of these involved the need to fly down the Red Sea, pass over the shoreline and enter the desert region using a method that would prevent early detection of the planes. The second was the particularly prolonged navigation at very low altitude over completely unfamiliar territory, following maps with which we had no experience and of whose accuracy we were not fully certain. The third was the flypast over a target de-fended by numerous anti-aircraft guns, at an altitude considered particularly vulnerable. Under these conditions, the element of surprise seemed to be a necessary and crucial condition. The fourth anticipated critical phase was the long flight back – after the planes would have been discovered, of course. Above everything hovered the question of performing a mission at such long range, when any effective control of the operational force on the part of Air Force Central Command would be minimal at best.

The briefing and concomitant discussions took several hours. Before we departed, Yacov took me aside and – using simple, direct language – expressed his confidence in our ability to carry out the mission, emphasising the need for absolute secrecy. When Uri and I set out on our way back to base it was already dark outside. Having been assigned a challenging mission, we were already burning with the familiar zeal – to execute it to perfection. As was our wont, on the way back to base we stopped at the 'Asa' steakhouse, where we were always given preferential treatment. We found it impossible to ignore the stark contrast between the routine of ordinary street-life and what was happening and about to happen in our own small circle.

The temperature at runway level at Ofir Airfield was close to 40°C. The two Mirages, painted in bright desert camouflage colours, had landed earlier that morning on the virgin black runway – the first operational landing of combat aircraft here. The flight from base to Ofir Airfield took place under strict radio silence. To prevent early detection, two other planes had taken off from base at the same time and then turned back north, at a high altitude that could be scanned by enemy radar, while from a predetermined point past Beersheba the two mission planes stayed at low altitude, hidden from the enemy's view. This manoeuvre was performed so that our two planes would not suddenly disappear, not to return, from the screens of the always-inquisitive Egyptian and Jordanian air controllers, thus arousing their suspicions.

Being the new squadron commander but a veteran Mirage pilot myself, I assigned Uri, the most experienced of the spyplane pilots in the Air Force, to be the leader of the formation, while I flew in the number two spot.

The head of the advance team of mechanics welcomed us at the parking lot and waited as we switched off the engines. This group of competent professionals, unconditionally devoted to their task, about twenty-five men altogether, took charge of the aircraft for the next thirty-six hours.

'How's the craft?' Ehud asked me, handing me the aircraft's logbook to sign.

'No problems!' I replied, as I removed the helmet from my head.

At the same time I saw Uri, in the cockpit of the plane parked on the other side of Ehud, give the thumbs-up signal to confirm that his craft was also serviceable. We knew, as do all veteran pilots, that our planes have souls of their own. Like the pilots so eager to fly them into battle, once they caught a whiff of combat these iron machines would perform flawlessly, without fault or delay. But, as always, we were surprised to discover how different their behaviour here was from their behaviour during routine practice . . .

The two of us stepped into the operations tent which had been pitched at the side of the aircraft parking lot. We opened the maps and sat down together to review the flight course and try to imagine what every minute of the mission would be like. We went over the details of the preflight briefing, devoting special attention to the table of 'events-responses' particularised for the mission: the list of mishaps likely to occur during such an intricate sortie, and the appropriate response to each. Uri, the formation leader, clarified some last details concerning the operation of the low-altitude camera system and kept at it until every loose end was tied up to his satisfaction. I carefully listened to everything he said like a dutiful number two, like a student, but also as his direct superior. He was the more experienced of the two of us, and the formation leader, but I had the responsibility of supreme command. It was a strange situation.

The torpid heat struck us in the face again when we stepped back out on the tarmac. The new runway was limited in length because of the terrain, and the combination of high temperatures and excessive take-off weight was turning a relatively routine take-off exercise into a problematic prospect. Another look at the take-off tables clearly showed that take-off, with the detachable fuel tanks absolutely full, would be difficult though possible. However, the planes could be expected to leave the runway near its very end, a situation that did not leave much room for error.

I handed my helmet to Yosko, the mechanic who greeted me, and did a routine tour of inspection around the aircraft. I clapped my hand against each of the gigantic fuel tanks beneath the Mirage's shiny wings, listening for the dull thud that indicated they were properly filled. I devoted particular attention to the jet's nose and the camera window in it, the shutters of which were open. The commander of photo-ops branch was at my side and handed me the camera logbook to sign separately, as required on such a mission.

As Uri and I were climbing up the ladders to our cockpits, two heavy CH-53 helicopters passed by east of the airfield, near the surface of the Gulf waters, making their typical dull roar. We knew that the helicopters were part of the mission force, and that their job was to take up position along the Red Sea, on standby to rescue us if necessary. Other forces, which we couldn't see, were deployed throughout the area to provide back-up communications, intelligence and control for our spearhead, the mission formation.

In the radio silence typical of espionage operations, Uri

slipped his plane over to the left side of the runway and stopped. I followed him and stopped to his right. An engine check at full throttle noisily shook the airfield's pastoral surroundings. I was satisfied with the check, which showed the engine to be working properly, and nodded my head at Uri, who was waiting in his cockpit for my confirmation. Two minutes of waiting and idling in neutral went by. At five seconds to take-off, the engines were revved to full throttle, and just as the second hand swept past its mark the leading plane shot forward, its afterburner making a thunderous noise as it immediately kicked in. I waited another ten seconds, and then I too began my take-off. As expected, the take-off run was especially long. At a certain stage some doubt even crept into my mind whether the length of the runway would suffice, or we'd erred in our calculations. I saw Uri's plane leave the runway right at its very end and stay at very low altitude. Now it was my turn. With the gentlest of touches I raised the nose of the long aircraft and left the runway not more than 200 metres (219 yards) from its end. I took advantage of the leader's turning a little to the left and then back right to join him in open formation, phased slightly backwards. Our journey beyond the dark mountains had begun.

We flew south down the middle of the Red Sea, a particularly spellbinding region because of the striking contrast between the blue, almost purple waters and the yellow cliffs of the shoreline. An unplanned left turn by the leader away from our course drew my attention. Looking ahead, I immediately discovered the reason for this diversion. Against the horizon I could make out a ship, over which our planned flight-course would directly have taken us.

'An old fox and experienced leader, that Uri,' I thought to myself. Such a ship could blow our mission's secrecy if it spotted us passing and reported us to the enemy.

The time had come to turn right towards land. I slipped from Uri's right to his left side as we turned west towards the shore-line. I saw Uri guide his aircraft towards a spot where the mouth of a large wadi interrupted the chain of cliffs along the shore. The two planes crossed the waterline and began to follow the rising terrain. This was at a point not far from Port Sudan, really off the beaten track . . .

We were both acutely alert to anything happening along the shoreline and in its immediate vicinity. A previously unspotted radar station, a squad of lookouts deployed near the beach, a military force that might happen to be there accidentally, even a citizen with a telephone or wireless connection – any of these could prematurely trigger a warning and arouse the entire Egyptian air-defence network. But there was only wilderness around us. Not a living thing could be seen, to our delight.

'Clock, map, terrain,' I recited the refrain I'd learned during my first navigation lessons at flight training academy. Clock – check the exact time; map – find the place on the map that corresponds to this exact time, and locate a feature suitable for identification half-a-minute ahead; terrain – identify your precise location in the terrain, in relation to the planned course and timetable. This procedure would be repeated another ten times, or maybe even twenty, during the next half-hour.

I divided my attention between navigating, which was more the leader's responsibility than my own, and the task of looking around and providing mutual cover that my role demanded. After all, where we were flying, nobody but us was in direct control of the situation. We were far beyond the range of the Israeli radar network, and even basic radio communication was doubtful. All around us lay wilderness: huge wadis, chains of hills, some of them rather high, and endless expanses of desert. In any event, twice during the long flight we discovered traces of a human presence. In one case it was a site that looked like an inoperative workers' camp, and in the second case, three vehicles raising clouds of dust in their wake, to our right at no great distance from the aircraft. That was it.

Now the terrain below us began to drop away, moderately at first, then more rapidly. A grey mist covered the entire landscape ahead of us. The southern, upper Nile Valley lay ahead, approaching at a speed of 750 kph (466 knots). The requirement to stay hidden at low altitude, which had been critical until now, was superseded all at once by our commitment to performing the mission flawlessly. This was the task at hand in the coming moments, putting aside all other considerations.

'Grey formation, pull!' Uri commanded, and his aircraft rose from close to the ground to an altitude of 800 feet (244 metres). I understood that the reasoning behind Uri's decision to climb slightly higher than planned was to achieve greater coverage, at the cost of greater risk. Now the planes passed all at once from the yellowish, denuded desert terrain to the dark, brown-grey lands on either side of the river. They passed precisely above the last map reference prior to the target.

'Grey, roll the cameras!' Uri commanded, and we both flipped the switch to operate the cameras.

Everything I had ever heard or read about the Aswan High Dam was now dwarfed by the sight that greeted me. It wasn't a 'big' dam – it was huge, of tremendous size, far beyond anything I ever imagined. A steep, towering wall, incredibly wide, dropped sheer to the north, a sprawling lake behind it to the south, and a camp for mechanical equipment and many other installations scattered throughout the surrounding area. A glance at the cockpit instrument panel showed me that the camera was operating as it should. The entire picture-taking course slipped behind us in a flash, within twenty seconds. Over, but not quite done yet.

'Grey, stop!' Uri ordered, turning right, to the north, in the desert wastes on the other side of the Nile Valley, putting distance between ourselves and the defences near the dam site. Then we completed another turn, this time to the east, retracing our course. At low altitude we once again crossed the Nile Valley, leaving behind us this entrancing region, enveloped in its grey watery mists, and returned to the barren wilderness.

So far as we could tell from our cockpits, we had achieved absolute surprise, and the mission had been accomplished without anyone having had time to respond at the time and place of its execution. The tension began to subside on the way back. Now we faced one final dilemma: on one hand, the fuel supply situation dictated that we seek high altitude as soon as possible, but on the other hand, the presence of Egyptian interceptors in their air force bases along the Red Sea shore compelled us to avoid discovery by Egyptian radar by continuing to fly at relatively low altitude. If they were to scramble due to accurate warning, they could easily block our course back home.

'Green leader, this is Grey, do you read me?' Uri called to the leader of the formation of cover and relay aircraft, now flying somewhere above the central Sinai peninsula.

'I read you, Grey. Emerald. I repeat: emerald.'

'Read you loud and clear: emerald,' Uri confirmed. Scanning the list of codes on his knees, he found the meaning of 'emerald': 'active enemy aircraft in the arena'. From my cockpit, I quietly followed everything that was being said and done.

Meanwhile, we continued to fly at low altitude despite the fuel problem in view of the notification just received, which meant that interceptors had been scrambled against us, apparently from the Egyptian airbase at Ardaka on the Red Sea shore, opposite Sharm el Sheikh. I knew that our ability to continue flying at this low, ostensibly safe altitude was limited in time. Twelve minutes later, Uri announced: 'Green, two minutes to *merkava*' – which meant that he would have to begin climbing in another two minutes.

'I read you, Grey. You are go for *merkava* in two minutes.'

It was clear to me that Green formation, a pair of Mirages from the northern squadron, would now be forwarded to our vicinity to lure away the Egyptian planes and even shoot them down if the situation should warrant it – anything to ensure the spyplanes' safe passage back to our airspace.

When the planes began to climb, the desert landscape fell away below and behind us and our field of view rapidly widened. The northern part of the Red Sea came into sight, its tip split into two 'fingers', the Gulf of Suez stretching north-west and the Gulf of Aqaba stretching north-east, and the island of Shadwan nestled down in the corner between them. At an altitude of about 10,000 feet (3048 metres), communication was established between the returning formation and the control unit. From that moment on the controller, after greeting us with a hearty 'Welcome back!', began to direct us on a course back to Ofir Airfield, keeping us away from any undesirable contact with the Egyptians.

On the secondary radio channel, to which I switched merely out of curiosity, I heard the controller guide Green formation in the direction of the Egyptian planes and prepare possibly to engage them. I heard the voice of Even, my friend and the commander of the northern squadron, and hoped for his sake that battle would be joined, as he so ardently wished. From the tone of the voices, it could be inferred that the situation was heating up. Our own aircraft were already above the Red Sea waters when we heard the controller instructing Green formation to turn away and break contact with the Egyptian MiGs. In a disappointed tone of voice, the Green formation leader confirmed his instructions and turned northwards back home.

We gently touched down our planes at the end of the shiny black runway in Sharm el Sheikh. We taxied and parked the planes in the lot. The mechanics, every last one of them, were waiting on the tarmac. Without asking questions that would have gone unanswered in any event, they all knew that a flight out of Ofir Airfield and return to it, lasting an hour-and-a-half, under a heavy mantle of secrecy was no trifling matter. To the extent that we could, the two of us explained to the crews that everything had been successfully accomplished, and we were accorded an enthusiastic reception. The strong embrace between myself, the squadron commander, and Uri, the formation leader and the squadron's ace 'photographer', served as ultimate proof to everyone there that a highly significant mission had indeed been carried out to perfection. While the planes were being re-fuelled, the two CH-53s arrived with a loud roar of their rotor-blades and landed on the runway. Nehemia, leader of the CH-53 formation, stepped inside the operations tent and joined the ranks of well-wishers greeting the operational force.

At ten o'clock that evening Uri, Asher and I got into the squadron pickup truck and drove to Tel Aviv. At the entrance to an innocent-looking house, we showed our credentials to a soldier on duty there. Two minutes later, a colonel in Air Force intelligence ushered us into the central photo-lab. After our eyes grew accustomed to the dim red light in the room, we were invited over to the deciphering desks. Together with the lab commander, the three of us bent over and examined the fresh photographs, stunning in content and in quality. There was no need for words: the photographs showed everything, but every-thing!

CHAPTER NINE

Mount Tabor, 1953

I held the letter in my hand and my heart leapt in excitement. Noa would be coming on Saturday. I read the letter, then reread it again and again. The memory of the touch of her flesh beneath my fingers that evening two weeks ago on the bank of the Yarkon, spread through my body like fire. The summer was at its peak. The students of the second form had finished their studies and gone their separate ways. A small group of those who had been first-formers until two weeks earlier, myself among them, stayed behind as caretakers of the school farm for part of the summer vacation. An atmosphere of high-handed proprietorship enveloped the handful of young men who had stayed behind atop the green-brown hill, surrounded by fruit-laden groves of trees.

Last spring, in the eucalyptus forest of Hadera, I had touched her for the first time. We had known each other for years already in the youth movement, taken part in activities, talked about this and that, taken trips and argued about the weightiest issues, but I had never gathered sufficient courage to express my feelings towards her. On Saturday nights we would both wait for a 'legitimate' opportunity to dance together hand in hand, but I always put off 'my petition' until 'next week'. At the agricultural school I dreamt about her at night and thought about her during the day.

I left the agricultural school in sandals, blue shorts and a pressed white shirt to attend the finale of the youth movement congress, which was held at the clubhouse in Hadera. As I approached the clubhouse courtyard, from afar my eyes were already scanning the boys and girls milling about inside it. I inhaled sharply when I caught sight of Miri, Noa's hulking 'bosom' buddy, 'cruising' around the court-yard. Like the swallow that is the harbinger of spring, so Miri betokened Noa's presence to me.

That night, when people began to scatter for bed, I went up to her. 'Shall we go?' I asked. With an understanding nod she immediately assented. We walked together quietly beside the railroad tracks, going west, at first a bit distant from each other, then closer and closer together. On our way we crossed the main highway to Haifa and continued to pace, to hover, through magical orange groves. Our legs took us farther and farther, all the way to the eucalyptus trees. The pleasant nip of the air and the fragrance of the trees wrapped around us and brought us close together. With barely a word exchanged, we found ourselves holding each other. We embraced, plunging together into the depths of a love we had never known before. Through touch, our hands felt our bodies' aching desire for one another.

I felt her back writhe around me. I smelled her hair, filling my nostrils, I felt her nipples rise in response to my touch, and a feeling of joy swept over me. We wordlessly shed our clothes, pressed against each other and became one body, in a supreme rush of sensations. For hours we stayed there, scarcely comprehending, perhaps dreaming, bathing in the scent of our bodies and the aroma of trampled eucalyptus leaves beneath us.

The first rays of dawning sunlight and the chirping of the awakening birds brought us back to reality. Hugging each other and radiant with love, we walked back to Hadera along the path through the orange groves. Smack in the middle of the empty, deserted Haifa-Tel Aviv highway, right in the centre of the roundabout, I gathered her in my arms and kissed her lips. We laughed at the thought of how crowded this very spot would be with people and traffic in another two hours.

I returned the letter to the pocket of my shorts and went over to the tractor. The Caterpillar D-2 had arrived at the school a few weeks earlier. I, like many of my friends and some of the school teachers, gathered around to see the new, advanced tractor being unloaded from the truck that brought it there. Bespectacled Dan, director of the crop-farming programme, was the man of the hour. He strutted about like a bridegroom, brandishing the wonderful piece of equipment's instruction manual in his hand, feeling like a giant despite his low stature, which was always a source of profound annoyance to him. When the truck went on its way, Dan took control of the proceedings, switched on the tractor, and drove it with appropriate dignity into the heavy machinery shed. Furthermore, soft drinks, cookies and fragrant muscat grapes were served to everyone present.

I was no longer a boy. I felt the great rapidity of the change in me from a boy to a young man, both outside and inside. Work in the fields had tanned my skin, burnt the ends of my hairs, broadened my shoulders, stabilised my feet's grip on the ground, and emphasised the light colour of my eyes against the background of my sunburnt face. Along with my external appearance came maturity and wisdom. As time passed, I easily felt how I was coming to gain recognition among my friends and teachers. To be truthful, this was a feeling I loved. I liked the feeling of having people around me listen to what I said, respect my opinion, trust me, and not hesitate to entrust me with particularly responsible tasks when necessary.

I took the flexible rope, wrapped it around the flywheel of the secondary engine, and breathed life into it with a single, powerful tug. The small engine began to run until its revolutions steadied properly. With an expert hand, I now opened the diesel fuel tap to the main engine. The plastic cup attached to the fuel-pipe immediately filled. I now gripped the Z-shaped steel handle and pushed it forward. The secondary engine's revolutions subsided somewhat, while the noise it made swelled due to the strain placed upon it. A light puff of smoke came out of the exhaust pipe. The tractor's primary engine groaned once or twice and began to run, all of the huge tractor shuddering beneath it. Now a heavy cloud of black smoke blew out of the pipe. When the main engine settled into its rhythm, the black smoke disappeared high above and the whole contraption began making a new kind of noise, monotonous and pleasant. I detached the handle connecting the two engines, closed the fuel tap to the secondary engine, and listened to it shut down.

Moyshik, who was standing beside me, climbed up to his post alongside the haystacker harnessed to the tractor. The piles of hay collected in recent days were arranged in rows down the length of the large field. I coupled the transmission to the stacker and the procession set out on its way. The flexible steel teeth of the rake tossed the piles of hay into the stacker's belly, raising a huge amount of dust. Moyshik, whose face and shoulders were already covered wth dust, slipped the dust-glasses over his eyes and kept watch over the stacker's operation. The two coils of yellow rope could be seen dancing and turning on their axles, the ropes snaking out from them and wrapping around the bales of hay being stamped and prodded, with regularly spaced blows, behind and out of the machine.

Our shift ended close to noon. From the direction of the school, Arnon and Gadi showed up to replace us. When they drew near, I stopped the tractor at the edge of the field. I gazed in satisfaction at the ground, which had been cleared of piles and filled instead with bales of hay scattered in rows, the product of our morning's labour. The four of us chatted a bit and then took leave of each other. As the rumble of the stacker drew away from us down the furrows of the field, Moyshik and I climbed the hill in the school's direction.

A hot noontime wind was blowing from the west. The hill stood swooning in the heat, and the farm was still. I excitedly strode down the path to the road. I passed the barn and cowsheds and saw Victor, the huge mule, shamble over to the half-full feeding-trough, swatting away flies with his tail.There wasn't much love lost between us. Two weeks after I arrived at the school, a raw first-former, I tried to harness him to a wheeled platform. Victor, who could smell a novice a mile away, planted a vicious kick to my ribs – the kind of blow that leaves a purplish-green mark and aches grievously for a couple of weeks. Thus I learned the hard way never to approach the backside of the recalcitrant mule, towards whom I nursed an enmity and desire for revenge . . . I continued down the path until the intersection, where I sat down in the shadow of two large oak trees, waiting for the bus from the direction of Mescha.

In the morning I had gone to Mrs Wax, who was in charge of the infirmary and fond of me for some reason, and asked her for the key to the infirmary that evening. I knew there was a wide bed there and I would be able to enjoy my privacy with Noa. I fell into a drowsy stupor and didn't hear the bus arrive. When I opened my eyes, I saw Noa's eyes smiling down at me. I was embarrassed and confused, and uncertain how to handle the situation

It was Noa who gathered her wits about her and took matters in hand.'Where to now?' she asked. We climbed the path up the hill and slipped away into the infirmary on the building's third floor. While she showered I stood there, half-naked, and looked out of the window towards Mount Tabor, which was growing dark as the shadows lengthened. On its lower slopes stood the white houses of the village of Arab al Shibli, which looked so pretty nestled among the thickets and fruit-groves surrounding them. I was tense and anxious in anticipation of the impending encounter, which I had ceaselessly pictured during the past weeks. When she emerged and came towards me, clean and fresh, drops of water still clinging to her body and a smile on her face, I felt my heart pound and my knees go weak. We embraced each other and sank down into the inviting white sheets.

In the evening, under the light of a half-moon, I took her to my magical secret hideout. Past the road we climbed a path that twisted up the hills. After two turns we left the familiar, everyday world behind us. I went on leading her down the path I knew so well. After circling the hill of oak trees we descended into a small gulley. To our ears came the sound of the spring waters, which collected there in a pool and flowed downward in a thin trickle. Around the spring stood fruit-laden fig trees, grapevines bearing luscious bunches of grapes interwoven among them in stunningly beautiful disorder. Ponderous pomegranate trees, cactus shrubs, a raspberry bush and two cherry trees completed the picture – a veritable Garden of Eden.

Until the moon dropped low in the west we lay there, in a cosy thicket that I'd discovered deep inside the garden. Our bodies were becoming familiar with each other and our hands avidly sought out their delectable mysteries, as together we experienced the heights of pleasure and grace. The yelps of jackals calling from faraway hills, the whoops of the wise owl and the gentle fluttering of bats' wings accompanied us as we walked and danced our way back down the twisting path to the white building on top of the hill.

CHAPTER TEN

Fire – 'Texas' Skies, 24 June 1969

Gilad and I were stretched out on our beds in the bunker beneath the old Egyptian control-tower, which had been demolished during the taking of Bir-Gafgafa, the Egyptian base we had renamed Refidim. Two hours of morning twilight standby – which obliged us to sit in the aircraft cockpits, harnessed to our seats and ready for take-off within a minute-and-a-half – were behind us.

Second Lieutenant Tamar, the new, brown-skinned, blue-eyed, stunningly beautiful operations officer, and Orna, our short, beaming wing secretary, joined us for the breakfast that the two of us prepared on the spot. A well-seasoned green salad, scrambled eggs, toast made from slices of army-issue bread and coffee with halva were a fitting rejoinder to the appetite we'd built up during the standby.

Since receiving my fighter pilot's wings in 1959 I'd spent many hundreds of hours sitting inside the cockpit – mornings, evenings, nights, periods of heightened alert, during missions, and every time the control network discovered a threat, real or imaginary, which required it.

Going into standby mode had become such a practised exercise that I was able to perform it flawlessly with my eyes shut. Over my body went a pair of light overalls, covered by the relatively heavy anti-G suit. In the pockets of the suit rattled a variety of rescue equipment such as a revolver, a 'Sara' wireless transmitter for locating a downed pilot, commando knife, small canteen or two of water, tiny flashlight, map and communication codes, and other items a pilot might find useful. In my left hand I held my helmet.

A pilot's helmet is a personal accessory of inestimable value to its wearer. From the start the helmet is moulded with its internal dimensions perfectly adapted to the pilot's head, in order to perform its job – protecting the skull from impact or injury. Over time the skull and the helmet become used to each other, like a hand and well-worn glove. Add to that your personal scent, and the picture of a growling panther or winged hawk that the artist among the squadron pilots has affixed to the white background, and what you get is a perfect bond between man and object . . .

We left our cockpits at 7.20 am. Over the runway telephone, which communicated directly with the control station, I asked for authorisation to stand down. I heard the controller's voice over the earphones, and authorisation was duly given. Another do-nothing morning, I thought to myself. I took off my helmet and laid it down on the cockpit canopy, without disconnecting it from the communication system and the oxygen pipe. This arrangement would save me fifteen seconds if and when the standby bell rang and the order was given to scramble immediately. From experience I knew that these few seconds could make all the difference between meeting or missing the enemy planes. I stepped across to the crew of mechanics in the shed beside the standby hangar, exchanged some banter with them, warmly hailed Hemy, the head of the team beloved by all, and slowly walked towards the bunker.

The smell of burnt toast and hot coffee greeted me in the doorway. We sat down, the four of us, on wooden chairs around the simple, army-issue metal table, and the room filled with the pleasant atmosphere of friendly conversation and the occasional outburst of joking laughter. On a crate in the corner of the room stood a transistor radio tuned to the IDF station, which was broadcasting familiar tunes, though the sound was of poor quality. The sedate group was joined by Zvika, base commander at the time. He brought with him the morning newspapers, which had arrived by cargo-plane a while earlier. I had known Zvika for a long time. He, a veteran himself, was happy with my appointment as head of the Mirage squadron. We enjoyed getting together and talking about our past, our future, and what was going on in the force and in the army. Tamar got up, stepped over to the radio and fiddled with the reception, which significantly improved the sound of Arik Einstein's voice.

> As I was talking with Zvika, I followed Tamar with my eyes. I'd be loath to admit it, but though I made an effort to appear nonchalant, I was bursting with admiration for this young woman, her comportment, her powers of expression, and her beauty.

The black field-telephone near the radio emitted a clipped series of rings. Gilad, who was closest to it, leapt as though bitten by a snake and picked it up. 'Scramble!' he yelled, tossing the receiver aside and galloping outside. I leapt to my feet and ran after him, sending bits of food flying in all directions. As we were passing the bunker threshold the siren went off throughout the interceptor station area. The mechanic, who had previously been lounging in the shade beneath the plane, greeted me with the rescue-jacket in his arms. I slipped my two arms into it in a single motion and, without stopping, climbed up the four rungs of the yellow steel ladder. As I was lowering my bottom to the seat, in my two hands I took the helmet from the canopy in front of me and placed it on my head. I could immediately hear the background noise of the runway telephone.

'Red one, on air!' I announced without preamble or supplement.

'Red, scramble, azimuth: two, four, zero!' replied the controller. With three metallic clicks I locked the ejector seat straps, which were thrust into my hands by the mechanic. He finished removing another two security pins and attaching another strap, tapped twice on my helmet, cleared the ladder in a single leap, slipped it out of the slots from which it was hanging on the plane's side, and moved aside. With a finger of my left hand I gave the ground crew the circular signal which meant 'ignition'. I noticed that the mechanic and armourer were already standing to one side and giving me the thumbs-up. I pressed the ignition switch. The familiar outburst of compressed air was heard immediately, but weakened and turned into a dull roar when I closed the canopy and shut myself inside the small, crowded, but immensely practical cockpit.

The tremendous engine turbine revved up, slowed slightly

and accelerated again, until the engine settled into its characteristic idling rhythm. Meanwhile, all the red warning lights on the
instrument panel went out, one after another, a clear indication
that all systems were functioning properly. I taxied towards the
runway. Out of the corner of my eye, I could see number two
begin to move behind me. Without slowing, I turned onto the
runway and aligned the plane's nose with it, opened up full-
throttle, and twisted the handle left to turn on the afterburner. I
felt the concussion of the afterburner and the aircraft's forward
acceleration. A gentle tug of the stick and the nose of the aircraft
rose, obscuring my view of the end of the runway in front of me.
Another tug and the plane left the runway. I threw the landing
gear handle, visually confirmed that the wheels had risen, and
turned left immediately in the direction of the Suez Canal.

Four minutes of flight-time at an altitude of 20,000 feet (6100
metres) allowed us to finish our preparations in the cockpit,
check the status of all systems and activate all armament
switches, as the situation demanded – an aerial dogfight being
likely to ensue at a moment's notice.

'Red, Tempo formation has engaged west of Suez. I'm taking
you there. Combat channel: fourteen green!' came the familiar
voice of the interceptor controller.

'Texas' was the code-name for the barren desert expanses
south-west of the town of Suez, an area where dozens of
dogfights between Israeli and Egyptian fighter planes took place.
The name came to me in a moment of inspiration during one of
the squadron's merry evenings, when we were all sitting
crowded together on a beach beside the Sea of Galilee, watching
an old, scratchy western projected on a sheet hanging from the
side of our truck. The name quickly stuck and was adopted
unconditionally by all the squadrons in the force.

'Red, prepare to drop detachable tanks. Channel fourteen green,
go!' I order. Over the radio I can hear the voices of the pilots
engaged in battle, loud and clear.
   'Tempo two, I'm above you, carry on.'
   'One, break away, he's behind you, range 2000.'
   'Eye contact, I can handle him. Carry on with yours.'

The voices resound excitedly, the speech is hurried – there is no time now for superfluities.

'Red, the fight is at your eleven o'clock, low, range six miles (9.7 km). They seem to be a quartet,' the controller reports.

'Red, drop tanks, check switches!' I order my formation.

'Tempo, this is Red. We're above you at 15,000, have made eye contact,' I now report to the leader of Tempo formation, who is engaged in combat below us.

'Roger, Red, I read you. We've got one down, three more still here.'

I recognise the voice of Oded Marom, my good friend and the commander of our sister squadron in Hazor Airbase. Far below me I catch sight of a Mirage in a tight turn facing a pair of MiGs, which are flying in very close formation.

'Tempo one from two, my MiG has disengaged. I'm turning back. Report your altitude,' Tempo two now calls to his leader, Oded.

The battle picture is completely clear to me now. The lone jet below us is the leader of Tempo formation, who is chasing after the MiGs in a tight turn. By my calculation, Tempo formation doesn't have much time left. In another twenty to thirty seconds they will have to switch off their fuel-guzzling afterburners and vacate the area. Furthermore, in my estimation no quick conclusion is imminent between the Mirage below me and the pair of MiGs. Number two and I continue circling above the three jets locked in a battle for their lives, 10,000 feet (3048 metres) of altitude between us.

'Red from Tempo one, I'm turning with the pair, but not in firing position. A bit short on fuel, will have to disengage shortly,' Oded's report to me fully confirms my suppositions.

'Roger, Tempo one. I'm coming down on them from above, watch out!' I announce.

I roll my plane towards an imaginary spot exactly in the centre of the turn of the MiGs and lower my plane's nose almost vertically downward, manoeuvring my way into a firing position from an unexpected direction, with which the MiGs, I figure, have no chance of contending. I switch off the afterburner and reduce engine power for a few seconds so as not to pass over my adversaries at much too great a speed.

'Red, this is Tempo one. I see you, I'm breaking contact,' comes the much anticipated notification from Oded.

'Red two, are you with me?' I ask.

'With you all the time. You're clear, carry on,' Gilad coolly answers.

The final and decisive stage is now rapidly approaching. It is clear to me that the fate of the two MiGs, which have already been thoroughly exhausted by their recent encounter with Tempo formation, is sealed. At a range of 700 metres (766 yards) I turn on the afterburner again and make my turn as tight as possible. Once again I perceive that slight greyness in my eyes, which appears due to the immense G-force stemming from the sharp turn at high speed. Now it seems that the MiGs have discovered the new enemy pouncing on them. Suddenly, without any warning, the nose of the rear MiG, the one closest to me, rises sharply and the aircraft immediately rears up perpendicularly and then rolls over and plunges downwards, apparently out of control.

'Two, take him!' I order Gilad and continue closing in on the lead MiG.

At a range of 400 metres (438 yards) the sights align with the front section of the MiG's fuselage, next to the cockpit. Still too far. I wait and allow the distance between us to shorten even more.

'This MiG's flying days are over . . .' I mutter to myself. At a range of about 280 metres (306 yards), I squeeze the cannon trigger and release a thundering, lethal burst of fire. Two flashes at the base of the MiG's right wing turn the entire jet into a flaming torch at blinding speed. I pull upwards and pass directly over the burning MiG. It's all over.

'Red two, your location and altitude,' I call to my number two.

'I'm low at your nine o'clock. My MiG's pilot ejected and the plane hit the ground,' Gilad reports.

'Red formation, your azimuth home: zero, seven, zero. All clear. Go to altitude 25,000 and report results,' the controller is heard again.

It is only now that I feel the intensity of my excitement. My throat is dry and raspy, my heartbeat is racing, and all my senses are extraordinarily alert. Gilad joins me at very close range, only a few metres apart, nods his head and raises his left fist in congratulations. I answer him with a gesture of folded hands. The few minutes it takes to fly back to base suffice to bring our minds and bodies back to 'normal'.

'Refidim tower, this is Red formation, asking permission to buzz you,' I request the control-tower.

'Red, permission granted,' replies the controller, who has immediately comprehended the impending report.

In close formation we pass only a few metres above the interceptor station next to the control-tower, raise our noses at a steep angle, and perform a precisely timed victory roll.

The group of squadron mechanics, joined by soldiers and officers from the base, crowd around the aircraft hangar and await our entry. Whooping and waving enthusiastically, they push the aircraft into their parking slots. Gilad and I are carried down on upraised arms and greeted by claps of congratulations on the back and handshakes from everybody there. As is my wont, I gather the mechanics together and tell them about the dogfight and its outcome. I know that in this way I can make them feel like an inseparable part of the collective accomplishment, and make their efforts seem meaningful. It is such a small effort on my part, but to what a fruitful end.

> As soon as I rose out of the cockpit, I caught sight momentarily of Tamar. She was standing together with Zvika and Orna, but slightly apart from them, and waved her palm at me in congratulations, though bashfully. We locked eyes for a brief moment.

The mechanics went about the business of refitting the aircraft. Gilad and I sat down in the corner with the intelligence officer to fill in a full debriefing report. We were interrupted by the telephone.

'The Air Force commander wants to speak to you,' I was told by Orna, who took the call first.

'Sir!' I said. On the other end of the line was General Motti Hod, Israeli Air Force commander. We spoke freely, without any hint of the distance between us in miltary rank. I described the incident to the commander in detail, was asked a few questions and gave him my replies, and hung up the telephone.

Zvika, the Refidim base commander, who had left the spot earlier after giving me a robust handshake, now asked for me on the telephone.

'Amos, the chief of staff, Haim Barlev, is visiting the armoured division based next to us, and he is asking you to report to him.' I summoned Gilad and the two of us got into the jeep at our disposal.

Five minutes later we entered the office of the division commander. Six or seven high-ranking officers, all of them veterans of the armour corps, were sitting around the table and relaxedly talking. Among them I recognised Haim Barlev and Shlomo 'Cheech' Lahat. I saluted, and the chief of staff invited us to sit down and tell them about the dogfight that had just taken place. Quietly, with precision and the requisite measure of detail, I reported on the battle and its outcome. I could easily sense the curiosity – in part professional and in part simple human interest – with which my report was received. We were asked another two or three questions on the personal level, saluted again, turned on our heels and went back to our lodgings.

During the twenty-four hours after the battle, the standby siren was heard several more times, and one time we were even scrambled to the Canal arena to mount an uneventful patrol down the length of it, without entering into any real hostile contact. I was witness to an increasingly complex situation that developed within the squadron. On one hand, the entire unit demonstrated a practical, professional and serious attitude towards the ongoing hostilities, which contributed to the quality of the debriefings and to constant and fruitful progress on the part of us all; on the other hand, among the pilots a sort of gung-ho atmosphere took hold, spiced with a measure of personal competition, which could relatively easily have deteriorated into a lack of control accompanied by disasters and defeats. I knew that only the right combination of aggression and discipline, of ardour for combat with an uncompromising professionalism and the restraint of personal whims, could maximise achievement and keep breakdowns at bay. I tried with all my might to locate the golden mean and not deviate from it.

*   *   *

That afternoon two other pilots arrived by Cessna transport plane to relieve us. I briefed Eitan, the replacement leader and my deputy squadron commander at the time, drawing his attention in particular to the 'heating-up' of the arena in the wake of the recent dogfight. I did not forget to mention additional technical details that might enhance our chances of achieving a decisive outcome in any coming engagement and improve the safety of our people, to whatever extent possible.

I picked up the telephone to the control-tower and asked for Tamar.

'This is Tamar speaking,' her melliferous voice came to my ear.

'Tamar, it's Amos.' We exchanged a few pleasantries.

'I recall from our conversation yesterday that you're supposed to be going north for the weekend,' I said. 'In another hour we'll be flying north in a light Cessna plane. You're invited to join us, if it suits you.'

'I'll check and get right back to you,' she said.

A short while later she called back and gratefully confirmed that she would be joining us.

Fear and excitement fused in my heart. I could feel how this servicewoman was taking possession of my entire being, and I had neither the ability nor the desire to stem the tide. On the way home, worldly-wise Gilad retired to the back seat and immediately fell asleep. Up front I talked with Tamar, who sat close to me, about a thousand trifling matters. I showed her interesting sites along our route north, which looked entrancing at this twilight hour, as we passed near them at low altitude.

There was a pleasant warmth between us, and the slight, seemingly accidental contact of hands contributed as well to the feeling of intimacy. When we touched down at Tel Nof Airbase, I drove her to the hitchhikers' platform. When I turned to drive away I could already feel the longing I was leaving behind. I wondered whether I'd ever see her again.

CHAPTER ELEVEN

Flight Training Academy, 1956

'Contact!' shouted the sweaty mechanic in a loud voice after a turn of the crank brought the flywheel to the necessary speed to turn on the engine of the yellow steerman biplane. With a peculiar creaking noise the engine engaged and the propeller began to turn irregularly on its axis. The gigantic round engine, which had been just a mute and clumsy lump of metal until an instant ago, uttered its first coughing noise, then a second and a third, and came to life. A cloud of grey smoke billowed out of the thick exhaust pipe. It covered the exposed pilots' cockpits in a gloom that smelled of partially burnt fuel, and immediately blew away to the rear in the blast of air from the propeller. The engine had survived the trauma of ignition and turned into a living creature, thundering with an ear-splitting but rhythmical noise.

I had already once had a taste of taking off in an aircraft – but of taking off without landing. Two years earlier, six times in the course of a week, I and thirty of my comrades in the Nachal paratroopers unit had been packed aboard a DC-3 Dakota aircraft. We had screamed 'Hi-ho, hi-ho' in masculine voices under the direction of a parachuting instructor as the plane took off, and had been thrust outside with a push ten minutes later on a practice jump to the sand dunes of Rishon Letsion. That had been the sum of my flight 'education' to date, and other than that I had never flown.

Now I paced excitedly towards the aircraft for my first real flight. I wore a pair of coarse khaki overalls, an old, worn flight-jacket and warm flight-boots. I advanced towards the plane with the pilot's parachute harnessed to my back, dangling beneath my backside and banging into the back of my legs at every step. All the preparations, all the lessons, all the exercises – none of it sufficed to prevent the feeling of confusion that held me in its grip during these moments. 'Familarisation flight' was written in my personal logbook, in the top row of the first volume.

Lieutenant Zvika, whose face I was glad to discover protruding out of the rear cockpit in the mirror above my head, signalled something to the mechanic with a thumbs-up gesture. The mechanic disappeared beneath the biplane wing, returning after a few seconds to stand beside the plane and flash the thumbs-up signal in our direction. I felt the steering rudder and the pedals moving in the cockpit and tried to follow their motion with curiosity mingled with awe. I noticed the throttle handle move forward. The engine's purr grew louder and the plane began to move towards the runway, jumping over the bumps. I could hear Lieutenant Zvika's voice from the earphones of the cloth flight-cap on my head. The voice, which came from the microphone attached to his neck, sounded like the cackle of a goose to me. I was embarrassed at not understanding a word he said, and I could only hope that this failure of mine would not lead to any serious mishap.

I turned to look to my left and felt really 'in the know' when I saw the green light of the 'Aldis' lamp flashing from the direction of the control-tower. I recalled from one of my lessons that an intermittent green light meant 'permission to straighten out on the runway'. Lieutenant Zvika lowered his flight-glasses, which now concealed the whole of his face, taxied the aircraft and straightened it along runway 32. The green 'Aldis' light stopped flashing and shone with a steady beam – 'permission to take off'. The roar of the engine, unexpectedly loud, enveloped us.

The plane began rushing forward, and after a very short while I saw the ground drop and fall away below us. It didn't at all resemble the scene I had so often tried to imagine. A strong gust of cold wind blew around and into the cockpit, giving tangible meaning to the concept of flight. Because of my embarrassment in the presence of Lieutenant Zvika, with great effort I held back the shout of joy inside me: 'I'm flying! I'm flying! I'm flying!' I knew – or hoped – that I would still have an opportunity to give full voice to that inner shout of mine when I made my solo flight.

After that first familiarisation flight came others. Following grim-faced Lieutenant Zvika came Lieutenant Gershon, a short and affable redhead. After six-and-a-half hours of flight exercises Lieutenant Gershon thought that I was ready to 'go solo' – to make my first solo flight. He was wrong. The solo test was dreadful, and only brisk intervention on the part of the examiner, who took command of the stick with a shout, saved the plane and its two pilots from a woeful end in an overturned plane. Tail between my legs, I came back to Lieutenant Gershon for supplementary training, full of doubt regarding my future as a pilot.

Major Shimon Ash, the flight examiner, climbed into his cockpit with ease. His body sank into the cockpit, only his head, covered in a cloth flight-cap, sticking outside. From the goose's cackle that came over the intercom system, I understood that the plane was in my hands and the way was clear. The turning of the crank and the creaking of the flywheel's engagement with the engine were no longer a novelty. The cry of 'Contact!' was accompanied by an announcement of 'Magneto on'; the groans of the stirring engine, the cloud of smoke escaping to the rear, and the feeling of the plane's vitality and animation – all of these transported me into a flying mood.

I taxied the yellow Steerman over to the designated runway. I was given the green light, opened up the throttle, and took off. After about half an hour of basic exercises in the nearby flight practice areas, I turned the aircraft back in the direction of the base, descended to low altitude, and circled to make my approach for a landing. Three times I touched the plane down on the runway and took off again, without coming to a complete stop. The fourth time we landed and cleared the runway. Major Shimon took over the controls and, with an incredibly practised touch, taxied the aircraft over to the side of the runway, stopped there, and instructed me to press on the brakes. In the mirror above my head I saw Major Shimon rise from his seat, fasten and tighten the seat straps, and get out of the plane with the parachute harnessed to his back. He stepped across and stood beside me, on the outside, offering some last remarks, which my feverish brain was no longer registering anyway. He gave me a final tap of encouragement on the head, stepped down to the tarmac, turned and gave me the thumbs-up: go for it!

After take-off, at an altitude of 1200 feet (366 metres), I turned the plane in the direction of the flight practice areas. I looked up, down and to the sides, glanced in the mirror as if to ascertain there really was no instructor with me, and let loose a shout of joy at the top of my voice into the chilly, blue, intoxicating air. I enjoyed feeling the plane respond to the movements of my hands and feet, and for a brief moment I thought of Noa, Ayala, Dan, and the rest of my gang. How happy I would be to share the feeling and the accomplishment with them. I felt that I had taken a significant step, if only the first at this stage, in my life's new direction – going up.

The descent back to lower altitude went smoothly. I joined the line of aircraft circling the field, making sure to identify them and other planes in the vicinity. A surprise was in store for me when I glanced in the direction of the control-tower. A rocket-flare fired from the tower informed me and everyone else that the landing runway had been substituted, apparently because of a shift in the wind. Pleasure stole into my heart when I found that I was in control of the new situation. I managed to identify the new designated runway's direction according to the large T-sign on the square signboard next to the control-tower. I stabilised the plane in its proper position in the line of 'ducks', the planes circling the field, and began the landing procedure under these new conditions. When I entered the final leg of the approach, and the runway was already getting wider and wider in the window in front of me, I received the green light from the 'box' – the trailer set up by the flight controllers near the beginning of the runway – and hunkered down in my seat for the landing. The plane's nose rose in front of me as my speed dropped. I regained sight of the runway's asphalt on either side of the fuselage and shut the throttle entirely, keeping the plane exactly parallel to the axis of the runway. There was a small squeal as the tyres made contact with the asphalt, and the aircraft, in disciplined manner, steadied upon the runway on all three wheels.

I cleared the runway and stopped to perform the necessary checks, and a hugely gratifying feeling of relief swept all through my body. Major Shimon was waiting for me where I'd last seen him. When I drew up to collect him, he broadly grinned at me, as though to say: 'Welcome to the club!'

El-Al captain Shimon Ash would be killed seventeen years later as a pilot in the reserves, flying a combat mission during the Yom Kippur War.

Along the line of aircraft in front of the green squadron shack, a crowd of flight cadets in overalls was waiting. I could easily discern their excitement, the pails of water ostensibly hidden from my sight, and the glint of mischief in their eyes. To the rear stood Lieutenant Gershon, the redhead with the face of a child, watching the proceedings. Our eyes met, and I felt great relief at having acquitted myself well and not disappointing my instructor a second time. Dripping with sweat, I got down from the plane and willingly submitted to the cascades of water showered upon me from every direction, accompanied by hearty congratulations, claps of encouragement and kicks to the backside, all in the finest flight academy tradition.

We left the green squadron shack as darkness was falling. We started to depart on foot, singly and in small groups, conversing and laughing with each other, as young people will. At the same time, in the aircraft lot opposite us the older cadets of the basic course were embarking on their nocturnal flights.

Layzik, 'Tsif-tsif' and I stayed behind the others and waited beside the carob tree to watch the happenings in the lot. The 'Harvard' planes looked very big and impressive. In some of them the lights at the ends of their wingtips were already on, green to the right, red to the left, and mechanics were bustling around them. Pair by pair, each consisting of an instructor and a cadet, the pilots arrived at their aircraft. Three of the aircraft had their engines switched on, and their powerful noise filled the air. Spellbound, we three young flight cadets watched the proceedings. One after another the aircraft taxied away from the line in a wide turn towards the runways, leaving behind a hot gust of wind. Mechanics with lamps in their hands marked the route, and the aircraft lights receded in the distance. To me it looked like a picture from another world altogether.

Troubling thoughts filled my mind: would I myself someday be able to fly these gigantic beasts? Did I have it in me? I wasn't sure.

The ranks of flight course cadets were rapidly thinning. Scarcely a day went by without one or two of the men hoisting the bulky kitbag to their shoulders, making the rounds of the rooms to say goodbye, and disappearing.

I certainly wasn't the most companionable of my peers. But I did make an effort, and largely succeeded, in establishing a positive relationship with all of my fellow cadets, although I didn't go out of my way to be liked by them. On the one hand my easy-going nature and seriousness, and on the other hand my sense of humour and relative maturity, being two years older than the others, endowed me with an established and recognised status within the course. Just as I did not have any intimate friends, so too I enjoyed the good-fellowship of many, and in particular I managed to avoid any personal rivalries. This helped me to survive this period of massive ejections from the course without difficulty or undue excitement. Quite naturally, the smaller the framework became, the tighter grew the personal relations between the 'survivors', and our company rapidly cemented into a close-knit and supportive unit.

Lieutenant Gershon, my beloved instructor, was killed. He had an emergency posting as the pilot of a Vautour, the twin-engine French fighter-bomber jet. The first squadron of Vautours was based at Ramat-David Airbase. At least once a week, Gershon would vanish from the flight academy and fly with his operational squadron. I always found it strange to imagine such a small pilot flying such a huge aircraft.

The Vautour that Gershon was flying suffered a mid-air collision with his number three, Gideon.

North of Mizpe Ramon, in the central Negev region, lies Ramat Mitrad. The Air Force appropriated this desolate spot and turned it into a gigantic target range for training the force's squadrons. The site's characteristics – its distance from inhabited areas, the desert terrain and the geographical location, which demanded precise navigation to the site – made it eminently suited for what was required of a good practice range. On the surface of the sun-baked expanse of earth, a perfect, full-scale model of one of the big Egyptian airfields was traced and drawn in black pitch, complete with runways, lots and scattered aircraft stations. Dummy aircraft and facilities were built and positioned realistically. The targets for bombing, cannon-fire and rockets were placed in such a way that precise data regarding hits could be collected and reported. A control station was also erected in a prominent spot to provide visual and radio control for the range officer, who would come down to the site during practice sessions. Sometimes, when large exercises were held, special target dummies were erected and fuel drums stashed behind them. This arrangement allowed pilots to see the results of their hits when the fuel drums exploded into flames in a most realistic fashion during the course of the attack.

Gershon led the quartet of Vautours in an attack at the range in Ramat Mitrad. Yacov, Gideon and Eli were with him in the formation. Those years saw the consolidation of the tactics for attacking enemy airfields, which would be put to the test and succeed so dramatically in the Six-Day-War. Underlying the standard plan of attack was a requirement to combine the heavy bombing of the runways with cannon-fire to destroy enemy aircraft scattered around the airbase, all this while providing appropriate mutual defence to our own aircraft. Different plans of attack were formulated and executed by various types of formations, from single pairs to complex formations of twelve aircraft. Gershon's quartet set out to practise one of the methods developed.

After the Vautours executed the planned bombing run in two separate pairs, the original plan broke down when one of the pairs took an unduly long time leaving the target and re-entering the range for the sniping runs. Without realising anything was amiss, the two pairs – Gershon and his partner and Gideon and his partner – went into their sniping runs literally facing each other. The range officer also had no inkling of the accident about to happen before his very eyes.

Gideon felt the terrible blow and his plane immediately began to spin on its axis at an altitude of about 100 metres (328 feet) from the ground, one of its wings having been ripped away entirely. He had time to think and comprehend in an instant that this was a mid-air collision and that he had to eject immediately from the aircraft, which was gyrating crazily. Luckily for Gideon, the plane had already passed the range area (which was elevated above its surroundings), flown over the steep cliff, and debouched above precipitous Wadi Ramon – which gave him an additional 400 feet (122 metres) buffer of protection. He swiftly and resolutely reached out for the ejector seat handle and was shot out of the plane, landing on his feet on the ground only seconds after his parachute opened.

The blow to Gershon's plane, however, was lethal and immediate. His plane was struck in the area of the pilot's cockpit, leaving him no chance. Both aircraft and pilot crashed to the rocky floor of Ramat Mitrad.

> This was the second time I was exposed to the chilling experience of losing a colleague in an accident or in battle. Since then, and in the years to come, the phenomenon would repeat itself. We would respond with a denial of the personal, intimate hurt in a sort of ritual, collective 'circling of the wagons', in a businesslike attitude towards the particulars of the accident, a heavy reliance upon friends, and even with cynicism and black humour. This was apparently the only way we could return without delay to our routine activity, which was dangerous in itself. Most though not all of us got through it without grave disturbance.

Short, squat Major Dror, with a round and slightly pock-marked face, was Gershon's replacement. With catlike speed he clambered into his seat in the rear cockpit of the Harvard. His flight cap, made of khaki cloth, was perched on his head at an insolent angle, and the parachute harnessed to his shoulders dangled beneath his backside. He tapped me lightly on the shoulder as he got into his seat. We had already completed the preflight briefing that morning, on the bench in the squadron yard. The aim of today's lesson was practising flying by instruments.

A light metal framework with a sheet of cloth stretched on top of it – the 'hood' – was installed in the back on both sides of my cockpit. This contraption could slide forward, whereupon the stretched cloth shut off the window of the cockpit canopy from inside, so that the pilot training beneath the 'hood' could be prevented from seeing the world around him. In this condition, unable to see anything but the instrument panel in front of him, the cadet was called upon to perform specific flying exercises, or to get out of peculiar flight situations and gain secure control of the plane, using the instruments only.

From his place in the front seat, Dror taxied the aircraft, contentedly humming to himself and drumming lightly with his fingers on the wall of the plane's fuselage from the outside, his hand spread open to the wind. From the depths of the front seat, I peeked outside and listened to the goings-on over the radio and to the hum of Dror's voice, transmitted through the mask over his mouth. The view from the rear seat, towards the runway in front of us, was extremely limited by the front half of the plane's fuselage and its nose with the fat piston-engine in front. I found it hard to grasp how the flight instructors could fly and taxi the planes and avoid the pitfalls set for them by the novice cadets, with their view forward obstructed so badly.

'Amos, shut the hood,' said Dror as soon as he got permission from the tower to straighten out on the runway.

I lowered the seat entirely and shut the hood. From this moment on all I could do was imagine to myself what was happening outside, beyond the cloth cage around me, and watch the instruments, which 'told' me, in their mechanical way, precisely what the aircraft's situation was in relation to the world. As I listened to the talk over the radio, I drew myself into the atmosphere of flying by instruments. In the centre of the panel in front of me was the artificial horizon – a ball-shaped instrument, its lower half dark and its upper half light. In its centre, parallel to the line which represented the horizon, was the figure of a tiny circle with two wings representing the aircraft. Arranged in a systematic manner around the artificial horizon were the rest of the instruments, such as the speedometer, altimeter, rate-of-climb indicator, compass and more.

On the 'three two' runway – I could see the direction on the compass in front of me – Dror opened up the throttle of the Harvard's noisy engine and began the take-off run. I saw the plane's icon on the instrument, which had been high above the horizon, plunge until it almost touched the line of the artificial horizon. The turning of the speedometer and the positive reading of the needle on the rate-of-climb indicator informed me that we had taken off and were airborne.

'Amos, take over. Continue climbing and turn left to azimuth two, seven, zero,' Dror said.

'I'm taking it,' I confirmed, taking over the controls of the plane.

Over the next hour I fielded a barrage of instructions: horizontal turns; turns while climbing or descending; turns limited in time; gentle turns and steep turns; and for an encore, intricate combinations of all these possibilities together. When this first session was over, I was asked to lock the artificial horizon. Now I was in a much greater predicament, since I had to repeat the same exercises, but this time relying only on the other instruments, and not on the sophisticated artificial horizon. This was no easy task. I was sunk inside the cockpit and completely riveted to the cluster of gauges in front of me, shifting my gaze from one instrument to another in a sweat-soaked attempt to avoid being transfixed by any of them at the expense of neglecting the others and thus losing control of the plane.

From time to time Dror would come to my assistance, calm me down a bit, and explain to me where I had gone wrong and how to improve my flying technique.

'Amos, you can switch the artificial horizon on again,' he said.

'Okay, it's open,' I replied, with an enormous sense of relief at flying with a full instrument panel again, which now seemed a luxury.

Over the earphones I could hear Dror exchanging disjointed remarks with the pilot of another aircraft, but I couldn't make out their content.

'Let's practise a few unusual situations,' Dror said to me, taking back the controls and beginning to toss, roll and turn the aircraft upside down. I completely lost whatever slight sense of orientation I still had regarding the plane's situation.

'You take it,' Dror notified me, in this state of confusion.

'I'm taking it,' I answered. Now it was incumbent upon me to restabilise the aircraft as fast as I could under controlled flight, wings level, in a more or less fixed direction and at 'normal' speed. After another three or four of these exercises, I was feeling completely drained and very close to vomiting.

'I'm taking it,' Dror announced. 'You can get out of the hood.'

I slid back the hood and was momentarily blinded by the

glaring sunlight outside. I felt that Dror was manoeuvring the aircraft very sharply. I glanced to the right, following the movement of his head, and the matter instantly became clear to me.

Below, to the right, I could see the nose of another Harvard rising towards us. Dror stepped hard on the right foot-pedal and, using the stick, rolled the plane wildly to the right and downwards. The plane appeared to stop on a coin, catapulted over the end of its right wingtip, and went into a vertical dive. The other plane, our 'adversary', now approached swiftly and passed us on the left, going up, only a few metres away. I was galvanised by the intensity of the experience. I had often heard, and participated in, conversations about what we cadets referred to as 'dogfights', but I had never comprehended the full significance of the term. Now, having been afforded an opportunity – clearly illicit – to get a small taste of what it was all about, I literally blushed with pleasure.

The battle continued for a few rather agonising minutes, ending finally with an elegant wag of both aircraft's wings.

Shai Egozi, the flight instructor in the other Harvard and the man whom Dror had been 'fighting', joined us in close formation on the way back. From the other plane's back seat protruded my classmate Mosik's face. We waved at each other as if we'd both become party to a new secret.

Egozi, a good man though a bit of an oddball and an especially madcap fighter pilot, would be killed several years later when his Mystère jet crashed near the landing runway in Ramat-David Airbase.

CHAPTER TWELVE

Fire – Cairo Skies,
17 June 1969

The two long-nosed Mirage jets, painted in yellow-brown camouflage colours, emerged from the depths of the western desert, flying in an unexpected direction *from west to east* at a speed of 580 knots, over 1000 kph, and at low altitude. Once again, our Air Force had surprised the Egyptians by employing a 'crazy' flight course. It began with the crossing of the Gulf of Suez in a particularly desolate area, continued with a deep penetration westward into the expanses of the western desert on the far side of the Nile. It culminated in a high-speed dash east to perform a spy-camera flypast over the Cairo-West Airfield, and from there a low pass over the city of Cairo to photograph Cairo International Airport, and then back to land at Refidim Airbase.

To this intricate and involved mission I unabashedly assigned myself as leader and Asher, my sterling deputy, as number two.

Immediately after completing our turn right, eastward, in the desert, at a point about 80 km (50 miles) west of Cairo-West, I ascended to an altitude of 200 feet (60 metres) for a few seconds and dropped the detachable fuel tanks, now empty. I glanced in Asher's direction out of the corner of my eye and saw him drop his fuel tanks too, which spun away behind the plane and, on hitting the ground, raised a considerable cloud of dust that trailed away to the rear and disappeared. Now, without those gigantic tanks beneath our wings, our speed rose to 600 knots (1110 kph), as planned.

The intersection of two dusty roads and a forlorn-looking camp of Egyptian armour informed us that the desolate desert expanses were about to vanish behind our tails. I pinpointed my location and prepared the jet for the spy-camera flypast, to be executed this time at an altitude of 800 feet (240 metres).

'Red, pull!' I announced, climbing to the designated altitude, not more than 250 metres (820 feet) altogether.

This time the notification wasn't for the benefit of number two, who was nearby in any event and completely aware of what was going on, but for the benefit of the southern controllers' station. What it meant was: 'End of radio silence. We are in position and on time at a spot just prior to entering the critical phase of the spy-camera pass.' The return confirmation from the station arrived within a few seconds.

At my command, we both switched on the special low-altitude cameras. As opposed to high-altitude cameras, those we were using were specially built to cope with the very high speed of transit over objects in the field, so that the pictures would not come out – as they would with ordinary cameras – completely blurred and lacking in intelligence value.

The gigantic airfield came into view directly ahead of my jet's nose. I dipped slightly to the right, leaving the northern part of the airfield to Asher, and steadied the plane on its photographic course to obtain the best possible results. I surveyed the airfield at a glance and did not find any activity that threatened our formation. The airfield looked petrified beneath the yellowish, dust-laden air typical of all central Egypt. The planes passed over it at enormous speed, flying in the direction of Cairo's southern districts towards their second target, Cairo International Airport.

'Red one, heads up! Heavy bogey at your eleven o'clock, same altitude,' Asher called to me over the radio.

I turned to look in the stated direction and saw it immediately. Just 3 km (1.7 miles) away to our left and near our flight path, I saw a cargo-plane in typical military camouflage colours, flying on a course that was converging towards us. The swift Mirage jets rapidly closed the distance to the cargo-plane. For Asher and myself – both of us 'red-hot' fighter pilots – the instinctive temptation was inevitable: bank slightly left, straighten back right, throw the air-to-air missile switch, and another 'easy' takedown of an enemy plane could be registered in the pilot's and the squadron's logbooks – all in all a handsome bonus for such an intricate and daring mission.

I could already see Asher's jet, which was closer to the 'heavy', inclining slightly to the left, as if he'd read my thoughts. Two seconds – that's all the time a pilot has to come to a decision at these crazy speeds. I knew Asher well; I knew he was a cool and level-headed pilot. But I still couldn't take any unnecessary chances.

'Leave him, two. Continue on course!' I vehemently barked at Asher, and at myself perhaps as well . . .

The objective of our flight had been defined in the clearest manner. I was well aware that we had to stick to our goal and not deviate from it. The missiles that our planes carried were to be used only in 'self-defence' or to ensure we achieved the defined objective. Personal gratification had to be put aside. There was no place for it here.

Asher descended and passed the cargo-plane to the right, very low. Had the cargo-plane pilots seen us? Had they identified and reported us to Egyptian control? I had to assume that the answer to both questions was affirmative. This meant that we had to try to shorten the time remaining by gaining speed.

'Full dry,' I announced over the radio, opening up the engine to its full power in 'dry' mode, without the fuel-guzzling after-burner.

The two jets, their wings cleared and their weight decreasing, added a notch to their speed, which was now in excess of 600 knots (1110 kph). A cloud of smog typical of any big city stood like a thick wall in front of us, partially covering the buildings of Cairo beneath it. To our right, the gigantic apices of the pyramids of Giza protruded above the smog, receding backwards. The jets smashed through the sound barrier as they passed the sprawling metropolis at an altitude of only 300 metres (985 feet).

I knew that our jets would make an earsplitting roar above the city, but I hadn't taken into consideration the ultrasonic boom that was generated when we passed the speed of sound. To tell the truth, it didn't worry me at all. I concentrated on navigating and got the formation ready for its spy-camera flypast over the second target. The flypast was executed, the cameras took the pictures, and the planes sped towards the open desert in the direction of the Suez Canal. The broad strips of film in the camera cartridges had now also been imprinted with images of the entire layout, facilities and aircraft at Cairo International Airport.

'Red, permission to climb to 30,000,' the controller notified us.

I was now waiting to hear the code-word 'Owl', which meant 'enemy planes scrambling to intercept you'. According to all my calculations, this should already have been happening and the delay seemed odd to me, for it contradicted the controller's instructions to climb. My surprise received an explanation a moment later.

'Red, code "Owl". Continue climbing, assume azimuth one, one, zero,' the controller announced, as anticipated.

'No surprises,' I smiled to myself in the mirror. I radioed confirmation and turned in the designated direction. On the secondary channel over the radio, I could now hear intercept instructions being given in a low tone of voice to a different formation, for a dogfight in the Delta area.

'He's a sly devil, the Force commander,' I thought to myself. 'He's used our flying mission as bait to draw the Egyptian jets into a trap and shoot them down.'

Our jets climbed to higher altitude. A few short vapour trails could be seen far away to the north, of the kind emitted by jet engines with afterburners on. I imagined that a dogfight was now taking place there, the addendum to our flight. In any event, I hoped that pilots from my squadron would be taking part in this battle, and in my heart I wished them luck.

A week after the mission there was a small notice in the newspapers, which didn't make the headlines. 'Egyptian President Gamal Abdel Nasser fires Air Force chief,' stated the notice, without further explanation or interpretation. Intelligence filled in the picture. It turned out that thousands of windows had shattered in the posh residential neighbourhoods of southern Cairo, caused by the ultrasonic boom from the squadron's two Mirage jets. In my quarters at Tel Nof Airbase, Asher and I acknowledged our satisfaction at our contribution to the livelihoods of Cairo's poor glaziers . . .

It would have been easy for the Egyptians to reconstruct our flight paths. Add to the embarrassments of that day the shooting down in dogfights of another two MiGs by Mirage pilots from Oded's squadron in Hazor Airbase, and the seat of the Egyptian Air Force commander would appear a relatively small price to pay.

CHAPTER THIRTEEN

Flight Training Academy, 1957

I could barely open my eyes. My temples were throbbing and I was blinded by the light. I shut my eyes again, fought to stay awake, and continued trying to understand where I was. Mosik, my roommate, uttered a loud groan. I swivelled my head to the left and half-opened one eye. Despite the headache, a broad grin spread across my face when I saw Baruch 'Buff' plastered to the floor, wrapped in a mixture of wrinkled uniform and military blankets with a pillow over his head. The memory of last night's drunken proceedings came back to my mind with reviving consciousness.

Nine flight cadets, myself included, had been summoned to see the flight academy commander, Shaya. We had been informed by him, each of us separately, that we had successfully passed the basic course and would be moving on the following day to the advanced course for jet aircraft at Ramat-David Airbase in the north.

At seven o'clock in the evening, we had assembled in a side-room of the officers' mess – the nine of us, together with our personal trainers, the course commander, and the commander of the basic flight training squadron – for a festive dinner. The 'formal' portion of the evening's entertainment went by relatively quickly. The atmosphere became more and more lighthearted and intimate, and the bottles of wine and vodka were swiftly drained and put aside, to be replaced by fresh full bottles. None of us, neither trainers nor trainees, was accustomed to drinking hard liquor, and the deterioration that might have been expected came sharply and swiftly.

By 9.30 pm everybody was already hugging everybody else. We danced together, trainees and trainers, and every once in a while somebody would get up on the large table, loudly announce how much he loved or hated his trainer, and invite all present to raise their glasses in another toast to eternal happiness and good cheer, or to the swift and savage demise of that self-same wonderful trainer.

At about eleven o'clock it was 'decided' that the time had come to distribute 'gifts' to the trainees of the junior courses. Crooning at the top of our voices – which sounded to us, the performers, quite buoyant and harmonious – we proceeded to the residential quarters. The 'gifts' – cheap candies, peanuts, chocolates, olives and other titbits – were distributed in the rooms of the sleepy trainees, whether they liked it or not. This gleeful procession went on for some time, stopping occasionally at 'fuelling stops' to maintain its momentum. None of the merry band of nine remembered, or would ever remember, exactly how the expedition came to an end. Only a few random pictures remained inscribed in memory, such as that of Dan, 'the skinniest man in the world', holding up Eliezer the White's head, both of them smiling stupidly in a small ditch beneath an outpouring of water from an open tap, or that of Reuven and I literally going through (!) the wooden door of a room whose occupants refused, for reasons known only to them, to open it to their uninvited guests with sufficient alacrity and courtesy.

I glanced at my watch. It was 8.20 am. Now I remembered that we had to prepare our quarters for a 'farewell' inspection supposed to take place at 10 am, after which we would be setting out for Ramat-David Airbase. I dragged myself out of bed, swatted my roommate, and went off to the showers with a towel over my shoulders. The cold shower brought me back to full consciousness.

The parade inspection passed uneventfully, more or less, except for a used condom that was planted at the door of room number two with the clear intention of confounding Shaya, commander of the flight academy, when he came to conduct the inspection. To the delight of the room's occupants, who could barely keep a straight face, Shaya picked up the offending article with the tip of his long stick and carefully placed it in the centre of the pillow of gangling, red-faced Baruch 'Buff'. The incident was quickly terminated, the parade inspection came to a close, and our company set about packing and preparing for departure.

The military bus stopped for inspection at the gate of the airbase in the heart of the Jezreel Valley, beneath a lovely landscape. A pretty female officer who was waiting for us climbed on board and was received with hoots, whistles and a torrent of questions, some to the point and others very much not to the point . . . The bus passed through the administrative area of the base and drove on, under the officer's direction, towards the building of the twin-engined Meteor jet squadron, which served in a dual role as a regular combat squadron and as a squadron for advanced flight training. The squadron building appeared empty and deserted. Our company of flight cadets alighted. We removed our luggage and piled it at the side of the road. The bus turned around and went back on its tracks with the officer inside it. A hot but pleasant north-western breeze, typical of the valley in the early evening hours, enwrapped us. We sat down in a row along the edge of the building's balcony, which looked out on the access road to the squadron, and waited for something to happen.

From the unexpected direction of a dirt side-road, a cloud of dust could be seen rapidly approaching. At the point where the road and cloud of dust converged, an open military jeep came into view driving at high speed in our direction. The dust scattered when the jeep hit the asphalt road, performed a fluid turn into the squadron parking lot, and came to a stop. A short, robust man, wearing shorts and a shiny red T-shirt, skipped down from the jeep.

'It's Yoeli, the squadron commander,' we exchanged to each other in whispers. The man approached us with a bounding, gait and a pleasant smile on his face. We got up and surrounded him, and he began a light, noncommital and welcoming introductory conversation. I gazed upon the man with obvious admiration. I scrutinised his appearance, body language and manner of speech, and I noticed he wore his wristwatch on his right arm rather than the left, as is customary. He invited the company to a short tour of the squadron building, gave us a short exposition of the place and its rules, and dismissed us to our new quarters.

The following morning, when we went out for our first full working day at the squadron, I was wearing my wristwatch . . . on my right arm, where it would stay.

I met Harry first thing that morning. He was a moustachioed Aussie of average height and compulsively hyperactive. He was so Australian that even his Hebrew, which was strewn with English words, sounded like broken Australian. Harry came up to me with smiling eyes, slapped me fiercely on the back, and informed me that he was going to be my personal trainer. I fell in love with Harry immediately, and I soon found out that not just I but everybody loved him. He was the type towards whom nobody could remain indifferent: warm, direct, with an over-flowing sense of humour, and quite free of the aloofness so typical of most of the trainers.

Without delay, we set out for the line of Meteor jets for me to have my first introduction. The transition from the slow and clumsy piston-engined Harvard, which we had flown until now in the framework of the basic course, to the Meteor seemed like going from a motorbike to a Formula One racing car. As we strode in the direction of the line, a pair of Meteors came flying from east to west with a tremendous jet roar, split up and – climbing to the left in a turn that exposed the planes' under-bellies – performed a sort of complete diagonal loop and came in to land on the main runway. Once again the same feeling of doubt flashed through my mind, which I knew from my first close encounter with aircraft: the doubt whether I, too, would ever be able to sit inside such a flying metal beast and control it.

Harry let loose a ripe English curse beneath his moustache when he discovered that a ladder hadn't yet been affixed to the side of the aircraft. The ladder arrived and I climbed it, entered the cockpit and sat down in the slightly intimidating ejector seat. Harry stood on the ladder beside me and gave me a minute to compose myself. There was a particular smell to the cockpit, completely different from the smell of the Harvard with which I'd become familiar. There was the smell of jet fuel in the entire area, partly from burnt fuel vapour from the exhaust pipes and partly from fuel that had spilled in various spots. I sat transfixed by the appearance of the cockpit interior. There were dozens of gauges and handles in every corner, distributed in a way seemingly meant to confuse the mind of the novice pilot.

Now came the flood. Harry started to explain the cockpit, and once he began he didn't stop. After fifteen minutes of solid, uninterrupted explanation, partly in barely understandable Hebrew and partly in rapid-fire English, a fog of helplessness descended on me. The shutters of my brain clamped shut and I felt a terrible incapacity. This went on for some time, ending when Harry finally left me alone in the cockpit, stunned, and went on his way.

I took a deep breath, tried to calm down a bit – without much success – and began working, by myself, slowly, on the complicated cockpit and its labyrinthine recesses. In the plane next to me I could see Mosik's head. The beads of sweat glistening on Mosik's brow amply testified that I wasn't the only one who was in a bit of a shock . . .

The two jet engines revved up to full power and Harry, who was sitting in the back seat of the two-seater plane, took his feet off the brakes. The jet shot forward at a speed that took me by surprise – I wasn't prepared for it and I'd never known anything like it before. In the small mirror in front of my eyes, I made out the dark helmet visor that completely covered Harry's face. The rate of acceleration was absolutely incredible to me. I cautiously rested my hand on the double steering stick, which operated in parallel in both seats, and felt Harry pulling it back to raise the plane's nose and take off.

'You take it!' Harry called to me over the intercom, which meant that the steering would now pass him to me.

'I'm taking it!' I replied, taking the stick under my control.

The Muhraka ridge of Mount Carmel was rapidly approaching. I raised the plane's nose and passed over the ridge at an angle of ascent that looked very steep to me.

'Turn left,' Harry said to me. I dipped the left wing a little, but the plane continued flying almost straight ahead. 'More, more!' yelled Harry from the back seat.

I went on dipping the wing up to an angle of fifty degrees. Still almost no response from the plane. Now Harry lost his patience.

'Stay with me on the controls,' he raised his voice. While I kept my hand on the stick, Harry dipped the wing to an angle of almost ninety degrees and pulled back hard on the stick. With unexpected power, the G-force of our acceleration pressed my body into the seat and pushed my hand downwards, momentarily completely paralysing me.

'Wow!' I muttered to myself. 'This is something from another world . . .'

When the immense pressure eased off, I looked around and discovered that the plane's nose was now pointing north-east. Intoxicated with this new sensation, I lifted the nose slightly above the line of the horizon and swung the stick sharply left. The response was immediate and intense. The plane spun on its axis, and then stopped instantly in dutiful submission to the braking pressure I now applied to the stick. I was making new and wonderful discoveries. Over the next half-hour, I was introduced to a completely novel airborne reality. The speeds and altitudes had been multiplied by a factor of four, or thereabouts; my new aircraft's manoeuvrability was unlike anything I had known before. A new world of flight was opening up – fast, high, exciting and fascinating.

In the evening, Lily, the squadron commander's energetic secretary, and Ada, the chubby, sharp-tongued operations sergeant, joined Foksy, Eli Mor and myself on the way to the cinema. The atmosphere in the squadron – and at Ramat-David Airbase in general – was easy and friendly. It was very different to that at the flight academy in Tel Nof Airbase. Servicemen and servicewomen, pilots and flight cadets, NCOs and female officers – all intermingled, treating one another without trace of aloofness or authority. When the movie ended, a few couples could be seen going off into dark corners. Others went to while away another hour at one of the clubs, or returned to their quarters. Eli and I said goodbye to the group and went back to our room. We had a navigational flight scheduled the next day and preferred to review our flight courses again.

As my eyes passed over the flight course marked on the map, from east to west, my gaze came to rest on Kibbutz Sa'ar, where my good friends from the youth movement and from the Nachal paratroop brigade had come to settle. A 'devilish' idea popped into my head . . .

The morning briefing at the squadron was routine. The plan called upon the six flight cadets, in six swift, one-seater Meteor jets, to perform a navigational exercise in succession, at a time interval of five minutes between each two planes. I was fourth in line.

North of the Sea of Galilee, I banked the aircraft in the direction of Nebi Yusha fortress, and flew westward from there. I passed beneath the summit of Mount Meron and continued west, following the surface of the terrain, which sloped downwards towards the coastal strip in the vicinity of Nahariya. When my plane passed over the houses of Kibbutz Kabri, I swung slightly to the left of the planned flight-path. With the sun at my back, ahead of me I could easily identify the flat grainfields and beyond them the large banana plantation of Kibbutz Sa'ar. With an ear-splitting shriek the aircraft swooped over the basketball court, near the dining hall at the edge of the hill. I knew that I had very little time before the next plane in line would arrive. I raised the plane's nose steeply upward and to the right, performing a sort of diagonal loop and exposing the aircraft's back to anybody watching from below. I made a complete loop and came back in a flat 'goodbye' flypast directly over the houses of the kibbutz. To make my identity clear to any of my friends who might be watching, I wagged my wings in farewell as I drew away from the kibbutz heading west, towards the sea. A wide grin spread over my face as I left the site with a roar of engines, in my grave 'concern' for the milk yield that day in the kibbutz's dairy farm.

During the following days I was filled with anxiety at the risk I had taken, and constantly awaited the telephone call summoning me to the commander for an inquiry. To my relief, my private air show went by without any repercussions. The 'offender' was never apprehended.

This is our last flight at the flight academy. Harry and we four soon-no-longer-to-be flight cadets leave the briefing room, pick up our flying gear and head out to the aircraft.

It's a cold winter's day. Rain and hail swept over the north before dawn, subsiding slightly when the sun came up. Mountainous, white-grey cumulus clouds, some of them highly developed, are drifting westward in the still jittery wind. Shoulder to shoulder, Harry and Mosik walk over to the two-seater lead jet. Eliezer, Eli and I scatter down the line towards our one-seater Meteor-8 jets. I'm just about floating on air. The feeling of anxiety in the face of the unknown, which consumed me only four months earlier, has disappeared, giving way to an alert but relaxed feeling of confidence. A routine turn of inspection around the aircraft, I sign my name into the logbook, a brief – but this time, particularly friendly – consultation with the head of the technical crew, and finally I can climb into the cockpit, with its special, familiar odour.

Take-off is uneventful, and the planes pass over the ridges of the Carmel range, glistening in the sunlight after the tempest. Harry's voice, in his prominent Australian accent, is calling on us to close ranks prior to passing through the cloud layer that covers large patches of the sky. I recall Harry's story of how he set out in a formation of Mustangs two years ago, when the Sinai Campaign began. Flying at very low altitude, they managed to sever with their propellers all the telephone lines that were spread the length and breadth of the desert, in effect destroying the Egyptians' communications network throughout the Sinai Peninsula. It was quite a feat.

All at once the formation bursts out of the shadowy grey environment beneath the clouds into the blinding light and clear blue sky above. In a single motion I lower my helmet visor, and the world immediately looks darker and softer, less harsh on the eyes.

The formation spreads out, climbs to high altitude, and starts practising various turns and manoeuvres. To the north, Mount Hermon rears up its summit, white-capped for the first time this year. Despite the festive mood of this last flight, Harry does not spare us any of his colourful comments and reprimands regarding our place in the formation, such as: 'Number two, move your ass and get in line!' or 'Three, for fuck's sake, are you trying to kill me?!', and other such gems.

'Close formation, go!' he now announces, calling on the

formation to stay very close together for the descent through the clouds and the landing. I, number two in the formation, take my place to the leader's right. Now I can see Mosik in the front seat, engrossed in piloting the plane. Harry sits at ease behind him, both hands on either side of the canopy a king on his throne. In close formation we descend and rapidly approach the cloud layer, this time from above, going down. In response to Harry's command, the formation switches to the control-tower channel.

The nearer we approach the clouds, the more pronounced the sensation of speed, as wisps of cloud fly past to the rear. Together the four planes sink into the woolly white cobweb. I quickly raise my visor before it becomes a dangerous encumbrance. Now the planes really crowd together. In this kind of milky mess – which starts out white and quickly turns a thick grey – you have to 'sit' in a stable position close to the leader, constantly maintaining eye contact with him. Stray only a few metres away and you'll find yourself on your own, at double the risk of collision.

'Permission to buzz runway 27,' the leader requests the control-tower. 'Permission granted,' comes the answer immediately.

'Phased formation right, go!' he orders the formation, and numbers three and four change their positions and move to the right. In phased formation to the right, closely aligned, at an altitude of 300 feet (90 metres), the quartet of Meteors passes over the airfield to the right of the landing runway. Directly above the squadron building, the leader 'breaks' upward and to the left, the other three planes following suit at briefly spaced intervals. One after another, we complete the round, lower the landing gear, and touch our jets down on the runway surface.

'What a wonderful way to end this chapter in my flying career,' I think to myself, as we clear the runway and head back to the line.

Of all the details inscribed in my memory, what sticks out in particular is the shoe-shine before the parade ceremony, at which I was awarded my pilot's wings.

As I was polishing the tall black shoes for about the twentieth time, I suddenly remembered the old Arab shoe-shiner, who used to sit at the corner of Rothschild Boulevard and Herzl Street in Tel Aviv in the early forties.

I would go with Father to send a package to Jerusalem at the busy 'Aviv' taxi-stand. When our mission had been accomplished, Father would stop beside the shoe-shiner's stall and seat himself on the stool. The practised shoe-shiner put on a wonderful show with his sleight of hand, his assortment of brushes, and the concluding spit on the shoe before the final polish. I, little Amos, had a hard time deciding who was the more entrancing – the amazing shoe-shiner or the tamarind vendor who used to walk along the boulevard, carrying his shiny copper jug on his back and accompanying his warbling cries with a rhythmical clanking of the copper cups between his fingers.

I spat twice on each shoe, in remembrance of the Arab shoe-shiner in Old Tel Aviv, and was pleased with the sight of the final polished result on my feet.

Three buglers sounded the familiar ringing call, and onto the parade ground stepped Air Force commander General Ezer Weizman and the chief of staff, Major-General Haim Laskov. Nine young new pilots stood with pounding hearts upon the concrete strip, which usually served as an aircraft parking lot. Two planes, a Mystère IV and a Vautour, both of them French-made, had been left at the sides of the strip, endowing the ceremonial occasion with a suitably fitting airborne background. The young men had seen their dream come true, and they were brimming with the experience. Three Meteor jets passed in salute above the parade ground with their typical shriek.

The flight academy commander called out the name of the winner of the award for best cadet. It was mine. I stepped up to the row of commanders and drew myself erect as the fresh pilot's wings were pinned to my chest by Major-General Laskov. From the Air Force commander I received the trophy for best cadet, and turned back to rejoin the row of course graduates. The entourage now approached this row and pilot's wings were awarded to each graduate in turn. My parents were there – I could see them out of the corner of my eye, waving to me.

'Where is Rachel?' I became slightly alarmed when I couldn't locate her. Once again I passed my gaze over the audience. There she was! Her large brown eyes were peering out at me from one of the rows on the left. I imagined she could see me looking, but I couldn't turn my head in her direction. Now my happiness was truly complete. It felt as if the silver wings pinned to my shirt were burning a hole in my chest. Every sinew in my body was overflowing with a feeling of pride and, even more, of satisfaction. I suddenly felt – actually for the first time in my life – the heady taste of an accomplishment that was entirely my own. It had begun as a dream, taken form as an idea, turned into decision and then into concrete action, and was now duly completed.

The whole world was there in my hands!

CHAPTER FOURTEEN

Fire – Northern Sinai Coast, 8 November 1969

'Immediate' evening twilight standby – which meant sitting harnessed inside the cockpit during the last two hours of daylight – was over. During the standby, I had been listening over one of the radio channels to the controller's monotonous instructions to a pair of Mirages from Hazor Airbase, which Yiftach was leading on patrol along the Suez Canal.

'Panther, left to one, seven, zero . . .' 'Panther, right to three, six, zero . . .' so it went repeatedly, every four or five minutes.

'Pair of bogies west of you, thirty-five miles, bearing south,' intoned the controller in that same, bored tone of voice, reporting an Egyptian patrol that was 'flat-ironing' the sky on the other side of the canal.

At other times such a state of affairs would have sparked general confusion, a much higher tone of voice, and the pre-battle tension of an almost inevitable dogfight. But it had become routine in the new situation regarding the skies of the Suez Canal and western Sinai, which developed during the War of Attrition. Like all routine, it had the effect of relieving tension, hiding beneath its unruffled surface the conflagrations liable to erupt at any moment.

One such conflagration took place four days previously. A pair of Mirages from Hazor Airbase, Oded the leader and Yiftach number two – the same man whose drowsy voice I now heard replying to the controller – had stumbled into a very difficult encounter with a quartet of Egyptian MiGs in an area known as 'Texas': those immense desert expanses west of Suez City.

In the dogfight Oded shot down one of the planes, while

Yiftach took off separately in pursuit of another MiG all the way to the approaches of the Nile Valley and shot it down there. In the heat of the chase, Yiftach momentarily forgot to calculate the fuel reserve he would need to return home. When he realised his precarious situation, he had no choice but to let his all but certain prey get away and continue west, while he turned back east. But now a fresh pair of MiGs spotted him and took up pursuit, aiming to shoot him down.

With the fuel in his tanks rapidly depleting, alone and lacking the mutual protection of a partner, under repeated attack by the MiGs, and without the ability to return fire effectively Yiftach continued his retreat. His head was turned backwards more often than to the front in order to elude the next assault. His situation appeared almost desperate, until another pair of Mirages drew near and apparently prompted the Egyptian controller to call off the MiGs' chase. With the fuel gauge pointing menacingly to zero, Yiftach's jet crossed the Canal. Returning to Refidim Airbase was already out of the question. There were two options remaining now. He could either eject from the plane as long as he was flying at a safe altitude, or he could attempt to land on the short and narrow strip at Ras-Sudar. Now the engine shut off! The plane became a glider, rapidly losing altitude and descending. Yiftach removed the gunsight camera from its stand in front of him and thrust it inside his anti-G suit. The film in the camera held irrefutable proof of the MiG he'd felled earlier, and that was something he wasn't going to give up easily . . .

With his remaining speed, which was just enough to keep the wings stable in controlled flight, Yiftach managed, due to a wonderful combination of skill and luck, to land his plane safely in Ras Sudar.

Listening to the seemingly unconcerned voices of the pilots and controllers, I recalled that feeling of a heavy jet fighter gliding under no engine power towards the runway, with only a hairsbreadth between arriving and ejecting. It was the memory of what I myself had experienced two years earlier.

The red skies of Sinai gradually turned black. The controller dismissed Yiftach's pair on patrol, authorising them to return north. A few minutes later, over the runway telephone, he also dismissed me and my partner from standby. The mechanics gathered around the plane to get it ready again, this time for nocturnal standby.

For several weeks now, squads of Egyptian commandos had been trying to cross the Canal and operate in Israeli territory. It had begun with intelligence-gathering operations, subsequently developing into sabotage acts, ambushes and the killing of Israeli soldiers. One of the ways adopted to deal with the problem involved the use of aircraft. Nobody was under the illusion that it was possible, under cover of darkness, to hit a small commando unit directly using jet fighters. It was decided, however, that when commando-carrying rubber boats were reported crossing the Canal, a plane would be scrambled from the standby wing at Refidim Airbase. It would drop flares above the suspect area, and perform a low-altitude flypast in an attempt to locate or at least frighten the commandos in the boats. It was assumed that any commando force, even if it wasn't really hit, would be deterred and be forced to withdraw without carrying out its mission east of the Canal.

It was for this kind of standby that the mechanics were now preparing the two Mirages parked in the standby station, as they hung illumination flares on their wings.

Nir, my standby partner, and I went to eat dinner in the base mess-hall, keeping with us a radio set in case we were ordered to scramble, which didn't happen. So we invited a few guests to our bunker, where we all watched a movie screened with a home projector placed at our disposal by the good 'Aunt' Leah of the Soldiers' Benevolent Association. The movie and subsequent small-talk came to an end, the company dispersed, and I lay down on my bed in my overalls and shoes. I was first in line to be scrambled during nocturnal standby.

The telephone call from the control station, with its sharp, insistent ring, came at about two am. 'Go into immediate standby mode, you'll get your briefing over the runway telephone,' said the controller on the other end of the line. After hundreds of nights of operational standby in general and flight standby in particular, I had become accustomed to awakening very quickly. I tossed on my G-suit and rushed over to the plane.

'Amos, this is Haggai, are you with me?' came the hoarse voice of the control unit's commander.

'I'm with you, carry on,' I replied.

'Our outposts in the vicinity of Baluza, along the northern coast opposite Port Said, have come under cannon-fire from the sea, apparently from one or two Egyptian destroyers which are in the arena, about 12 km (7.5 miles) from shore,' he said. 'The Pit is requesting that you fly there – we'll guide you to the ship – and drop flares above it, which we expect will make it beat a hasty retreat.'

As I listened to the controller, I was already twirling my finger to signal that I was about to switch on the engine. As usual, the mechanics swarmed around the plane to remove the security pins from the cannon and flares and to draw the chocks away from the wheels; now they were already giving me the thumbs-up. The engine's powerful blast turned into a relatively dull roar when I shut the cockpit canopy. All the flight instruments had already been dimmed before when the planes were put into readiness, and only a few last adjustments to the light outside were required now.

I pushed the throttle handle slightly forward, and the plane gathered some momentum. I exploited the momentum to turn right in the direction of the runway. A glance to the left brought the runway lights into view, arrayed in two long, precise lines leading towards the 'black hole' beyond the end of the runway. I straightened the plane between the two rows of light and, without stopping, opened full-throttle in 'dry' mode and jerked the stick to the left to switch on the afterburner. I knew that outside, throughout the base and its immediate surroundings, the engine's thunderous roar was deafening. I was bemused by the fact that here, in the very centre of the storm of sound all around me, the noise was very subdued, not to say pleasant.

The runway lights flashed to the rear and with practised skill I lifted the plane from the runway. The passage from the illuminated area into darkness was by no means a surprise, but it was always accompanied by a short-lived sensation of 'loss', which needed to be overcome by drawing on additional resources of spirit. I stuck my head inside the cockpit and concentrated on flying by instruments in a precise and controlled manner. The green wheel lights flickered and then they all went out, indicating that the landing gear had retracted and everything was functioning properly.

'Red, climb to 10,000, azimuth three, five, zero,' said the controller.

'I'm going to high altitude, approaching the coastline. Continue directing me to the target area,' I replied.

At an altitude of 3000 feet (910 metres), I raised my head and began to look around me. It was a dark, moonless night, and wisps of cloud were scattered here and there at 5000 feet (1520 metres), but you could only see them if you passed through them. The sky above was clear and black, and the stars were out in their thousands, glowing like lanterns from horizon to horizon. On the ground, pale clusters of light could be seen, indicating the whereabouts of military outposts or units deployed in the field, with huge expanses of inky gloom between them, punctuated only by the occasional glow of what was probably a solitary Bedouin encampment. Farther away, towards the north-west, I could see a pale halo of illumination, which was the cloud layer reflecting the lights from the Egyptian town of Port Said.

Two bright flashes of light suddenly appeared, emanating from a spot out to sea, north of the coastline. 'Controller, I'm in eye contact with the hostile vessel, and I'm approaching the spot. Will report further developments,' I notified the control station over the radio.

The blazing flashes of the ship's cannon were an excellent substitute for the controller's guidance, which was now rendered unnecessary. I aimed the plane to make a pass at a distance of about a kilometre (0.6 mile) from the source of the fire – the enemy vessel, which meanwhile had once again been swallowed up by the darkness. I glanced back inside the cockpit and threw the armament switches in order to perform an illumination run over the target. When I passed opposite the ship's conjectured location, I pressed the stopwatch, continued flying directly north for exactly twenty seconds, and then performed a measured, lateral turn back south. I pressed the stopwatch again, and again counted to twenty seconds, this time heading south.

When the hand of the watch reached its mark, I pressed the

flare release switch. I felt a slight jolt, and a cluster of three powerful flares began to plunge downward. Another thirty seconds of darkness ensued, which I took advantage of to get away from the ship and turn back in order to identify it from a sidelong view. One after another the three flares ignited, rocking gently beneath their parachutes and forming a pool of light underneath them in the middle of the murky sea. In the northern portion of this illuminated watery surface, the destroyer could be seen cruising north, which was prominently indicated by the wake of foam trailing south behind the ship's stern.

'I am in eye contact with the target and preparing to attack it,' I notified the controller.

Now it was my intention to swiftly deploy my second cluster of flares in front of the destroyer, so it would be unable to escape from the illuminated area before being hit. As I was once again passing beside the target, worried lest it should escape into the dark zone too early, the destroyer's captain himself came to my rescue, opening up with anti-aircraft cannon-fire from the deck. It could have been a charming sight if it hadn't involved the risk of being hit. Bursts of tracer shells exploded like a gigantic fountain of fireworks. I made a mental note to myself that as long as I stayed really high above the destroyer, the fire was ineffective and could even help me precisely identify the ship's location. This situation could change, however, once I started making my strafing runs. 'We'll cross that bridge when we get to it,' I said to myself.

The second and last cluster of flares at my disposal had been released, and I reckoned the destroyer would now be caught in the illuminated trap for about three and a half minutes. I had no bombs, which would have better suited my purposes. All I had at my disposal were the two rapid-fire 30 mm cannon, which were lethal to soft and sensitive targets.

I activated the cannon safety release switch and, as I was losing altitude, turned and straightened the plane's nose in the destroyer's direction in a steep flypast. I aligned the centre of the gunsight with the midship deck, glanced at the altimeter, which gave a reading of 1300 feet (396 metres), allowed the deck to grow a bit wider in my view of it through the gunsight, and squeezed the trigger, firing a long burst of shells. At this point the anti-aircraft fire, which was shooting directly upwards, became rather alarming. I pulled the stick hard to climb upwards and didn't have time to get a look at the hits. I knew that the flares' extended duration and my reserve of shells would allow me one more run, and I decided to take full advantage of the opportunity. I executed a wide turn in the dark area above the descending flares and prepared for a second flypast from south to north, leaving Port Said's halo of illumination behind to my left. This time I took care to make my approach down the length of the destroyer, in the direction it was sailing. This would give me more time and a larger exposed target area, increasing my chances of inflicting serious damage.

Again I aligned the gunsight with the midship deck. The cannon trigger was unsheathed and ready to shoot, while the target was rapidly filling the gunsight in the plane's front window. A fountain of incendiary fire began to spout tracks of light, emanating from the dark hulk in the centre of the illuminated circle of water. 'Don't pay any attention to the anti-aircraft fire now. Ignore it!' I tried to convince myself.

> When I eventually got around to replaying this moment to myself, I couldn't remember any element of fear. Was this foolishness on my part? Unfounded insouciance? To a large extent, yes. But I was in a fight – an Israeli fighter pilot locked in battle with the captain of an Egyptian destroyer. Nothing more, nothing less. And I was determined to win the battle. After all, that was my job, and this was all just 'business as usual' for professionals, who had no time nor place for second thoughts. All we needed and aspired to was to win!

This time I opened fire at an altitude below 700 feet (213 metres), and I kept squeezing the trigger for as long as my nerves continued to hold. I could already see the flashes of my cannon-fire hitting the decks when I pulled the plane sharply upward, dipping my wing in order to keep the ship in my sight as it flowered with exploding fragmentation shells.

The plane abruptly left the illuminated area, entering complete darkness.

I looked backwards in the direction of the receding destroyer, and for a few seconds I was transfixed by the sight. When I turned to look forward, however, I completely lost any sense of my whereabouts in space. The stars in the sky, the halo of light from the city that now reappeared, the scattered clusters of illumination on land on the other side of the shore – everything was confused. I felt my insides shrink with the sensation of a complete loss of orientation.

'Amos, pay attention! You're in vertigo!' I screamed to myself, actually aloud this time. By force of logic and training only, against all intuition, I huddled inside the cockpit and forced myself to look at the flight instruments and function accordingly.

From vast previous experience, I was familiar with the eerie quiet that descends on a plane when the speed is too low. The speedometer inside the cockpit gave a reading of zero: z-e-r-o. This wasn't a plane anymore, it was a lump of metal stuck in the sky and about to fall. On the ball of the artificial horizon, I could see that the plane was upside-down on its back and inclined upwards at an angle of seventy degrees. The stick was very soft, as is typical at very low speeds, and I knew that the last thing I should do now was pull it to lower the nose. This would almost certainly put the plane into a tailspin, out of which the only way home, if there was any, would be strapped to the ejection seat and in a lifeboat, at best . . .

'Behave nicely, please,' I whispered to the plane, as if it were a living and attentive being.

I gently shut the throttle and watched as the nose gradually descended in the direction of the horizon behind my back. For a few seconds, which seemed like an eternity to me, there was a feeling of complete weightlessness in the cockpit, until the plane's nose dropped gently. The speedometer gave a reading of 60 knots (110 kph) – the first number on the scale – and the plane slowly gathered speed. At around 200 knots (370 kph), I performed a roll and balanced its wings according to the artificial horizon, switched on the engine again, and brought it out of the dive. The altimeter gave a reading of only 1500 feet (457 metres), which was about 500 metres from the sea surface. I straightened the plane on a southerly course. Behind me to the right, the remains of the last cluster of flares were still visible, until they finally went out and let the murky shadows conquer the sea, hiding the drama that had just occurred.

At three o'clock in the morning I landed my plane back at Refidim Airbase. I got down from the jet and made my way to the residential bunker. Over the telephone I delivered a brief report of the incident to Air Force headquarters in Tel Aviv. After I had completed the requirements with a laconic intelligence report, I lay down as I was on the bed, which was unmade as I'd left it. All in all, I thought to myself, it was just another routine operation: I had been scrambled, mounted an attack whose true results would probably never be known, landed and reported, and that was that. I had time to think about the Egyptian ship and its captain. I wondered what had happened there, on the deck, and what was happening there right now.

In two hours I was due to get up for first light 'immediate' standby, I thought to myself, and fell into a deep slumber.

CHAPTER 15

Hazor, 1958

Foksy and I met in front of the 'Habima' theatre, as we had arranged in advance, at 9.30 pm on a Saturday. We were both riding our motorcycle of choice – Foksy on his Matchless and myself on the Triumph. We were both in uniform, with second lieutenant bars on our shoulders and shiny new pilot's wings pinned above our left breast pockets. We had arrived at Hazor Airbase seven weeks earlier and begun flying in the operational training course, the purpose of which was to prepare us to carry out airborne combat missions.

The course was conducted using French-made Ouragan fighters. We young pilots, who thought that the burden of cadet-ship had ended when we'd received our wings, quickly found ourselves in a strict framework of discipline and rather harsh rules of conduct. We had to pass daily and weekly examinations, to be fastidiously punctual, and to make sure we got enough hours of rest and sleep, while every leave ended by 11 pm back at Hazor Airbase.

The Ouragan was an uncomfortable, recalcitrant, hard-to-fly, one-seater aircraft. It was equipped with all the weapon systems in use at the time, and had been chosen for training young pilots mainly because no more suitable plane was available. The regime at the squadron was meant to achieve two goals: first, to instill in the pilots those habits of diligence and precision that would stand us in good stead in future; second, to ensure the highest level of flight safety, especially in view of the challenges posed by a new and formidable aircraft, flying ever more complicated and dangerous missions.

The previous night, Friday evening, I had left my home in

the city at 9 pm, wearing black trousers and a light shirt. Having slept well for two hours, I went down to the yard, got on the brightly polished motorcycle, and felt like I was on top of the world.

Rachel was performing in Shefayim that evening. The troupe's performances throughout the country had become legendary, and young people thronged to see them. I would occasionally accompany the troupe and was always delighted by their performance. I particularly enjoyed Rachel's performance. We had only started going out together a few months previously, and our meetings had been infrequent due to the nature of my service. When I approached Shefayim, the show was already in full swing. My heart was pounding furiously as I arrived. I parked the motorcycle and strolled backstage, where I was greeted warmly by two members of the troupe who were standing there and recognised me. On the stage the troupe was in the middle of the 'fishermen's dance', of which I was particularly fond, probably because of Rachel's lovely solo part at the end of it.

A wave of loving warmth carried me towards her as she left the stage. She was barefoot and walked very upright, which emphasised her stunning back. Another pair of dancers got on stage now to perform a different dance. Backstage, the entire troupe was getting ready for the finale. Rachel suddenly caught sight of me. She left the others and flew into my arms. We embraced for a few lingering moments, whispering sweet nothings to each other.

'Please don't move, I'll be right back,' she said in her modest way, which captivated me so much, and then she left me to return to the company of the dancers who were about to go onstage.

After the curtain fell, a general commotion of dismantling and preparation for departure began. The troupe of dancers and musicians, all of them perfectly charming men and women, gathered in the backstage area and traded their impressions of the performance and of a thousand other matters with each other. There were giggles, glittering eyes, cajolery and half-joking kisses and hugs, and then things began to wind down. I stood slightly apart, enjoying the sight and returning a greeting to those among the troupe who knew me, and greeted me with a word of welcome and a slap on the back.

Rachel climbed on the backseat of the motorcycle and pressed herself against my back. I kick-started the motorcycle and drove away, filled with pride at my flair. It had been a hot spring day with a hamsin wind blowing. The warm air was filled with the intoxicating fragrance of orange blossoms from the citrus groves in the area. We drove to my home in the city. At home everyone was already asleep, and we went straight into my room. I closed the door and put a Platters record on the turntable. By the light of the small table lamp, we undressed each other very, very slowly, as if we were trying to absorb the very essence of joy of these fleeting moments.

Embracing each other, we fell into bed. Every inch of her smooth body touched every inch of mine, solid and muscular. We breathed in tandem and rejoiced in each other's smell, until our bodies united in a tempest of passion. We fell asleep, then woke again, and each time we were overcome by surging ripples of love. At 10.30 am, when we got up and emerged from the room, washed and radiant, my parents joined us for morning coffee to talk about world affairs. Nothing was said, but it was already clear to everyone that our relationship was solid and unshakeable.

Two young pilots, we set out on our motorcycles. The streets of Tel Aviv leading south were almost empty. We quickly left them behind and turned onto the main highway to Rehovot. The fragrance of orange blossoms that enveloped us the entire way, from Rehovot to Gedera, revived memories of the previous day, still fresh in my mind. As we passed the darkened houses of Bizaron, an agricultural settlement, we encountered several of the village dogs, which ran alongside us barking for a few dozen metres, then gave up. We passed through the gate of the airbase, parked the motorcycles next to the residential quarters, and went to our rooms.

Already sitting on the floor of the building's balcony, their backs to the wall, were three of our group who had returned from leave early. Reuven, who hailed from Kibbutz Maabarot, opened a tin of canned fruit that he'd brought with him from home, and we all traded stories about our experiences during the short leave. As usual, Mosik told the tallest tales. To our howls of amusement, he related how he had (once again!) stumbled into a steamy love affair, lasting exactly twenty-four hours, with a well-known beauty from Haifa, who had exhausted him in her charming cabin on the heights of Mount Carmel, and who had driven him in her luxurious car, this very evening, all the way to the Hazor turn-off. Nobody went to the trouble of ascertaining exactly where fact ended and fiction began. The group dispersed, each to his own room. Before I lay down to sleep, I devoted a while longer to studying the plan of one of the aircraft systems, on which we were due to be tested the next morning.

At 8.15 am the next day, a Sunday, the morning briefing in the squadron-room ended and the pilots stepped across to the safety equipment rooms to pick up their gear and set out on the first session of flights for the day. The topic of today's training flight was 'sequential pursuit', with cameras to stand in place of actual armaments. The course trainees and trainers split up into pairs; each pair was to carry out the exercise in its allotted flight area. Some were mixed pairs in which the leader was the trainer, while others consisted of two trainees, without a trainer.

Reuven and I were paired together; I was assigned to be number one, the leader, and Reuven number two. The two of us huddled together for a few minutes in the briefing room, and I reviewed all the details of our planned exercise: take-off and landing procedures, the flight area, flight-paths back and forth, and radio frequencies and communications protocols. Then we set out on our way.

We strolled over to the two planes, which were parked in the lot adjacent to the squadron building. I checked and signed my name at the bottom of the appropriate column in the logbook, handed my helmet to the mechanic who was in charge of seeing me off, and performed a turn of inspection around the aircraft. I tapped on the detachable fuel tanks hanging from the wingtips, listening for the hollow sound that indicated they were empty, as planned. I stepped over to the ladder, climbed up and slid inside the narrow cockpit.

The cockpit canopy was shut and locked, permission to start the engine was granted, and the roar of the jet engines deafened the entire surrounding area.

'Grey, do you read me?' I performed a quick communications check with Reuven, who was in the plane parked next to mine, engine running.

'This is Grey two. I read you loud and clear,' came the immediate reply.

'Grey, taxi,' I addressed the control-tower, and received permission to use the runway for take-off.

The two planes set out, one after the other, and taxied to the end of the runway. I waited for a few minutes while the two formations ahead of us took off, and then received permission to straighten out on the runway. After performing a routine engine check prior to take-off, we both stood ready for take-off, engines idling in neutral.

'Grey, take-off,' I requested.

'Grey, you are at liberty to take off,' the controller responded.

I let go of the brakes, opened full throttle, glanced at Reuven's upraised head, which was bobbing up and down to signal 'ready,' and then my plane shot forward.

Banking left after take-off, the planes fell into formation and climbed to their flight area. Permission to enter the flight area was received from the control-station, and I instructed number two to get in line and begin the exercise. About ten minutes went by, during which I flew the aircraft in a steady turn, ascending and descending between 15,000 and 25,000 feet (7620 metres). I occasionally glanced behind and saw Reuven's plane sitting on my tail at various distances, at times gaining on me and passing above me outside the perimeter of the turn, getting ready to perform another photographic run.

When Reuven's turn was over, we traded places. I raised the nose of my aircraft, put some distance between myself and number two, and began my first run. At a range of 800 metres (875 yards), I aligned the 'peeper' – the aiming point of the gyroscopic gunsight – with the fuselage of the target aircraft. I rotated the drum of the throttle and tightened the ring of 'diamond' lights around the image of the plane. This was supposed to determine the exact distance to the target and ensure hitting it accurately with the cannon in actual combat. At a range of 700 metres (766 yards) I squeezed the trigger, which in today's exercise activated only a camera, of course, rather than the cannon. I continued flying towards the target, snapped another picture at a range of 400 metres (438 yards) and another one at 250 metres (274 yards). I then broke away left and climbed to higher altitude to begin the next run.

As I approached a range of 400 metres (438 yards) and gazed at Reuven's plane through the gunsight, I noticed a plume of black smoke behind him. I stopped snapping pictures and moved a bit to the right.

'Grey two, there's smoke coming out of your engine!' I notified Reuven as I drew closer to him, above him to his right.

'The fire warning light is on!' Reuven cried excitedly.

Now I could actually see the flames shooting out of his engine, which was located in the heart of the fuselage, and several metres to the rear. Panic began to take hold of me too.

'Two, activate the fire extinguishing system,' I said. This was a stupid blunder on my part. The Ouragan had no such system. I instinctively tossed out the command due to the memory, still fresh in my mind, of the twin-engine Meteor, which was equipped with a separate fire extinguishing system for each of its engines. Long after the event I would still be troubled by my conscience, whether I might have diverted Reuven's attention at this critical moment and robbed him of precious seconds,

'Grey two, your plane is on fire. Bale out!' I called to Reuven, trembling in excitement myself.

'Grey one, what's going on?' butted in one of the trainers, who was leading another formation somewhere in the vicinity and had overheard our talk on the radio.

'Number two's plane is on fire, and he's not responding,' I replied in an anxious voice. Reuven's aircraft, which I was accompanying at close quarters, banked left slightly and lost a little altitude, the manoeuvre appearing to be routine and under control. The flames hadn't abated at all, and I was expecting to see the ejection seat shoot out at any moment.

'Grey two, bale out! Bale out!' my own cries were now augmented by those of the trainer, who understood that the situation was critical, despite not being near the event himself. Reuven's moderate turn gradually steepened, looking more and more like an uncontrollable dive.

'Grey two, your plane's on fire. Bale out!' I screamed at him now at the top of my lungs over the radio. 'Reuven, bale out!'

No response. Reuven's plane was plummeting rapidly. I was forced to break off my close surveillance now and remained locked in a turn at a steady altitude, circling above the plane that kept plunging to earth.

A mushroom cloud of fire and black smoke welled up from the spot where the plane hit the ground. I kept looking around again and again. In my heart I was praying that Reuven had abandoned the aircraft at some moment when I might not have noticed it. I circled the area another two or three times, but no parachute could be seen. Over the radio came the voice of Joe Alon, squadron commander.

'Grey one, return to land. Do you read me?'

'I read you. I'm coming back,' I replied.

A lone Ouragan jet passed over the end of the runway at Hazor Airbase. It touched down, continued down the length of it, cleared the runway and came to a stop.

'Don't start losing your marbles now!' I muttered to myself. I performed the requisite checks after landing and taxied over to the parking lot. Now I felt that my knees were trembling a little and my throat was very dry. I parked the aircraft in its slot and couldn't help but notice that the slot next to mine, which Reuven had left only half an hour earlier, remained empty.

Two hours later, I set out as the number two in formation for a repeat flight exercise. Joe, the squadron commander, was number one, and he was determined to give this flight all the appearance of 'business as usual'. I fully comprehended the situation and willingly cooperated. The exercise went by without incident. For many years I would hold Joe in high regard because of that flight.

We sat, eight pilots, on either side of the flag-draped coffin inside the military truck and drove north to Reuven's kibbutz. The silence and consternation at the start of the trip gave way to casual conversation and even a few joking remarks. We were all putting up a defensive wall to overcome or deny death, which now seemed only a hairsbreadth away.

The funeral procession to the kibbutz cemetery was long, quiet and mournful. Coming back from the funeral, we stopped at a kiosk by the side of the road. We ate and drank our fill and relieved ourselves, in open defiance of the emotional burden with which we had been saddled.

When we returned to the airbase that night the accident and death were behind us. We had matured, having been personally exposed – for the first time – to the death of a close friend. Reuven had been a close friend, and now he was no more.

The next morning we would fly again.

CHAPTER SIXTEEN

Fire – Golan Heights Skies, 2 April 1970

The skies of the northern frontier were blazing. The sky had been aflame ever since combat operations, limited in scope but numerous and of daily occurrence, had resumed on the ground. This was termed the 'Syrian war of attrition' to differentiate it from its Egyptian counterpart, which began earlier, lasted longer and was of greater extent, though no more belligerent.

The two planes, mine and Gilad's (my number two), passed over the Yavniel Valley, heading north-east towards the Golan Heights.

As soon as I switched to the second radio channel to listen to the northern control-station, I heard the loud and discordant voices of pilots engaged in a dogfight. My keen, experienced ear could easily distinguish between the voices of pilots in command of their situation and those who were defending themselves under heavy pressure. I found it hard to identify the pilots involved in the fighting by their voices over the radio. Most of the Mirage leaders had learned to recognise their colleagues in this way, and the difficulty I encountered in this case led me to assume that those doing the fighting were Phantom crews. At any rate, the voice of 'tiger one', the leader in combat, seemed to me to be that of Gideon, a veteran pilot of the northern Phantom squadron.

'Red, pepper go!' I gave the command to open up full engine power in an attempt, seemingly, to reach the spot and intervene in the battle, which had been raging for two minutes already, 40 miles (about 75 km) away. I decided to soak up as much fuel as possible from the detachable tanks and discard them only very near the site of battle, on the slim chance that we would be able to make it.

'Tiger one's been hit. We're ejecting!' came the grave announcement of the leader over the radio.

'Gold from Red. How far away are we now?' I addressed my question to the controller.

'About 30 miles [48 km], azimuth zero, three, zero,' came the immediate reply.

My formation was already east of the 'Purple Line' opposite the southern Golan Heights in Syrian territory. I banged my fist in anger and frustration on the framework of the cockpit canopy. Only two minutes, I knew well, had stopped us from arriving at the scene and intervening in the battle, perhaps in time to prevent the downing of one of our crews.

'Red, this is Gold. Meet your date at azimuth three, five, five. Your target looks like a pair, at altitude 8000,' the controller's voice informed us.

The phrase 'meet your date' was actually a codeword for the benefit of the formation leader. It meant, 'I'm now sending you into a dogfight with enemy planes to shoot them down' – pure and simple. Fighter pilots everywhere may wait days and even years until they hear such a summons, which immediately electrifies the atmosphere and hones all their senses to a fine pitch.

'Roger, Gold. Red, drop detachables, check switches!' I ordered Gilad, who was right up close to me on my left.

When engaging in a dogfight, the side that sees its adversary first enjoys an enormous, sometimes crucial, advantage. At the interception stage, it is the control network that is supposed to provide pilots with this advantage. A small, select group of controllers – who functioned as intercept controllers in the control-stations facing the southern and northern fronts, respectively – had through hard work, persistence and talent arrived at the highest levels of skill in managing both the interception and the battle. Pilots and controllers had joined forces in thousands of training sorties, hundreds of operational flights, and dozens of discussions, briefings and studies, which led them to an excellent mutual understanding. As was only natural, at times voices had been raised and rather harsh criticism spoken on both sides, but so it usually goes with such active and congruent systems. However, all of this only contributed to improving the performance of the Air Force's interceptor squadrons.

My eyes were almost jutting through the transparent cockpit canopy in front of me. Any fragment of extraneous thought was now put out of mind. Every cell in my brain, every movement and every action were now devoted to the sole objective before me – to catch sight of my adversary, outmanoeuvre him into a firing or missile-launch position, and shoot him down. Maximum concentration; quick and clear thinking; attention to the voices and accurate reception of information from the outside; full exploitation of all mental resources; and practised execution – a combination of all these was the name of the game now. Interception – the stage at which the pilot and the controller must cooperate – was now put to the ultimate test.

'Bogies at nine o'clock, a bit low. Two, come with me!' I gave the word over the radio.

I had spied two MiG-21s flying in open formation, extended backwards, in a north-easterly direction. Their behaviour told me that the MiG pilots weren't aware of our Mirages, at least for the time being. In a very sharp motion, the G-force rocketing, I raised the plane's nose almost vertically. Out of the corner of my left eye I noted that Gilad, an excellent and disciplined pilot, was glued to his seat performing the same manoeuvre.

In about ten seconds I had managed to bring the pair of Mirages, both of them upside-down, in a gigantic roll to a point directly above the two MiGs, 7000 feet (2134 metres) higher than them. My immediate objective was to get our formation into a good position for the final assault, even as we hid right above the scalps of the MiG pilots, where it's extremely difficult to discover your adversary.

'In another two or three seconds we'll know whether they've seen us or not,' I said to myself, keeping my eyes focused on the two enemy planes in order not to lose them. The manoeuvre appeared to have succeeded. The two MiGs continued flying in a rather heedless manner, banking right in a moderate turn. The pair of Mirages now went into a steep dive, and I brought my plane into position to launch a missile. I took it into consideration that an air-to-air missile can also miss its target; in fact, just such a 'calamity' had already overtaken me seven years earlier . . . and I had lost an almost certain kill. If there was one thing I hated, it was repeating the same critical mistake.

Now the MiGs discovered our formation behind them. All at once their turn became sharper and the two of them split up.

'Two, you take the one in the rear, I'm going after the leader!' I notified Gilad.

'This is two, I'm taking him. You're clear, one,' Gilad replied.

I muttered to myself, 'You found us too late, there's no way you're going to get out of here!' I raised my plane's nose beyond the arc of the lead MiG's turn. I went a little outside his turn to the right and up, and came back, from the outside in, to what now seemed an excellent position for launching a missile.

I brought the centre of the sights on the glass in front of me into alignment with the MiG's exhaust pipe. The range was 800 metres (875 yards) when I heard the typical gurgling noise made by the Sidewinder missile. This was the missile's way of telling the pilot, 'I can sense the heat emanating from the target plane's engine. If all else is in order, launch me'. The range was right, and I waited another second or two until I saw that the MiG was easing up a little on the turn, which would make it easier for the missile to hit it.

Having uncovered the cannon trigger, with my thumb I pressed the small launch button, exposed beneath the trigger at the upper end of the stick. The missile leapt towards its target with the whining shriek typical of a rocket. A red flame, which quickly disappeared, could be seen burning through its exhaust nozzle. The missile left a curling plume of grey-white smoke as it sliced the MiG's turn at an angle. For a moment it seemed to have lost its way and missed the target.

An orange, blazing ball of fire covered the spot where the leader of the MiG formation had been. What had been an elegant jet fighter until only a moment ago instantly turned into a jumbled mess of metal fragments, some large and others tiny, enshrouded in fire and smoke.

'Small comfort maybe, but at least a little payback for our Phantom crew that was downed a few minutes earlier,' I thought to myself.

* 　 * 　 *

'Red, this is zero-zero. Do you read me?' It was the voice of Anat, squadron operations officer, speaking to me from the operations room back at the base.

'This is Red. I read you, carry on,' I replied.

'Red, please return right away. We need you and the planes here, pronto!'

I confirmed the notification and our formation sped back to the base. This time I declined to perform the customary victory roll, landing quickly and hurrying over to the squadron building instead.

I tossed my helmet and yellow rescue belt on the wooden bench in the equipment room and rushed down the stairs to the operations room, still wearing my sweaty grey pilot's overalls. I hadn't even removed the anti-G suit with its swollen pockets. Anat raised her blue eyes at me as she listened on the telephone and jotted down data in the large operations log on the edge of the table in front of her. At the head of the table sat Menachem ('Menn'), talking with Asher over the radio. From their conversation I understood that Asher was on 'immediate' standby inside the cockpit, waiting for the order to scramble from the control-tower.

'Anat, what's happening?' I asked, as soon as she hung up the telephone.

'There's nonstop activity in the north. The "Pit" wants us to keep one pair on "immediate" standby and another on "five-minute" standby all the time. Asher and Dror have just been scrambled north, so you and Nir have to get in your planes right away, and Eitan and Yossi will be on "five-minute" standby behind you.' As usual, she was succinctly clear and confident.

Through the aperture in the wall of the operations room I could see Alon the 'Chef' and two senior NCOs, sitting bent over and managing all the activity of the technical branch from their room. My eyes and the 'Chef's' met for a moment. He raised his hand in a reassuring gesture, as if to say: 'Not to worry, everything's under control.'

'Menachem, who was in the Phantom crew that fell up north?' I asked.

'Gideon and Pini. They were seen ejecting,' Menachem reported, adding nothing further.

The fate of the pilots who had ejected would be uncertain for a long time. Gideon, I recalled, was the Vautour pilot who several years earlier suffered a mid-air collision with the plane flown by Gershon – my personal trainer, who was killed in the accident – but managed to eject in time. I prayed for their wellbeing.

'Menachem, stay here and don't leave until a replacement duty officer arrives,' I said.

'It's alright, Amos. Reuven is on his way here. Don't worry, you can head out. Nir is already in his plane, pick him up on the radio.'

I leapt up the stairs in four bounds. I grabbed the belt and helmet, the inner lining of which was still damp with sweat from the previous sortie, and ran over to the minibus waiting to drive the pilots to the aircraft hangar. Panting from exertion, I climbed the ladder and sat down inside the cockpit. When the mechanic handed me the helmet, I placed it on my head and switched on the radio. Nir was already tuned in and listening on the channel, as planned. We received the order from the tower to scramble after waiting for half an hour in 'immediate' standby, which allowed me to gather myself together.

As we approached the Golan Heights for the second time that day, there was relative quiet over the radio. Clouds of grey-black smoke were billowing up from a number of locations in the centre and north of the Heights.

'Red, this is Gold. Keep a close watch around you. There may be MiGs at low altitude in your area,' the controller announced.

'Roger, Gold, I read you,' I confirmed.

The pair of Mirages flew in a north-westerly direction, at an altitude of 20,000 feet (6100 metres) and at a speed of 450 knots (834 kph). My eyes were directed downwards in a constant search for the MiGs, which apparently were flying in the vicinity. From the fact that the controller stopped directing us in a confident tone of voice towards an identified target, I deduced that if there was an enemy in the area, he had to be flying at a low altitude, hidden from the electronic eyes of the radar.

'Red, drop detachables! Two, come with me!' I cried, diving like a hawk towards its prey. Nir, my number two, was momentarily startled by the swiftness of my action, but he managed to follow me at a range of one kilometre (0.6 mile).

'Quartet of MiG-17s below us,' I notified him. 'I'm going after the one farthest to the right. Two, stay with me!'

'Red one, eye contact with you and the targets. Carry on, you're clear!' Nir replied, in the customary lingo of formation members.

It is no easy thing for a Mirage to take on a MiG-17. Although the MiG-17 is inferior to the Mirage in terms of speed, firepower and the quality of its weapon systems, it is clearly superior to the Mirage in its manoeuvrability at low and intermediate speeds. It is also able to climb better than the Mirage at low speed.

Since I was familiar with these characteristics, I tried to take them into consideration as I prepared to attack the quartet of MiGs. The MiGs had identified their assailants relatively early and began banking in a wide turn, called an 'Indian circle'. I chose one of the MiGs, which appeared to be in the most inferior position relative to myself, and rapidly began closing the distance between us. The pilot of the MiG that I was closing in on went into a tight left turn, but still by no means the kind of extreme manoeuvre appropriate to his rapidly deteriorating circumstances.

At a range of 500 metres (547 yards), I aligned the centre of my gunsight with the MiG's thick, truncated fuselage, lowered the cannon trigger into place, and squeezed it. Nothing happened!

'Either the cannon has misfired, or it's my mistake with the switches,' I analysed the situation in a flash. I lowered my gaze to the switches: 'Switches all in order,' I could only conclude from what I saw.

My distance to the MiG had decreased meanwhile to only 200 metres (219 yards), very close range, which necessitated breaking away to the outside. 'I refuse to let him get away,' I said to myself.

Emotion triumphed over reason! Any battle is too serious a matter to be entrusted to human feelings, which distort the picture of reality – the world of cold facts. That kernel of passion, wishes and desires, which drives the fighting man, has to be wrapped in the strong protective armour of clear and rational thought. Otherwise, chances are that the former will be smashed to smithereens in the face of a hostile, often deadly reality.

I banked my plane a little to the right, outside the arc of the MiG's turn. I opened my air-brakes for a second or two to lessen my excessive speed, shut them again, and resumed my tight turn towards the MiG's tail.

I employed the few seconds that I was now afforded to inspect the row of electric fuses belonging to the cannon system, and even had time to remove and accurately reinsert the cannon fuse, projecting above all the others. Now I was sitting on the MiG's tail in a firing position that left my quarry no escape. When I again arrived at a range of 200 metres (219 yards), the MiG's entire wingspan filling the circle of my gunsight, I squeezed the cannon trigger again and waited for the immediate, overwhelming outcome. Nothing happened! I was flying a jet fighter with no cannon. How humiliating!

'Red one, break away! They're on you!' Nir shouted at me.

'Damn the son of a bitch!' I yelled aloud to myself, desisting from the chase. I threw my head back, gazing down and to the left, and saw the thick, truncated snout of another MiG-17, which was sitting on my tail and coming directly at me. Just as I watched this frightening spectacle – every fighter pilot's worst nightmare – I saw flashes of gunfire emerging from the front of the MiG's underbelly. I knew (how well I knew!) exactly what it meant. The MiG's cannon were firing, and this time they were firing at me!

I now faced a critical dilemma. The initial, instinctive reaction was to veer wildly in an even tighter turn, to break away to one side and cut short the MiG's run. In that case, I knew, any reasonably proficient MiG pilot would exploit his plane's superior manoeuvrability, stay behind me and begin another run.

The second, more calculated response was to stop the turn, lower the nose, open full afterburner, and utilise the little altitude I had left to gather speed and escape ahead of the MiG outside the effective range of his guns. This tactic carried the risk of leaving the MiG in pursuit for several seconds while still inside his effective range, which he would undoubtedly exploit to continue firing at the fleeing Mirage.

I chose the second option. I pushed down the plane's nose hard, straightened the wings, gathered speed to the best of my ability, and prayed to my Maker . . .

A few bloodcurdling seconds went by; the explosion I was expecting at any moment never came, and my trusty aircraft continued flying, all in one piece. I flew on ahead some distance to make sure I was safe, and only then did I turn back, the controller helping me to rediscover the clutch of aircraft fighting among themselves. I even managed to catch sight of the flames bursting from one of the MiGs and the parachute of the pilot who had ejected from it. It was Nir who was responsible for the positive outcome of this dangerous battle. I knew that I had survived by the skin of my teeth. I also knew that the mistake had been mine, and mine alone. It was only my good fortune that brought me safely home that day, rather than to a prison cell in Damascus . . .

Harsh reprimands were heard that day by the squadron's technical officer and its weapons officer from their commander – me – regarding the condition of the squadron's cannon.

CHAPTER SEVENTEEN

Nitsana, 1959

My heart filled with pride when I saw my name posted on the board in the operations room as number two in the formation on duty for interceptor standby. At the end of 1958, less than a year after receiving our pilot's wings, my classmates and I were awarded the coveted status of 'operational pilot'.

The Air Force's most advanced interceptor, in which we had trained, was the French-made Mystère IV. This plane was of the same generation as the American Sabre and the Russian MiG-15. They were the first jet fighters to feature the prominent swept back wings, and the first also to approach and ultimately break through the sound barrier.

The new operational pilots performed the complex drill of scrambling on an interception mission five or six times, in 'dry' mode. This meant that each time the ear-splitting bell sounded inside the squadron building, we pilots grabbed our flight gear at a run and rushed over to our planes. We climbed into the cockpit, harnessed ourselves, dismissed the mechanic who assisted us and removed the security pins from the weapon systems and the ejection seat. We then shut the canopy, and signalled 'Ready!' over the radio. When we arrived at a level of execution that satisfied Ethan, the squadron's demanding operations officer, it was time to practise the real thing. Twice we performed the entire scrambling procedure, this time including full ignition, taxiing, and ultimately actually taking off, which culminated in a routine training flight.

A bottle of whiskey was whipped out from somewhere, all the pilots gathered in the clubroom, and the squadron commander welcomed the three young pilots. Ethan and Yehoshua, the veterans, kicked us all in the backside to mark the occasion, the squadron's servicewomen plied us with kisses, the glasses were emptied, and the ceremony was wrapped up to the satisfaction of everyone concerned.

Wearing my uniform, decorated with the pilot's wings and the lieutenant's bars, and slightly dizzy with pride, I set out for the servicewomen's basic training camp at Training Base 12 in the Sarafend military complex to visit Rachel. At the gate, I explained the nature of my mission to the female officer on duty there and was admitted to the base. I waited in the shade of a eucalyptus tree and beheld, in open bemusement, the whirlwind of activity that broke out inside the camp in an effort to find Rachel.

Operation *Rachel* took the better part of five minutes until its objective was located. From afar, between two rows of tents, she advanced towards me, walking at first, then running, wearing a green uniform two sizes too large for her and a wide-brimmed tembel hat. Despite my best efforts I couldn't help laughing at her appearance. Rachel, who could see the humour of the situation, joined me and we embraced each other, in the shade of the tree, peals of laughter paralysing our ability to speak.

We slowly drew away from the camp and were swallowed up in the shrubbery nearby. The sun had already set, giving way to the evening twilight. The voices of irate commanders and hysterical trainees, all of them female, could be heard from the direction of the camp, though somewhat muted because of the distance and the surrounding shrubbery. The two of us sat on the edge of an old trench and drew near each other. I was a little surprised to rediscover the beauty of her face and the flexibility of her body, concealed beneath the ridiculous uniform. Rachel pressed against me, eager for contact. The two weeks of basic training that had separated us had turned into the tension of longing that was about to be relieved. The regimen at the basic training camp, the discipline demanded, the loneliness and harsh treatment – all of these fed her longing for love and warmth.

Her hands slipped beneath my shirt and caressed my

muscular back and shoulders. I took off her shirt and mine and laid them both at the bottom of the trench, and we rolled down and lay upon them. Her full breasts pressed against my bare chest, and I felt her delightful and inviting warmth with my fingers. She helped me take off my trousers as I continued caressing every inch of her flesh. When I penetrated her, she clung to me with all her passion, responding to my slightest movement. When the wondrous storm subsided, we stayed joined together for quite some time. Now, as our spirits revived, we noticed how close we were to the camp, and to what extent our mutual longing had deranged our minds and made us throw caution to the winds. We pounded our clothes to dislodge the grains of sand, and burst into laughter again when we saw how they looked now. This time what drew the brunt of our amusement was my uniform, which was left wrinkled and dishevelled in complete contrast to its former neat appearance.

On my way back from Sarafend, I knew it for a fact: Rachel would be the mother of my children.

The first Mystères that scrambled south were those of Ethan and Dan, followed by those of Yehoshua and Oded. The encounter with the quartet of Egyptian MiG-17s took place only 5 km (3 miles) or so west of Beersheba.

Egyptian combat squadrons were stationed regularly at the Egyptian airfields in El-Arish, Jebel Libni and Bir-Gafgafa. The Egyptian planes were not averse to crossing the lengthy border, stretching from Eilat in the south to Nitsana in the north, or even to traversing Israeli territory in the direction of southern Jordan and Saudi Arabia. Israel's Air Force planes found it hard to block their path or catch them over Israeli territory because of the very brief available warning. Dozens of times our planes attempted to hunt down these trespassers by surprising them with aircraft hidden from Egyptian control's radar network in Sinai. Most of these attempts failed, usually developing into an Israeli pursuit into Egyptian territory over Sinai, stopped by order of Israeli control. A complaint would then be sent from the UN Inspector's Office to Air Force headquarters and a letter of 'reprimand' would be sent to the squadron, which was filed away . . .

I was one of those Israeli pilots who spent many hours flying on patrol (which we called 'flat-ironing') down the length of Israel's south-western border with Egypt. Dozens of times we heard the controller tell us, 'Bear left to azimuth one, six, zero', or 'Bear right to azimuth three, four, zero', as we flew actually along the border-line, with Egyptian MiGs flying opposite us at a distance of about 30 km (18.6 miles) from the border inside Sinai. In those days there wasn't an Israeli pilot who didn't dream about his chances of getting into a dogfight with the Egyptians in this area.

On rare occasions the Egyptians, in a premeditated demonstration of power, would dispatch a pair or quartet of MiG-17s to perform a flypast over the Gaza Strip. These flights almost always involved crossing the Israeli border, at least when turning back to the south-west. On even rarer occasions these penetrations into Israeli airspace went even further in this area, which was only two or three minutes' flight time away from the Air Force's bases in Hazor and Tel Nof. During the years between the Sinai Campaign and the Six-Day-War, several dogfights took place in this neck of the woods. On some occasions smashed MiGs were left lying near the border, on either side of it.

I, like almost all my comrades in the squadron, had in my possession, among the other flight manuals upon my shelves, a thin, handbook written by Israeli pilot Yacov Nevo, 'Yak'. It contained articles that dealt with innovations in the doctrine of aerial combat using the new jet fighters – a doctrine the like of which we were unable to find in any other source, external or internal.

'Yak', who was a fine and exceptionally creative pilot, had devoted much thought and time to analysing and developing aerial combat tactics for jet fighters. He also put the theories he'd developed to the test in actual flight, achieving very impressive results. He didn't find it easy to convince others to follow in his path, but eventually his mounting successes – at first in training flights and subsequently in actual combat – made him a sort of Delphic oracle to all the combat pilots of that era. On a certain Saturday in 1959, when the tracks of several MiG's were discovered in the Nitsana sector, 'Yak' and Shlomo Beit-On managed to draw a pair of MiGs into a trap: two Mystères feigned retreat while two others sneaked in at low altitude, zoomed up at the right moment and downed both of the MiGs.

I was number two in Shabtai's formation when we received the order to scramble from the Hazor Airbase control-tower. By the time we retracted our planes' landing gear, it was already clear that all the forces engaged in combat were breaking contact, and that our chances of taking part in the battle were close to nil. The main radio channel was throbbing with the cries of the pilots who had participated in it.

'Black one, break away! A MiG behind you at range 800,' the frenzied number two was heard to say.

'Damn the fool!' came the reply from Ethan, the leader, who was busy at that moment shooting down another MiG, and refused to let his quarry get away.

Ultimately the quartet of MiGs left the carcass of one of its members lying embedded in the ground near Rafah, and withdrew to El Arish. Shabtai and I crossed paths with one of the Mystère duos returning north to land. Bitterly disappointed at the tiny delay that had prevented us from participating in the battle, we shifted our armaments switches back to 'secure' mode. Again, as on countless previous occasions, the controller was heard intoning his routine instructions: 'Yellow, south at azimuth one, six, zero, altitude 20,000.' On the other side of the border, at a distance of over 30 km (18.6 miles), a pair of MiGs, whose appetite for battle had clearly diminished, took up position opposite us. A whiff of combat came to my nostrils! So very close, but still beyond reach.

That evening, in Rachel's room in Tel Aviv, I told her about the day's events. I was almost despairing – and I must have sounded so as well at my chances of joining that group of individuals who had taken part in aerial combat and had the good fortune to down an enemy plane. At the time it seemed to me that the opportunity was fast fading, never to return, and the thought of it was cause for bitter frustration. There was nothing for it but to drown these feelings of frustration in the surging tide of my love for Rachel.

CHAPTER EIGHTEEN

Fire – Port Said Skies, 25 April 1970

W hile the entire country was celebrating the arrival of the American Phantom F-4 jet fighters and their inception into the Air Force, feelings inside the Force's Mirage squadrons were somewhat mixed. After all, following years of absolute hegemony in the skies of the Middle East, and of smug superiority inside the Force itself, past glory was about to fade. Nobody cast doubt on the quality of the new plane and its advantages in combat, in every respect. It was clear to all the pilots how vital and justified taking this significant technological leap forward had been. Nevertheless, to us, the Mirage pilots, it was a heavy blow, and we were not overjoyed to be vacating the summit.

Asher, now my deputy commander, sat in my room, the office of the Mirage squadron commander. We were discussing an innovative method of photography and its adaptation to our purposes when the secretary gave notice that Shmulik Hetz, commander of the southern Phantom squadron, was on the line. I took the call, which began, as always, with jovial informalities, spiced with vignettes of gossip and mutual jests. When we got down to business, Shmulik asked me to perform a series of aerial combat exercises, simple at first and growing more complicated, in order to study the new plane's characteristics in depth and to prepare the Phantom crews for their aerial combat missions in a thorough and comprehensive manner. I acquiesced immediately, of course, and promised every possible assistance in the preparation and execution of the programme, and in drawing conclusions afterward. After we'd said our goodbyes, Asher and

I spoke for a while on the topic, drawing up a framework for the requested series of flights.

The next day I summoned Asher and three other veteran Mirage leaders to my office to discuss in greater depth the advantages and disadvantages of the Phantom and the Mirage, in head-to-head combat. The Phantom had immense power, superior speed, a highly sophisticated weapons system, and the four eyes of its two crewmen. On the other hand, the Mirage's advantages included its small dimensions, which made it difficult to pick out with the naked eye during combat, its superior manoeuvrability, and the vast experience accumulated by its pilots in the field of aerial combat.

After two relatively lacklustre flights just for the sake of comparison, I assigned Asher Snir to carry out the third flight of the series. On this flight the plan called for the full simulation of a dogfight between the Phantom and the Mirage, head-to-head.

Tension took hold of our squadron when Asher set out for his plane. I went down to the operations room to sit beside the radio set, even though we all knew it was impossible to understand what was really going on up there from the radio communications. We heard Shmulik, who was flying the Phantom, establish contact with Asher and proceed to meet him in the designated flight area. We heard his announcement, 'Outside turn', followed by the expected announcement, 'Inside turn'. The two contestants would then have turned nose to nose, closed the distance to each other, and gone into their combat manoeuvres. A silence fell upon the radio channel after the last announcement, which lasted a full five minutes. We, the handful of pilots inside the operations room, knew that during these moments the two pilots and lone navigator were huffing and puffing, corkscrewing and wheeling in the air. They would be turning their heads from side to side to avoid losing the adversary, and fighting mightily to achieve a single objective: to place their gunsights on the fuselage of the opposing plane and hold them there for just two seconds, which would suffice to 'shoot down' their adversary.

'Cease combat. Cease combat,' Shmulik's breathless voice was heard on the radio.

'Roger, cease combat,' Asher immediately confirmed.

From their communications it was possible to infer that they were gathering themselves together, climbing back to high altitude and getting ready to repeat the exercise. After another few minutes, we again heard the announcement, 'Cease combat'. The two pilots took leave of each other with a casual 'See you soon' and returned to land, each at his own respective airbase.

On its way back, Asher's plane would have to taxi along the narrow runway right next to the squadron building. Upon the balcony stood the group of Mirage pilots, together with several mechanics, a female officer and the squadron operations clerk.We all stood there, leaning on the balcony railing, burning with curiosity to see Asher's face when his plane passed the building. The roar of the engine was heard as the plane approached, and then the plane itself emerged from behind the corner. When it got to within 30 metres (33 yards) of the spot, Asher stood, his torso protruding outside the cockpit, and waved his fists in the direction of the spectators in an obscene 'French' gesture, a broad smile plastered across his face from ear to ear.

We needed no further explanation. It was already clear to us that for the time being the Mirages weren't about to vacate the aerial combat arena in anyone's favour. A couple of hours later, when the roll of gun-camera film that Asher had brought with him from the plane was screened in the darkened briefing room, we saw the irrefutable proof in the form of the Phantom's silhouette with the Mirage's gunsight superimposed on top of it, staying there and not wavering for several long seconds. I was well aware that this state of affairs could not last. I knew that the odds were sure to be evened once the learning process gained momentum and more experience was acquired with the new planes. But for now it was clear to us that the Mirage squadrons still had lots of life left in them. Our role, winning the dogfights and ruling the skies of the Middle East, was not yet over.

All was quiet in the on-call interceptors bunker at Refidim. Ruvik and I had concluded 'last light' standby about an hour-and-a-half earlier. We took turns showering, so that one of us would remain on '15-minute' standby throughout the night, as required. We put on shorts, T-shirts and sandals, and took the mobile communications set with us when we went together to the dining hall. We chatted with friends for a while, then drove back to the bunker in the on-call jeep. On 'Voice of Israel' radio we heard the rather routine news broadcast, warning of fog expected that night along the coastal plain. The news gave way to light music and I sank into a thrilling, new novel.

The familiar ring of the duty-phone shattered the silence. After years of serving on standby the response to the sound had become instinctive and rapid. My left hand instantly took up the receiver. The controller, on the other end of the line, sounded calm enough.

'Amos, there's some kind of intricate scenario unfolding in the north. It seems some coastal targets in the El Arish area have been attacked from the air, and Phantoms from Hazor are scrambling towards the hostile aircraft. In any event, I want you to go into a state of "immediate" standby. Call us from the cockpit and we'll see what develops.' I confirmed the order and went out – just as I was, in my gym-shorts and sandals – to the interceptor station.

At heart I didn't believe that anything serious would ensue. The Mirage's nocturnal interception and kill capability was woeful, mainly because of the poor performance of its French 'Cyrano' radar. It was a very innovative radar system in its technical conception, but the most routine atmospheric noise would fill the screen with green reflections that concealed the blip of any real target worth pursuing. This was especially the case when the radar's antenna was pointed downwards, towards land or sea.

It was clear to me that the Phantoms, with their sophisticated weapons systems and radar, would successfully finish off the job on their own, and that nobody would be needing my services. Two drowsy mechanics climbed towards me and helped me into the cockpit. They activated the external generator, gave the aircraft an electrical charge, and called in the rest of the team in case I was ordered to scramble.

Going through the motions, I fastened the 'anti-G' belt over my bare legs, a ridiculous sight. I sat in the cockpit, pulled on my helmet, and made contact with the controller.

'Red on air, what's happening?' I asked over the telephone line, which linked me directly to the control-station.

'According to our information, one hostile was apparently brought down near El Arish. Two Phantoms are giving chase to one or two additional aircraft, which are retreating west. The

"Pit" doesn't think they'll be needing you, but they want you to stay on "immediate" standby for the time being.'

I acknowledged the report. The Phantom's far-advanced weapons systems, including a superb radar, radar-guided missiles, and a special navigator and systems operator in the seat behind the pilot, plus the fact that the chase was taking place over the sea, which caused much less difficulty in target acquisition than over land, all seemed to justify leaving me out of the picture. At least for the time being!

'What now?' I asked, after another minute had passed.

'The chase continues. One Phantom has returned to base and a third is being scrambled,' I was told in reply. I tried to locate and listen to the combat channel on the radio, but all I managed to hear was snatches of conversation in excited voices, from which I couldn't reach any reliable conclusion.

'And now?' I began to apply pressure.

'Nothing new,' replied the controller.

'Notify the "Pit" that I'm gunning the engine!' I told the controller, without asking for any authorisation. This took a bit of chutzpah . . .

'Roger,' replied the controller, in some resignation, unwilling to get involved in matters of authority. I gave a hand signal to the mechanics and pressed the ignition switch.

Ceaseless friction with the enemy in the Middle Eastern skies had turned me into an almost perfect hunter. The creativity and adventurous spirit that I inherited from Mother, and the will to win and ambition that I received from Father, had combined to form a constant aspiration to contend and triumph. These combined with combat experience, familiarity with the enemy, and control over the flying fighting machines that I commanded. I persistently sought and chased after violent contact and the sweet taste of victory, with all my heart and soul.

In my feverish mind I traced all the options that seemed available to Egyptian aircraft retreating from their target area, under pressure from their pursuers. 'If I were an Egyptian pilot under these conditions, I would fly as low as possible in the dark, head far out to sea and away from the land to avoid the Israeli outposts along the Sinai shore, and fly west, and of course . . . I would also pray fervently for deliverance!' I thought.

'Controller, ask permission in my name from the "Pit" to take off and patrol the Beluza area,' I requested.

I quickly received a negative answer. By now the Phantoms were drawing nearer in their chase from east to west, towards the central Sinai coast. I managed to monitor the radio communications, from which it became evident that the pursuers had no contact with the retreating aircraft – apparently only a single one.

'Requesting permission again to take off. Put some pressure on them up there!' now I actually raised my voice. I was sure that some of the harshness in my voice would also be communicated to central command in Tel Aviv.

'Red, scramble north!' the hoped-for command finally arrived.

Within twenty-five seconds I was in the air. I retracted the landing gear, turned on the Mirage's antiquated radar, and looked outside. A half-moon flooded the Sinai desert with a magical light and the sky was absolutely clear and bright. I adjusted the instrument lights inside the cockpit to the bare minimum, and lowered as far as possible the intensity of the green 'smears' moving from side to side on the radar screen.

'Red, you are not authorised to go north beyond the shoreline. Stay on patrol at 15,000 above land,' said the controller. I confirmed the order.

'Do you have contact with the target?' I asked the controller.

'We have intermittent contact. Last at 6000 feet (1830 metres), heading west.' This description tallied well with my suppositions, and I concluded that the Egyptian aircraft was already flying at low altitude and trying to hide somewhere 'out in the surf'.

'Request permission to patrol ten miles north of the shoreline!' I went on pestering the controller, while in actual fact I began edging northward.

'Negative, for the time being!' came the answer, but by this point I wasn't following instructions to the letter exactly.

'Red, heads up. Gold [the pursuing Phantom] is breaking contact. Assume a course, zero, two, zero, and descend to 10,000. I'm sending you in to intercept!' the hoped-for announcement from the controller finally arrived.

'Roger, keep feeding me data,' I replied. Now began the familiar process of interception, the purpose of which is to bring the interceptor into radar contact with the target aircraft. I followed the controller's instructions, my eyes scanning the screen for any sign of a suspicious blip. Futile seconds went by, and the controller's instructions sounded slightly hesitant to me as well, not unequivocal as usual. I glanced outside again and saw that there was enough moonlight to fly almost wholly by sight.

At this stage I came to the conclusion that the radar was only hindering me. With one decisive motion I simply switched it off. With that the last luminous distraction inside the cockpit was eliminated, and within seconds I felt my eyes adjusting to the new conditions. I decided to descend to an altitude of 5000 feet (1524 metres) and fly in a north-south direction, at right angles to the conjectured course of the Egyptian, who would have to fly from east to west, at least if he wanted to make it back home tonight . . .

I flew about twenty-five miles out to sea and banked left, southward, the moon in front of me and to my right.

A glimmer! Far below, ahead and to my left, I thought I saw the reflection of bright, metallic paint under the moonlight.

'Controller, don't bother me now! I may have eye contact!' I ordered imperiously, silencing the entire radio channel. Everything went quiet. I was on my own!

The tiny bright spot came closer and closer to my left; at any moment it would pass behind me.

'Once he gets behind you he'll stop reflecting the moonlight, so pay attention!' I admonished myself. I was already putting together a plan in case I should lose eye contact with the target. But was this the target?

Just as I had forecast, and to my great disappointment, the 'spot' passed behind me to my left and disappeared. My stomach was pinched with worry lest I'd lost him, perhaps altogether. I banked my Mirage, which was much faster than the target aircraft, to the left, northward. My plan was to place my aircraft, when I had completed my turn southward, once again in the identical situation relative to the target aircraft. I hoped that the moon would play the crucial role it played before and illuminate the target.

It took almost an entire minute until I arrived at the same position again, the nose of my aircraft pointing south. I was close to desperation and didn't think I'd find him again. I strained my eyes, scanning the seascape in front of me, searching for the 'spot' engraved in my memory. Another ten seconds went by when suddenly, as if he'd been waiting just for me, the 'spot' reappeared.

'Now you're finished, my friend. I'm not going to lose you!' I said out loud, in part to myself, in part to the Egyptian pilot.

I manoeuvred my aircraft, quite steeply this time, on to the rear of the Egyptian. I banked tightly, right and left, losing altitude and dropping under control to an imaginary point several hundred metres behind the target aircraft. Now I could make positive identification. It was an antiquated jet bomber, an Ilyushin IL-28, easy to identify by the two large jet engines hanging from its wings. It was a cumbersome aircraft. I estimated its speed at 250 knots, about 420 kph.

This low speed wasn't at all suited to the swift Mirage. The situation was made more difficult by the low altitude to which the Egyptian, and I in pursuit had descended. The water's surface was dark, and I knew that the altimeter in my aircraft wasn't calibrated to provide an absolutely accurate reading. Although it felt as though I were close to dipping my bottom in the water at any moment, I resolved that I should be able to follow whatever level the Egyptian descended to – and so I did.

The critical moment approached. The air-to-air missile hanging from my wing started crackling, which meant that the missilehead had begun to sense the heat emitted by the Ilyushin. I could already begin to discern the two dull rings of fire from inside the exhaust pipes of the Ilyishin's two engines. The crackling of the missile grew strong and stable. I now estimated the distance between the aircraft at 500–600 metres. (547–656 yards) I just had time to remark to myself that the Egyptian crew almost certainly had no idea I was there, or how desperate their situation was.

The missile set out on its way, leaving behind a blinding trail of fire. For safety's sake I almost instinctively pulled upwards and to the left as I followed the missile's flight. It was a very short flight, and it seemed to me that the missile directly penetrated the right engine and blew it up. For the Egyptian there was no escape. The low altitude left him no room to manoeuvre, and the plane fell into the water in only a few seconds, vanishing beneath the dark surface of the sea.

When I switched off the engine back at the interceptor station in Refidim and clambered out of the plane, the officers and soldiers who had gathered there couldn't help laughing. I got out of my seat, took off my helmet and handed it to the mechanic, and stepped outside dressed for summer camp – in shorts, a T-shirt and sandals!

As I have continued to do since then, I gathered together the mechanics and other soldiers of the on-duty squadron and told them about the battle and its outcome. When I reached the end of my story everyone cheered; somebody broke out a bottle of champagne, and there was great jubilation. After all, to successfully hunt and shoot down a plane at night, with the pilot employing only his eyes and mind, is no ordinary accomplishment for the Israeli Air Force, or anywhere else in the world for that matter.

When I stepped into the residential bunker, I was even more surprised to find another two pilots and two navigators there, the crews of the Phantoms from the base at Hazor. I immediately identified these unusual guests, old friends of mine, as the ones whose voices I'd heard a half-hour earlier, when they unsuccessfully gave chase to the Ilyushin Il-28, which was downed by a missile from my aircraft. The reason for their arrival in Refidim, as immediately became clear to me, was the heavy fog covering parts of Israel, which had forced the shutdown of runways in the north. I recalled that the weather forecaster on the radio had predicted fog.

That night the telephone lines between Refidim and all the Air Force bases in the north were working overtime. There wasn't a commanding officer, friend or fellow squadron commander who didn't call to quiz and congratulate me. Yoram, a senior Phantom fighter pilot and one of my nocturnal guests at Refidim, informed me that the other Ilyushin Il-28, the partner of the one I'd brought down, had been shot down by Shmulik Hetz, commander of the first Phantom squadron, along the coastline near the Nahal Yam settlement. This news made me even happier, especially because of my friendship with Shmulik, but also because of the kill's importance for the morale of the pilots and navigators of the new Phantom squadrons.

When everything calmed down late at night, I called home to Rachel. I told her all about this exceptional mission, about the great good fortune and accomplishment that had fallen to me. She listened and congratulated me. But when I lay down before dawn to sleep for a bit and recalled our conversation, I realised how unsuccessfully I had conveyed the true intensity of my enthusiasm and pride.

Before I fell asleep the thought passed through my mind that there has never been, and probably never will be, a fighter who can fully and authentically convey the impressions of his victories and defeats to another person, unless that person happens to be a fighter like himself. A stranger couldn't possibly make any sense of it . . .

CHAPTER NINETEEN

Hazor, 1962

Zorik, commander of the Ouragan squadron, was the first to alight from the Norde cargo-plane that flew us to Chateaudun, a French airbase about 70 km (43.5 miles) from Paris. Half-frozen from the cold inside the noisy and uncomfortable aircraft, the other six Ouragan pilots and I descended after him. We had arrived in France in order to pick up eight old Ouragan jets consigned to the Israeli Air Force, and fly them to Israel.

We were all knowledgeable and experienced regarding the aircraft, but our mastery of French, especially with respect to military aviation, was very poor. Although we had devoted several hours to studying the language using voice recordings, only a few of us had arrived at anything like a truly sufficient understanding of it. The only one who was able to speak fluently with the French was Danny Shapira, the 'champion' of aircraft transfers to Israel, who joined our company in Chateaudun to direct the operation, giving us the benefit of his vast experience.

The planned flight course was to take us from Chateaudun to Eastre, a military airfield in southern France near Marseilles; from there to Brindisi in southern Italy; from there to Athens in Greece; and from there to Hazor. To perform the long legs of this itinerary, the planes were outfitted with particularly large detachable fuel tanks at their wingtips. To check the aviation systems, especially the fuel system, it was determined that we would carry out a few long-range test flights from Chateaudun, and that only after the planes were found fit would we set out on the long journey.

Of all the planes that were examined, one was found to have a problem that required an additional test flight. Zorik, the senior officer in our group, assigned himself to perform the flight.

On 20 June 1962 the skies over France were covered with a thick layer of clouds. We saw Zorik head out for the plane, his chubby body rolling from one stubby leg to the other as he marched, happy and good-natured as always. He climbed into the cockpit, switched on the engine, and taxied out to the runway. Just to make sure, two of our pilots went over to the control-tower, in case their help should be needed to communicate with Zorik. After a few minutes the plane took off, carrying enough fuel in its tanks for about forty-five minutes' worth of flying time.

In routine fashion, after take-off Zorik switched from the tower frequency to the national air traffic control channel. He climbed above the clouds, emerged at an altitude of about 25,000 feet (7620 metres), and began to carry out the necessary tests.

'Something's wrong with Zorik. Tell Shapira to come over to the tower right away!' came the call from Amnon in the control-tower to the offices, where we were all milling about with nothing to do. Danny immediately set out for the tower at a run.

Forty minutes had gone by since take-off, and by now Zorik should have been asking for landing instructions, but all contact with him was broken. Shapira, who in the meantime had arrived at the tower, got in touch with air-traffic control. He was informed that contact with Zorik had been lost ten minutes earlier, and that the plane had disappeared entirely from the screens. Another five minutes went by, and then another five, and by any calculation the fuel in Zorik's plane should have run out. The atmosphere inside the tower became extremely gloomy, and the news rapidly made its way to the other members of our team. Telephone calls streamed in every direction in an effort to ascertain the facts, while grave concern spread among the men. Zorik's plane had vanished! Experienced pilots know that only rarely does the initial notice of calamity in the air turn into 'good' news. On the contrary, it usually gets worse.

There had been a serious electrical fault in Zorik's plane. Both his radio sets were knocked out of action, as well as the only homing device he had onboard. With only 180 litres (40 gallons) of fuel in his tanks – enough for twelve minutes' flying – and not knowing his exact location, Zorik decided to descend below the clouds. He knew from memory that the surface of the terrain to the north was relatively flat, whereas the area to the south was more mountainous. Using a simple but inexact magnetic compass, he banked his aircraft north and began descending through the clouds without any control to guide him.

At 5000 feet (1524 metres): clouds! At 3000 feet (914 metres): clouds! At 1500 feet (457 metres): still clouds! He decided that if he couldn't make eye contact with the ground at 500 feet (152 metres), he would stop his descent, climb back to 2000 feet (610 metres), and eject.

At 850 feet (260 metres), just before reaching the critical altitude, his plane emerged below the base of the cloud. But his situation was far from over. In the greyness beneath the cloud Zorik now found himself in a most embarrassing situation. He knew that he had enough fuel left to fly for only about eight more minutes, but he had no idea where he was, or where for that matter he was supposed to land.

Zorik was known to be a cat who always landed on his feet, regardless of the circumstances. He coolly began to survey his surroundings and spotted cars in the vicinity. He turned in that direction and began flying alongside a road that looked like a major thoroughfare. As he approached an intersection, he descended to only several metres above the ground. From a distance he caught sight of a traffic sign above the road; passing directly over it, he saw 'Paris' with an arrow indicating the direction. In the hope of improving his chances of finding an airfield near the big city, he decided to follow the arrow. Who knows what drivers along that road might have thought when they saw a jet plane 'shave' their heads beneath the level of the treetops . . . but certainly they never imagined that the 'renegade' pilot was simply trying to read the road signs!

Another minute went by, and Zorik's eyes spotted a rural dirt runway for light aircraft, beside the road to his right. According to his calculations he had six minutes of flight time left. Zorik pressed the stopwatch. He'd decided to continue in the direction of the city for another two minutes, just in case he should be lucky enough to happen upon a more substantial airfield. If not, he planned to turn back, and land the plane on its belly on the dirt runway.

One of the two minutes he'd allotted himself went by, when his sharp eyes spotted a sizeable building that looked like a large aircraft hangar, igniting a spark of hope in his heart. Another ten seconds, and a long, broad asphalt runway came into view on the left side of the road: pure magic! There was no time left for questions or enquiries. He swiftly banked right and up, then back to the left and down, reduced his speed, lowered the landing gear, and landed. Luckily for him, the runway was empty of traffic along its entire length.

Zorik's plane rolled all the way to the end of the runway, turned left, and came to a stop in a lot there, where his engine expired from lack of fuel . . .

Two dark, khaki-coloured vehicles quickly arrived beside the plane, the white stars-and-stripes ensign of the American Army prominently emblazoned on their sides. Two officers went over to Zorik and informed him that he'd landed at an American military airfield.

'Danny, this is Zorik,' came his raspy voice from the telephone.

'Zorik!!! Where are you? What happened to you? Are you really alive?' replied Danny from the control-tower, where he'd been trying to conduct the search operations after him. The rumour quickly circulated among the men who, to tell the truth, had already been expecting the worst. Smiles began to spread on all our faces. Several hours later Zorik arrived back at Chateaudun by car and told his amazing story to the rest of the pilots.

Zorik and I had a very special relationship. For a long period, Zorik was my commander in the Ouragan squadron, where the two of us conducted the operational training course for fighter pilots who'd graduated from the flight academy. About two years after I'd transferred to the first Mirage squadron in Hazor, Zorik joined the unit as squadron commander, replacing its first commander, Joe Alon. Zorik didn't conceal his eminent satisfaction with my execution of all the tasks with which I was entrusted. In the periodical assessments he wrote over the years, he didn't hesitate to write my name in the highest possible evaluation category, beneath the printed caption, 'I would prefer him (under my command) over all others'. To tell the truth, this column was usually left blank . . .

Although we didn't rub shoulders with each other too closely, I always felt that Zorik was willing to lend me his ear. We also had a common background, having gone to school together at 'Kaduri'. In time Zorik – whose father, an old-time farmer from Kfar Bilu, was a veteran bee-keeper – helped me acquire a few swarms of bees and set up a small apiary, which I kept by myself as a hobby in the citrus groves near the runways of the Hazor airfield. It's no wonder, then, that the tale of Zorik's flight in France remained engraved upon my heart for years.

Eleven years later, towards the end of the Yom Kippur War, Colonel Zorik, commander of the Ramat-David Airbase, was killed during an operational sortie into Egyptian airspace, flying a Skyhawk jet.

Dinner that evening, in the centre of the town, was an exceptionally joyful affair. On 27 June the eight Ouragan jets landed in Hazor. A few days after returning to Israel I rejoined my operational squadron – the Mystère squadron.

The three Mystère jets stood in take-off position, one beside the other, their canopies open, ready to take off. I was the formation leader. I leaned my right arm on the cockpit railing, supporting my helmet against it. On the intersecting runway the process of harnessing the Ouragan jet to the 'drogue', a towed target for aerial shooting practice, was nearing completion.

'Eggplant from Edibles zero four, about to take off,' the Ouragan pilot notified my formation of Mystères.

'Roger, zero four. We're ready,' I replied over the radio.

'Rome from Edibles zero four, take-off,' the Ouragan pilot asked permission from the control-tower, which was promptly forthcoming. The Ouragan opened up its engine full-throttle and raced down the runway.

A 300 metres (274 yards) long steel cable had been attached to the plane's underbelly. At the other end the cable split into three strands, to which a 3 metres (2.74 yards) long iron pole with a single weight and two pulleys at one end of it was harnessed. Tied to the pole was a rectangular sheet of cloth, 2 metres (1.8 yards) wide by 12 metres (11 yards) long. The cloth was made of nylon thread interspersed with metal, especially strong to be able to hold up while being towed for a good length of time at a speed of 320 kph (173 knots). The point in the plane's underbelly to which the 'drogue' was attached was connected to the plane's weapons system, so that by pressing the bombing switch the pilot could release the 'drogue' at any moment it should become necessary.

The Ouragan lifted up from the runway after a slightly longer than usual take-off run and raised its nose at a relatively high angle, so that the towed target would rise faster and not be dragged along the rocky ground beyond the asphalt runway. The three of us saw the target leave the runway and shift into a position vertical to the ground caused by the weight at one end of the iron pole. The cloth rectangle could now be plainly seen, white with a black frame and another black circle in the middle. I pressed the stopwatch hanging in front of me. In another five minutes exactly it would be time for us to take off.

At three in the morning Rachel awakened me.

'Amos, we've got to drive to the hospital. The contractions are getting stronger and more frequent.'

My stomach turned over with excitement, which I tried to conceal, but with little success apparently. We left our small cottage in the family residential neighbourhood and walked hand in hand towards the brown pickup truck parked nearby. We were wrapped in a bubble of love: she, myself and the unborn infant, the new member of our family. I kissed her, switched on the engine, shattering the silence typical of that hour, and we made our way to the nearest hospital.

I took my feet off the brake pedals and opened up the throttle as far as it would go. With a glance at the instrument panel, I made sure that the rpm gauge read '100 per cent' and the engine temperature gauge, 680 degrees. At a safe height after the plane left the runway, I pulled the landing gear handle. Within a few seconds the light thumps were heard, testifying that the landing gear had locked into place in raised position. As I climbed I banked slightly to the left, then right again, to allow my numbers two and three to join me swiftly in formation.

'Rome, this is Red formation, going to work with Edibles zero four,' I notified the controller.

'Red, this is Rome. Assume azimuth two, four, five, altitude eight,' came the immediate reply.

Over the sea, at a distance of about 20 km (12.5 miles) from the shore opposite Ashkelon, I discovered the Ouragan creeping along at an altitude of 10,000 feet (3048 metres), the 'drogue' dangling behind it. I climbed above him, my formation with me.

'Zero four, this is Red. We have eye contact with you. Permission to head out north.'

'Roger, Red. When I'm aligned you can start shooting,' replied the tow.

'Red, single file, go. Red one going in,' I announced.

I lowered the plane's nose and went into pursuit of the target, losing altitude in a wide turn. When I saw the Ouragan and the target behind it directly ahead of me at a distance of about 2 km (1.24 miles), I changed the tilt of my wings from left to right. I aligned the 'peeper', the round pinpoint of light in the centre of the gunsights, with the target and continued the chase, my distance to the target rapidly decreasing. The 'peeper,' which was of fixed dimensions and at first covered most of the target, seemed to be shrinking, as if it were sinking into the target, which just kept growing in front of my eyes.

'Red one, cutting out,' I announced when I passed above the target, in close proximity to it, and broke away to the left and upwards, back to the point from which I would start the next flypast.

'Red two, going in,' number two announced.

'Red three, going in,' number three announced fifteen seconds later.

After two dummy runs without any live fire, I inserted the cannon fuse that allows electrical current into the system. I shifted the switch to 'active' position, and unsheathed the trigger. This time when I steadied the 'peeper' over the rectangular cloth target, and when the size of the 'peeper' relative to the width of the target indicated the correct range – about 300 metres (328 yards) – I gave a short pull on the trigger. A short burst of about eight shells was fired towards the target. Sometimes, in exceptional weather and visibility conditions, we were even able to see, with the naked eye, the cluster of shells rushing ahead and passing beside or through the target.

The routine of going into and out of our runs went on for the planes of my formation. When the tow reached the northern end of the shooting range, the pilot notified us to cease fire and turned back south. When he was again on course in a new direction, the exercise continued as before.

'Red, this is zero-zero. Do you read me?' came the voice of the squadron commander over the radio from the special transmitter installed in the squadron operations room.

'Zero-zero, this is Red one. I read you loud and clear,' I replied.

'Red one, *mazel tov*! You have a baby boy!' the commander announced in an uncommonly celebratory manner.

'Thank you, zero-zero, from Red one,' I replied.

On this run I didn't venture to shoot at all. I felt that if I were to squeeze the trigger now, the shells might make it all the way to Cyprus, but not one of them would hit its target. I retracted the trigger, turned the switch to 'inactive', passed near the tow to his left and performed three consecutive rolls in the air, in honour of Rachel and my firstborn. The pilot of the Ouragan tow and the other two members of my formation bent the rules a little, departing from strict radio communications protocol to add their own congratulatory remarks.

Forty-five minutes later, at the hospital, I kissed Rachel and was allowed to approach my firstborn son, Noam.

That day I didn't even bother to ask the squadron's shooting range officer how many holes tinged with blue – the colour of the cannon shells – had been found in the target brought back to base by the tow.

CHAPTER TWENTY

Mirages – The Beginning, 1962

The Mirage was the jet with the delta wings, diminutive and shiny in its bright aluminium colouring. It was the summit of every fighter pilot's aspirations from the moment of the first rumour of its impending arrival to the Israeli Air Force, and so it continued to be throughout the 1960s. Worldwide, the Mirage represented the pinnacle of aviation technology and constituted an immense leap forward compared with the planes that preceded it. Its maximum speed, twice the speed of sound, was also twice that of its predecessors in the air, such as the American Sabre F-86, the Russian MiG-17, and the French Super Mystère – all of them Mach 1 (speed of sound) planes.

The breakthrough in airspeed, however, wasn't the only dowry that the Mirage brought with it. The structure of the fuselage and wings, the power of its engine and afterburner, the aviation instruments, the weapon systems, the ejection seat, its manoeuvrability in the air – all these and more were at a level unprecedented in aviation history. The Mirage also had another endearing quality: it was French, which meant it was beautiful. It was a plane with French chic, which captivated the hearts of the world's aviators.

The acquisition of the Mirages for the Israeli Air Force must be credited primarily to Ezer Weizman, then commander of the force. When the rumours regarding this sophisticated plane began to spread through the Air Force, they were received with scepticism by the rank and file pilots. The plane's price tag seemed inconceivably high, and nobody believed that Israel would be able to shoulder such a burden. It was Ezer who realised, and who made sure others knew it, what an impact these aircraft could have. They could shift the balance in our favour come war. He put all his energy and ability into his efforts at persuasion. In the background, the French–Israeli 'love affair' flourished under the leadership of Ben-Gurion and Shimon Peres, filtering down to the lower levels in the higher echelons of both countries' military establishments and eventually opening the door to that incredible Mirage deal that brought the planes to Israel.

I parked the car in the lot in front of the hangar and paced down the concrete ramp to the underground yard. At a slow, deliberate pace, I drew near my dream – physically drew near it. There it stood in the yard, noiseless. Many security wrappings, marked with red tape to draw attention, were hanging at various points – on the wings, fuselage and landing gear. I advanced towards the plane with respectful humility.

Viewed from the front, the black radar nose protruded from the plane's front end. Rising from it was the metal-coloured pitot tube, which senses the air striking the plane and translates that pressure into airspeed. In almost all aircraft, including the Mirage, the pitot tube projects forwards ahead of the plane in order to be exposed to a 'clean' airflow, before it has been diverted and disrupted upon striking the plane's fuselage or the wings themselves.

I touched the plane's nose with my hand, not breaking contact with the fuselage as I advanced down the length of the plane. I enjoyed the cold, hard feel of the aluminium alloy from which the fuselage skin was constructed. I peeked into the dark interior of the air intake pipe, through which air flows into the engine, some of it for combustion and some of it to ventilate and cool the engine and its accessories. The opening of the intake pipe was partly blocked by a metal cone called a 'mouse', which really did look like the body of a giant mouse, its head and mouth pointing forward. From the little I'd already learnt, I knew that the 'mouse' could be moved back and forth by an electric motor, thus regulating the volume of air that was funnelled into the engine in accordance with flight conditions.

Another two steps brought me to the leading edge, the front edge of the wing. The innovative triangular wing, which had been dubbed the 'delta' wing, was the most exciting development in aeronautical engineering at that time. The horizontal stabilisers, those flat projections on either side of the tail that look like small wings themselves, had simply disappeared. Instead, the surfaces at the back edge of the wing – the trailing edge – were built so that they could move up and down. In the delta wing these surfaces, interconnected in a sophisticated manner, fulfilled all the steering requirements that previously had been provided by stabilisers, rudder and ailerons put together.

I continued my 'trek' around the steely silver bird and stopped in front of the exhaust pipe's huge funnel in the rear end of the fuselage. Around the opening I could see the intricate exhaust nozzle system. Dozens of metal plates, interconnected with steel rods and spring-like components, some of them overlapping, were arranged like a black corona around the circumference of the exhaust pipe. The metal parts looked charred and scorched by heat, proof of what they had to endure when the engine was running. I stuck my head inside the opening partway into the black void, letting my eyes grow accustomed to the dark. Now I could see the wheel of engine turbine blades and the compressor in front of it. I could only imagine the inferno that raged inside there when the pilot activated the immensely powerful afterburner.

Four months earlier, a few days after the first Mirages arrived in Israel, the rumour had spread among the pilots at the base: 'This morning Joe (Alon) is going to take off on the Mirage's first flight in Israel.' Together with two or three of my buddies among the trainers in the Ouragan squadron, I set out for the edge of the runway to witness this exceptional event. From the few pilots who had gone to France to study the new plane, led by the two designated squadron commanders, Joe Alon and 'Johann' Shtoper, we'd heard hair-raising stories about its performance. We'd been told, among other things, about the extremely high sensitivity of the innovative delta control surfaces. During take-off, it was said, the sensitivity of the elevation controls could lead to dangerous jolting when the plane left the runway. It was no

Amos Amir when a
Flying Cadet in 1957.

The author, standing on
the extreme right, when
on Flying Course No 24
during 1958 seen in front
of a Gloster Meteor.

Three remarkable gun-camera photographs taken from the author's Mirage during a strafing run on 5 June 1967 during the Six-Day-War. The Egyptian Tupolev Tu-16 was standing at Cairo-West Air Force Base when it was destroyed. The aircraft was a Russian-built medium bomber, codenamed 'Badger' by NATO.

Two gun-camera photographs taken from Amos's Mirage during a strafing run against a retreating Egyptian armoured division during the Six-Day-War. A truck can be seen to the right of the explosion and the dust kicked-up by the Mirage's bullets below the target.

Another Russian-built aircraft is destroyed by the author's cannon. This MiG-21 met its fate during September 1969 over Egypt – the War of Attrition. Codenamed 'Fishbed' by NATO, the MiG-21 was a single-seat fighter capable of Mach 2.5 and was a formidable adversary.

This combat sequence of photographs shows an air-to-air missile attack by Amos on a MiG-21 over Syria on 2 April 1970. In the first picture the MiG can be seen as a black speck at two-o'clock to the cross-hairs and the second picture shows the attacking missile's plume at twelve-o'clock as it races to its target. Photo 3 shows its initial strike and the final lethal explosion is captured in photo four.

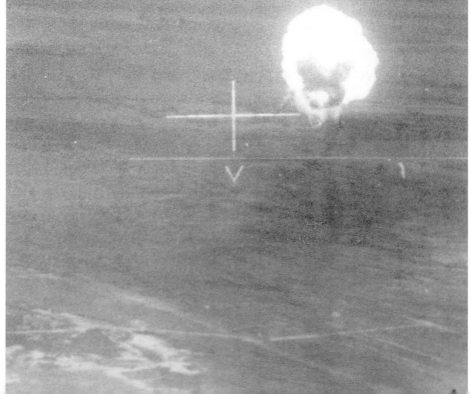

The famous Israeli Minister of Defence, Moshe Dayan, wears his characteristic eye-patch as he reads a briefing report from Amos concerning a dogfight over Suez during June 1969. The photograph was taken at Refidim Airbase in Sinai looking over the author's shoulder and with the Chief of Staff, Haim Barlev standing on the left.

The pilots of Israeli Air Force No 119 Squadron seen at the closing parade during August 1970. Lieutenant-Colonel Amos Amir, the Commanding Officer, stands fifth from the right.

'Pilots, man your aircraft.' No 119 Squadron's aircraft prepare to depart their base at Tel Nof for the last time. The French-built and designed Dassualt-Breguet Mirage was one of the most successful fighter aircraft of the '60s and '70s and was the author's favourite type. It was fast and versatile and could act as an interceptor, fighter-bomber or intruder. Note the victory roundels on the port side of each aircraft.

Colonel Amir, when Commander of Hazor Air Force Base in 1976, having just completed his first solo flight in the newly introduced Kfir fighter built by Israel Aircraft Industries.

Brigadier-General Amos Amir, Commander of the Eighth Air Force Base on the right, with General Gur, Chief of Staff IDF and General Peled, Commander of the Israel Air Force on the left, seen in 1977.

17 February 1977. The author about to take command of Tel Nof Air Force Base (No 8) as Major General Benni Peled takes the official emblem onto the podium.

The Parade at Tel Nof on 17 February, 1977.

The author after his first solo flight in an F-15 Eagle in April 1977.

The Bell Huey Cobra attack helicopter was one of the aircraft flown by the squadrons based at Tel Nof AFB. Here the author is seen in the cockpit prior to lift-off in September 1977.

Father and son. Amos seen at the controls of a Cobra helicopter in 1977 and a photograph, taken by his son, from the front seat of an F-16 trainer in which they were both flying. Son followed father into the Air Force and is now an operational fighter pilot – in the best family tradition.

wonder, then, that curious pilots set out to see this ground-breaking take-off for themselves.

Joe's plane approached the runway, waited beside it for a few minutes, and finally straightened out at the start of the runway, smack in the middle. A powerful roar was heard when Joe opened up full throttle for inspection. The engine roared for a few seconds, then quietened when he shifted back to neutral. A lot of dust was thrown up and hurled backwards by the exhaust gases, indicating that no planes had taken off from this runway for quite a while.

Now the engine was opened up full throttle again. The entire area behind the plane turned hazy because of the dust and hot exhaust gases, through which everything looked like fluid in motion. A small shudder of the nose indicated that the brakes had been released, and then the jet shot forward. We were standing about 1000 metres (1094 yards) away at the side of the runway where it was intersected by another at right angles to it, watching the approaching jet.

Glittering in its silvery metallic sheen, the Mirage zoomed towards us at tremendous speed. Directly opposite us the plane raised its nose very fast, to a height that none of us had seen before, which is only typical of delta-winged aircraft. We saw the plane leave the runway and its nose continue to rise.

What we next saw took our breath away! In a drastic – but clearly too drastic – reaction, the upraising of the nose was checked. However, instead of remaining stable in the requisite climbing position, the nose dropped and the plane appeared to descend towards the ground. It fell low enough to raise a cloud of dust from the sandy ground beyond the end of the runway, and then once again raised its nose up high. This rise and drop was repeated three times before the plane stabilised in a secure climbing position and disappeared. That evening, this take-off was the talk of the day in the squadron clubhouses and the pilots' residential quarters.

For us, the pilots who'd witnessed the event, it was an insightful and unequivocal lesson in the aerodynamics of the delta-winged plane and its oversensitive controls. *Pompage* (the pump phenomenon) was what the French called this phenom-enon, which was the result of overreaction on the part of an inexperienced pilot handling the sensitive controls. I made an effort to remember every detail of the thrilling performance for the sake of the days to come . . .

Now I completed my 'trek' around the Mirage and returned to the ladder leading to the cockpit. Armed with diagrams taken from the plane's manual, and with a spiral notebook of 'vital tests', I climbed into the cockpit and began the systematic process of learning the aircraft.

In two weeks' time I would be performing my first solo flight on the most advanced jet in the world – the Mirage.

CHAPTER TWENTY-ONE

Love of Rachel, 1963

The gigantic Stratocruiser, under the command of Oz, commander of the transport squadron, flew south by moonlight at very low altitude, following its planned course in the middle of the Red Sea. Two hours earlier the pilot had left the lights of Eilat behind. On both sides of our course, the shores of the Gulf of Aqaba, like those of the Red Sea beyond it, belonged to dangerous enemy countries. There was a suspenseful quiet in the pilots' cockpit when I stepped inside to pay a friendly visit. Oz was sitting in the captain's seat on the left side of the cockpit. In hushed voices, more in English than in Hebrew, the crew members exchanged information. I immediately felt the tension inside the cockpit. Oz greeted me with a desultory 'Hi' and turned back to his work, as did the other crew members.

'Giora, can you still read Port Sudan?' Oz asked the navigator.

'No, we passed them eight minutes ago and now there's no further reception from there,' replied Giora, the squadron's senior navigator.

For me, a fighter pilot who'd already spent many hundreds of hours in his narrow, one-seat cockpit, this kind of flying – as the well-managed and coordinated effort of several crew members working together as a team – was a new and fascinating experience. For the first time I saw how the cockpit activities were distributed among the crew members; how each of them performed the duties he was entrusted with; and how, ultimately, there was one person who had the last word and upon whom the full and undivided responsibility devolved – the captain.

Through a side-window I tried to catch sight of any lights

along one of the shores, but in vain. In a whisper I asked Giora for an explanation of the route we'd followed and what still lay ahead. Giora spread out the map in front of me and pointed to the marked course with the tip of the compass in his hand. For a good hour or so I stayed and watched the proceedings inside the cockpit and was deeply impressed by the crew members' calm and seriousness. When my curiosity was satisfied, I returned to the spacious cabin in the rear and sat down in my passengers' seat. It was the first time in my life I'd ever sat in one, on a quasi-civilian aircraft. 'It's just like in the movies,' I thought to myself, pleasurably stretching my limbs. I'd never sat in such comfort on an aircraft before, and the delightful feeling lulled me to sleep.

At dawn, before sunrise, the door of the plane opened onto a parking lot. Through the window beside my seat I saw a large sign written in French and English: 'Djibouti' was the name of the place. A hot wall of air slammed into my face when I approached the door. Considering the early hour, this was an utter surprise to me. Oz drew up next to me and smiled broadly:

'It's a bit hot in Djibouti, ain't it?' he said in the tone of a seasoned veteran.

The plane was approached by two military jeeps, from which alighted several grandly decorated officers, all of them black, and two French-speaking white civilians. After a brief huddled conference, the passengers – all seven of us – and some of the crew members were allowed to disembark and wait inside the 'terminal', a hot asbestos cabin, while the plane was being re-fuelled. I was enchanted by the atmosphere of mystery in this place I'd never dreamed I would see, and by the colourful characters, black and white, who milled around us; my imagination began to run wild. After a few large cardboard cases were unloaded from the plane, and after dozens more handshakes and sly smiles had been exchanged, we all got back on board the plane. The engines were started, and at a temperature of 45°C, the Stratocruiser took off to continue its journey south, to East Africa.

Rachel was waiting for me in Nairobi. After several years of hard work – gruelling flight practice, and two years' flying the new plane, the Mirage – and three years after the birth of Noam, our first son, it was time for a break. My father Aryeh had got an official job as an adviser to the government of newly independent Kenya. My father and my mother Anda settled into a formerly British colonial residence in a lovely, wooded suburb of this exotic town. The Air Force Stratocruiser let me off in Dar es Salaam on the Indian Ocean coast and continued on its way to South Africa. Rachel flew with El-Al on its route to South Africa via Teheran, and had already landed in Nairobi a couple of days before I arrived.

I saw her face first. There she was, standing in the area behind the customs counters with Father beside her and another man, a tall and slender black man with a good-natured face. A pleasant warmth spread through my body when our eyes met. I longed for her touch and her voice, and impatiently awaited the end of the formal arrival procedure. When I finally got through customs, we fell into each other's arms and embraced long and hard. I gave Father a hug and was introduced to Tony, my parents' chauffeur and personal assistant. The square, brightly polished black Austin took us 'home'. I was stunned by the gigantic bougainvillea shrubs along the sides of the road, and by the rows of coffee-bushes and green-leafed trees beyond them, which could not conceal the uniquely typical reddish tint of the East African soil. Together we drove up a hill outside the city and arrived at the yard of the big house. Squirrels busy gathering food there had to scramble aside to avoid the approaching car. A gust of pleasant chilly air, greeted us when the car door opened. Mother, looking the same as always, was standing in the doorway and smiling in welcome.

Tony, came into the guest-room carrying a huge platter with two large pineapples, neatly sectioned into slices, and a jug of cold mango juice. From the other side of the room wafted the fragrance of excellent Kenyan coffee, while thin slices of English cake waited patiently for deliverance. I held Rachel's hand in mine and found it hard to believe my eyes. This had to be Paradise itself! We chatted with my parents for a while, until we were able to get away to the pleasant bedroom we'd been assigned in the back of the house.

I stepped into the bathroom to take a shower; after my long journey it was not only requisite but most pleasurable. As I was enjoying the flow of the water over my body, the door opened. Rachel was standing there, nude and smiling. She pulled aside the shower curtain and joined me beneath the running water. Her wet black hair fell down the length of her neck, and her enticing body pressed against my bronzed body. The water kept on flowing and flowing and flowing. We flowed with it and kept flowing and flowing . . . Flushed and sparkling with love, we wiped each other dry – not entirely, only a little. Our bodies still slightly damp and chilled, we stretched out on the wide bed, on the starched sheet that smelled of cleanliness. I felt that all my nerves were on afire again. Electricity flowed between our bodies, between fingertips and patches of skin. I kissed her breasts, caressed her stomach, and felt her body slide against my manhood. Slowly, as if to prolong these moments of joy, I penetrated her. She moaned and threw her head back, giving herself entirely.

When the sun set, as the last light was fading from the sky, we quietly left through the back door of our room, which looked out on the yard, and walked about among the gigantic trees, arm in arm. A few monkeys and squirrels joined us on our enchanting evening stroll.

That evening we stayed at home. Tony, who also turned out to be a great cook, prepared the meal, and we sat down with my parents at the table, which was set with unfamiliar fastidiousness. I wasn't surprised to discover that Mother, with her openness and her ability to communicate with any living being on the planet, was already running a local women's club, speaking a few words and singing in the Zulu language. She seemed to be as proud of the achievements of Kenyan independence, the 'Ohuru,' so recently won, as if they had been the fruits of Israel's own War of Independence.

This was our finest hour together. We travelled from the heights of Mount Kilimanjaro in Tanganyika (*now Tanzania*), past Lake Manyara and the awesome Ngoro Ngoro nature reserve, all the way to Murchison Falls near the source of the Upper Nile. We toured the land of the Masai, so enthralling in its colours and smells, and in the life which flourished in its untamed landscapes. There, for an entire month, we felt as if we were the discoverers of a new and wonderful world.

In Kampala in Uganda, we boarded a boat for a two-day voyage around the shores of Lake Victoria. I was reminded of all the adventure stories I'd read in childhood about the discoverers of Africa and the continent's marvels. I hadn't been able to get Lake Victoria out of my head ever since, and the opportunity I was now afforded to sail around it fired my imagination. When the boat embarked on its journey, it was accompanied along the pier by a crowd of black Africans. We were given one of the few cabins in the forefront of the boat, which were reserved for 'pampered' tourists. The rest of the passengers, local people, were crowded on the foredeck, scattered with their bundles and belongings in a big, colourful and often noisy jumble. The boat sailed between three or four anchorages around the shores of the huge lake, and our entry into each port and departure from it were especially thrilling.

When night fell the voices from the aft deck quietened, too, turning into the typical, monotonous sound of African singing, which my ears attuned to over time. After feasting our eyes on the view of the surrounding shores, we both entered the cabin, where we tumbled into each other's arms.

'Amos, I want another child, a brother for Noam – here and now,' Rachel whispered in my ear.

'My Sweet, I'm all for it,' I answered with a laugh.

The voices of the African choir from the deck outside contunued to sing all through the night, accompanied by the dull thumping of drums.

CHAPTER TWENTY-TWO

Fire – Hazor Skies, 11 November 1963

At a certain point along the northern Sinai coastline, between the Bardawill lagoons and the town of Port Said, there's a place called 'Rumani'. An Egyptian Army camp with a radar station beside it had been built there. All the Sinai coastline, but this area in particular, was of immense importance to Israeli activity in the peninsula, and our intelligence dearly wanted to obtain photographs of the site. This mission was assigned to the Air Force.

As early as mid-1962, Air Force engineers began planning the assembly of an airborne camera for vertical photography, to be installed in the nose of a Mirage. Although the camera they had available was big and heavy and not particularly sophisticated, it could deliver good intelligence so long as the weather and flight conditions and the navigational accuracy were absolutely perfect. It quickly became apparent that the plane's original nose, which had been designed to hold the interception radar, was too narrow to accommodate this camera. The engineers who had been assigned to the task didn't throw up their arms in dismay. They designed and built a new nose, the internal dimensions of which precisely conformed to the camera's size and shape. This nose was much larger than the original; it was asymmetrical and extremely ugly. When first fitted to the plane, it was the source of great anguish to all who admired the plane's beauty, and who were now obliged to accept this ugly 'wart' at the front end of it . . .

Ran was the pilot overseeing this project, and after several months' work – including numerous flight tests and lots of

158

engineering and laboratory work – the job was nearing completion. Acceptable results from the flight tests were beginning to arrive at the photo-labs of Air Force intelligence, but the higher echelons had lost their patience and the vital need for updated intelligence overrode the desire to achieve a technically perfect system.

The mission to photograph the Rumani shore was postponed three times because of bad weather and cloudy conditions at the target site, so a new date was set for the late afternoon of 22 November.

I was hugely enthusiastic when I was assigned to be number two in the formation performing the mission. For me this would be my first deep penetration behind enemy lines. It was an experience with which Ran, number one and formation leader, was already familiar, having flown a few operational missions during the Sinai campaign in 1956. Nevertheless he, too, was tense and nervous as the time drew near. My own plane was equipped with cannon and the regular radar-bearing nose. The camera, inside the ugly nose, had only been installed in Ran's plane.

Dozens of times the two of us, together and on our own, went over our projected flight course and the variety of possibilities and complications that might occur. Every possibility, complication and malfunction required certain actions to address it. We learned by heart every minute of the flight, every feature of the terrain in our path, and every detail of what we had to perform along the way. The possibility of encountering enemy aircraft was broached and examined time and again. In effect, the mission required avoiding, at almost any cost, coming into contact with enemy aircraft during the flight. But to tell the truth, I was rather hoping that exactly such an 'undesirable' meeting might indeed take place . . .

The two Mirages, one beautiful and the other unbecoming, straightened out silently along the runway oriented to the southwest. We ran our engines at full power to check the systems, particularly the fuel system. I surveyed the various gauges inside the cockpit. Fuel began to flow from the large, detachable fuel tanks hanging from the wingtips to the central tank inside the fuselage, and from there to the engine, just as it should.

Ran swivelled his head to the right and looked in the direction of my cockpit. I concluded my preflight checks, took down the throttle to neutral, and raised my gaze to the left; our eyes met, and with just a slight nod of our heads we exchanged mutual confirmation: 'All set.'

Ran raised his left hand towards the stopwatch and pressed the switch beneath it, and the loud roar of his engine opening up to full power was heard immediately. Two seconds later his plane began to hurtle forward. Ten seconds after him my plane also took off, employing the full power of both its engine and afterburner.

This time the planes didn't head out west, towards the sea, but continued banking left and southward, in the direction of the Halutsa sand flats. At the scheduled spot, and exactly on time, the planes turned right towards the Egyptian border, about 20 km (12.4 miles) south of Nitsana. The point of penetration along the borderline had been chosen with particular care. The Egyptians had placed aerial lookouts all along the line, in regular positions; their job was to warn the Egyptian control system of border violations by low-flying Israeli aircraft. When determining our flight course, the planners looked for a spot at which the lookout stations were particularly distant from each other, and where the terrain made it possible to hide from the lookouts' eyes in a saddle of wadis. The planners hoped the torrid afternoon heat would also have its effect and put the bored lookouts to sleep.

Ran was famous for his ability to fly low, and he always managed to alarm all his wingmen in formation when he descended to only a few metres above land or water, a hairsbreadth away from impending disaster. I was already familiar with this ability of Ran's, and I descended to very low altitude too. Even so my guts were wrenched as I saw Ran descend even lower below me, and lower, and lower . . .

The two planes were literally lapping at the earth's surface as we passed over the borderline at high speed. Hundreds of times, I recalled, I'd flown in this vicinity on those endless north-south patrols, parallel to the border. This time it was a different story: now we were flying at right angles to the border, directly into the heart of Sinai, enemy territory.

Most of my efforts were devoted to two main objectives: first, to maintain my position at the proper distance within the formation, as well as stable eye-contact with the leader; second, to look around the entire expanse above and behind us in order to guard our tails from enemy aircraft that hadn't been discovered earlier by Israeli control.

From time to time I thrust my left hand into the recess between the canopy front window and the wall, took out the navigation chart, glanced at it, and looked up again in order to identify our location in the field. With the objects around me flying backwards at a relative speed of about 1000 kph (715 knots), and my plane flying at no more than 50 metres (160 feet) above the ground – this was no easy task.

Sites and places, whose names I'd heard many times in the context of the 1956 Sinai campaign, came into sight before my eyes, completely real this time. We passed north of the Abu Ageila junction, saw from afar the mighty silhouette of Jebel Libni and banked right in the direction of the coastline, performing a large and safe detour around El Arish airfield, from which two Egyptian fighter squadrons operated.

Only once along the route did I spot another aircraft in the sky.

One of the primary abilities a good fighter pilot has to have is the ability to spot and identify targets in the three-dimensional space around him. This ability is in part an innate ability, and in part the fruit of long training and practice. Like many of my fighter pilot colleagues, I found myself discovering targets in fields of view and at ranges that were inconceivable in everyday life.

'Nine o'clock, high altitude, not dangerous!' I broke radio silence to notify number one of a twin-engined cargo-plane flying about 10,000 feet (3050 metres) above us, about 10 km (6 miles) to the left, which, to me, appeared to be standing in the air. I knew that the plane itself didn't pose any danger to us. It was a matter for concern if one of its pilots should happen to spot us and pass on that information.

'Roger, eye contact,' Ran replied confidently and we continued on our way.

'Blue, I'm pulling!' Ran announced over the radio, straightening his plane on a course parallel to the shore, about 7 km (4.3 miles inland from the waterline. The shimmering expanses of the Bardawill lagoon now came into view in all their beauty, and I had a couple of seconds free to make a mental note of the spot's extraordinary magnificence. It even seemed to me that I caught a glimpse of a huge flock of flamingoes covering part of the blue-green lake. To my left and slightly ahead of me I saw Ran wag his wings alternately left and right, and I knew he was now preparing for a precision flypast over the target ahead of us.

'Blue, going into operation!' Ran announced that he was operating the camera.

Ran's plane stopped rolling from side to side and stabilised on its final set course. I almost sprained my neck from glancing to the sides and backwards as much as I possibly could. The sky looked empty and absolutely peaceful. The planned course for taking the pictures was exactly two-and-a-half minutes long. I noticed that Ran added an extra half-minute at either end of the course. 'The man just wants to make absolutely sure,' I thought to myself.

'Blue, I'm done. Two, come with me, right!' he ordered.

The two planes banked sharply right and down, towards the blue waves of the relatively secure sea. The yellowish Sinai coast swiftly disappeared to the right and behind us as we returned to low altitude, near the waves. Even if we had been spotted by the cargo-plane, and even if the information had been forwarded, it was too late for the Egyptians to catch up and intercept us. Flying close to the waves, far from shore, both of us felt right at home.

'Blue, this is big dog. Do you read me?' came the rasping voice of Air Force commander Ezer Weizmann over the radio. It was impossible not to recognise it.

'I read you, big dog. Carry on,' replied Ran.

'Blue, well done! Welcome home!' said Ezer, from his station inside Air Force headquarters in Tel Aviv.

'Roger. Thank you, big dog,' replied Ran.

Nobody had any idea yet what was about to happen.

'Hazor tower from Blue formation, we're landing,' Ran notified the control-tower as the two Mirages approached Ashkelon from the direction of the sea.

'Blue, runway two-niner, in use. You are free to join, the circuit's clear,' the flight-control officer answered him.

I reduced my engine power and left my place at the head of the formation to move into single file, opening up a distance of 1000 metres (1100 yards) or so from the leader. Both of us stretched out in our seats and entered the downwind leg of the circuit prepared to land, at an altitude of 2300 feet (700 metres). We were flying parallel to the runway, in a direction exactly opposite to the landing itself. The dark runway could be seen to our left, empty and waiting to receive us. Peforming the circuit of the field and the landing was a routine matter to us. There was nothing complicated about it, in utter contrast to the high tension we'd undergone only twenty minutes earlier during the course of our intricate and dangerous operational flight.

'This is Blue one, I've lost my engine!' came the cry from Ran in his cockpit. His plane could be seen beginning to lose altitude, but under stable control.

'I'll try to approach. Get ready to eject, one!' I announced in reply, right away. I knew for certain that with the altitude Ran had at his disposal he had no chance of completing a 180-degree turn and straightening out to land on the designated runway. Such a manoeuvre would have required another 8000 feet (2438 metres), while the 2000 feet (610 metres) he did have were rapidly dwindling.

'I tried to restart the engine. It's not working,' Ran announced, taking his plane into a moderate left turn so that it would crash in an open area and cause no damage. I exploited the small turn to approach number one's plane, managing to get within about 400 metres (438 yards) of him. We were now at an altitude of 600 feet (183 metres).

'This is Blue one. I'm ejecting!' announced Ran.

I saw the cockpit canopy rise, separate itself from the fuselage and fly backwards. Immediately afterwards I saw the blaze of the rocket that hurled the ejection seat to a height of 20 metres (66 feet) above the plane. I anxiously followed the seat with my eyes as the descending plane drew away from it, and breathed a sigh of relief three seconds later when the pilot left the seat and a colourful parachute canopy bloomed over his head. I could plainly make out Ran's stocky body beneath the canopy of the parachute, dangling between heaven and earth.

'Hazor tower, this is Blue two. Blue one ejected 8 km (5 miles) north-east of you, open parachute sighted. I'm continuing to circle the spot as long as I've got enough fuel left. Scramble a helicopter out here,' I notified the tower.

Now I turned my eyes back in the direction of the abandoned plane and an extraordinary spectacle came into view. Instead of going into a tighter turn, spinning and crashing into the ground, the plane went on descending at what appeared to be a moderate and controlled pace, drawing near the ground at a flat angle as if an unseen but practised hand were still at the controls. With its wings and fuselage almost perfectly level with the surface, the plane ploughed into a field. Clouds of dust were thrown up, and then the plane could be seen lying in the field, its wings still attached and the entire fuselage, from nose to tail, perfectly intact.

I glanced back in the direction of the slowly sinking parachute. I went into a wide turn around the parachute, which was prominently visible, and followed it until I saw it touch the ground, collapse and lose its characteristic hemispherical shape.

'Blue two, this is the tower. Helicopter on its way, location clear. You are free to join the circuit and land'.

I noted in my mind the green plot of land beside which I'd just seen the parachute come to earth. I performed another wide turn, and flew back in the direction of that green plot at relatively low speed and at an altitude of 300 feet (91 metres). When I passed over the spot I could already see Ran standing there in the field and waving at me. I wagged my wings a little to say hello and breathed a sigh of relief. Then I turned my plane back in the direction of the runway, joined the circuit and landed.

That evening a small party was held at one of the pilot's homes in Hazor; the star attraction was Ran, of course, limping slightly but otherwise unhurt. Even Weizmann came, bringing with him a bottle of whiskey that had an original limerick of his own hand-written on the label. In the middle of the party the Force's head of equipment department and the commander of the base's maintenance squadron arrived, broad smiles plastered across their faces. Miraculously, the abandoned plane had, on its own, performed a near perfect crash-landing in the field. All the major sections of the plane remained relatively intact, and it would be possible to determine exactly what caused the engine to shut down in flight. But they brought even more sensational news: the camera and all its contents had been retrieved in whole from that special, ungainly nose.

Later we were also joined by the head of intelligence, who'd got the photos he wanted so badly. Mission accomplished.

During the first three years of the Mirage's operation no fewer than seven pilots ejected from their planes, three in France and four in Israel, mostly because of engine malfunctions. This was cause for growing concern in the upper echelons of both countries' air forces, especially in light of the plane's enormous price tag, which weighed heavily on defence budgets and fuelled criticism of the decision-makers responsible for military procurement, headed in Israel by General Weizmann.

Now, with an almost wholly intact plane, whose pilot had ejected, in their hands, everyone was hoping that the mystery of the accidents would be solved swiftly. The planes of the two Israeli Mirage squadrons, based in Hazor and Ramat-David, were grounded until the results of the investigation into the most recent accident should arrive and the planes repaired. Indeed, the investigation was completed within three-and-a-half weeks and its technical conclusions were adopted by both the Israelis and the French. A method was determined to fix the fault that had been discovered, and one after another the planes were taken to the workshop to be repaired.

At the beginning of December King Mahendra of Nepal, came on a state visit to Israel. At that time not many heads of state came to visit, and the government went to great lengths to impress the distinguished guest and make his visit a great success. The King was also invited to visit the Air Force for half a day, and it was decided to put on a special air show of jet fighter firepower. The performance was set to be held at the Air Force range near the seashore, between Palmachim and Ashdod. The powers that be were especially anxious to show off the Mirages – the pride of the Air Force and of Israel's friend France's defence industry.

Two days before the date of the display, which was set for 11 December 1963, the first two planes left the repair line in the Hazor workshop and were released to fly. A third plane was released the next day, and so it was decided that a pair of Mirages would perform the shooting exhibition, while the third would be kept in reserve in case of malfunction.

Exactly one month to the day after 'Blue' formation, with Ran as leader and myself as number two, had set out on that operational mission, the two of us were assigned to perform the air show.

'Blue, permission to straighten out,' came Ran's voice over the radio, sure and confident as usual.

'Granted, Blue. Runway 23, wait for authorisation to take off,' came the reply.

'Blue two, I read you loud and clear,' I notified number one.

'Blue formation, take-off,' requested Ran.

'You are go, Blue. Wind on the runway is at 15 knots (28 kph).'

The two planes began their take-off run. Two non-explosive practice bombs were hanging from the wings of each plane, and our 30-mm cannon had been loaded with seventy practice rounds each. It was a very short distance from the airfield to the range. Ran had the formation switch to the range officer's channel, and checked communications both with me and with the range over the new channel; everything seemed perfectly in order.

In single file, one behind the other, we passed over the range officer's hill, on which a shady tent had been erected and benches set out for the benefit of the air show's spectators, the King at their head.

Communication was established, and the range officer authorised us to go into our bombing and sniping runs. Both of us readied our weapon system switches, opened our engines full-throttle, and climbed to an altitude of about 8000 feet (2438 metres) from which to go into our runs. I could see Ran in front of me, rolling his plane and going into his bombing run at a very steep angle. I glanced at the flight instruments, checked the switches one last time, and went into my own first bombing run. As I was diving towards the target, which was marked by circles of old, empty barrels around it, I had time to see a cloud of sand rising near its centre and marking the spot where the bomb dropped by Ran had hit the ground. It was a good hit, only a few metres away from the target's geometric centre.

With the gunsight lying steady on the centre of the target, I glanced at the altimeter. Its dial was spinning backwards as the aircraft descended. At 3000 feet (914 metres) I pressed the bomb release switch and felt the slight concussion, which accompanied the bomb's detachment from the wing. I pulled back the stick and raised the plane's nose up and to the left. The G-force of my acceleration pulled all my limbs and organs downwards until I eased off on the stick. Craning my neck backwards to the left, in the direction of the tail, I just managed to see the sand bomb hit very near the bullseye of the target: a heap of barrels in the exact centre of the concentric circles.

After dropping our four bombs, for which we were rewarded with cries of admiration from the range officer, both of us began making passes at lower altitude to demonstrate our cannon-fire. The targets consisted of canvas sheets spread between two thick wooden posts.

Like most of my fighter squadron mates, I was very fond of these sniping practice sessions. First, the proximity to the ground greatly intensified the sensation of speed; and this, together with all the fun of squeezing the trigger and hearing the cannon go off, always made for an increased flow of adrenaline. Second, the fact that the sniping results were scored and publicised among the squadron pilots always lent these proceedings a dimension of competition, and with it a degree of tension, but generally of a positive nature.

Each of us performed three passes at low altitude over the row of targets. Three times the cannon triggers were squeezed, the roar of the bursts of shells sounded, and smoke rose from the ground behind the targets.

'Blue, winding it up. Request permission to pass in formation above you from east to west,' Ran notified the range officer, and received confirmation over the radio.

'Blue, tight formation, go!' Ran commanded.

Speedily and with practised skill, as was my wont, I joined Ran and took up position to his right, only three metres separating the wingtips of our two aircraft. Ran glanced briefly in my direction to make sure I was in place, then turned to look ahead again. I fixed my gaze on an imaginary line between the tip of the aileron and the edge of the lead plane's cockpit. From now this would be my entire world. There was no looking away, no turning my head. Any diversion, any uncontrolled movement or needless wagging of the wings could spell disaster.

In a nicely tight formation, at an altitude of 150 feet (46 metres), the two Mirages passed directly over the heads of the dignitaries gathered on the hillside with a powerful roar of their engines.

'Blue, well done!' the range officer congratulated us.

'Thanks, see you,' Ran replied, after which he directed me to shift into a more open formation and switch radio channels as we flew along the coastline in the direction of Ashkelon.

At an altitude of 3000 feet (914 metres), as we were passing over the outskirts of Ashkelon in a south-easterly direction, my plane's engine suddenly shut off without warning! I couldn't help but wonder instinctively at the tricks Fate plays on people.

'Blue one from two, I've lost my engine!' I exclaimed over the radio.

I looked at the instrument panel inside the cockpit. The first suspicion that came to mind was that my fuel had run out; this was immediately refuted. But the readings that began to appear on the instrument panel were something I'd never seen before, nor ever dreamt I'd see. The engine rpm gauge dropped at a fantastic pace, stopping at a low and meaningless value. Red warning lights lit up one after another.

The plane's speed began to drop, and I had to put almost all my efforts into keeping it in a state of controlled flight/glide. I shut down the throttle and then tried, in the most orderly manner possible, to restart the engine in mid-air. I didn't think I had much chance of success, and indeed there was no sign of life from the engine.

Out of the corner of my eye I caught sight of Ran not far away from me to my right. I could hear him telling me something over the radio but my mind was too occupied to pay notice to it. My speed dropped to about 250 knots, which is slightly more than 400 kph. The altimeter was approaching 1000 feet (305 metres).

'At 800 feet (244 metres) I'll ditch the plane,' I told myself.

I didn't have the feeling that more time would bring better news, and so I prepared myself for ejection. I sat straight and erect, my back flat against the backrest, my legs tucked in – an exercise I had practised hundreds of times in the past and now had to perform for real.

When the altimeter needle touched 800, I pulled the yellow-black handle above my head all the way down, and a thick cloth screen that was tripped by the handle descended over my face. A loud blow was heard when the canopy separated from the fuselage and flew away. I didn't even notice the one-second delay before a huge, invisible force hurled me, together with the seat, out into the open air. There were two or three twists in the air, and then I felt a sharp and sudden deceleration. When I raised my eyes I saw the parachute canopy spread above my head, and a stunning silence all around me took hold.

Up ahead I saw my plane flying away from me toward the east, sinking more and more, until finally it crashed into a ploughed field. I couldn't restrain myself from making an obscene gesture in the direction of the treacherous jet, followed by a Russian curse.

The recent rains had left the fields of Ashkelon wet and full of mud, which pleased the region's farmers no doubt. But not me.

When I reached the ground, all set to perform a proper parachutist's roll, both my feet got planted and stuck in the deep mud. I lay down on the spot and rested for a moment on the damp earth. When I sat up I saw Ran's plane approaching. I began gathering up the parachute and waved to the jet passing above me. Ran caught sight of me. Now it was his turn to wag his wings at me in goodbye . . .

After a ride back to base in the helicopter, and after winning my argument with the doctors who wanted to keep me under supervision in the clinic, I returned home, limping on my left leg – the one which had got stuck in the mud first.

Just like a month earlier, a party was held in one of the pilot's homes. Again Ezer Weizman arrived, and again he brought with him a bottle of whiskey adorned with an original limerick – something along the lines of 'To Amos the brave / Whose ass has been saved . . .'

A story that was making the rounds among the Mirage pilots came to my attention. The Martin-Baker company, eminent maker of the ejection seats, had apparently promised to award a small gold decoration to pilots who'd made operational use of their equipment. I diligently applied in writing to the company.

Two months later the gold 'caterpillar' emblem, which I received as a gift from the seat manufacturer, was pinned to my shirt lapel.

However, the process of mending the Mirages wasn't finished yet.

CHAPTER TWENTY-THREE

Hatserim, 1966

With its characteristic, grating whine, the Fuga-Magister jet taxied into the aircraft line of the flight academy in Hatserim Airbase. It was straightened out in its slot, came to a stop and the engine was switched off. Before the whistle of the engine even had time to die down, the rear canopy swung open and the flying instructor rose from the cockpit to leave.

With a hop and a skip I dropped to the concrete tarmac, wearing my grey flying overalls and a yellow rescue belt, a major's bars on my shoulder. Without removing the helmet from my head, I signed the aircraft register and went off to the nearby open shed. I found a shady corner, sat down on the railing, and laid the rescue belt and helmet on the concrete floor beside me. I passed my fingers through my hair and let the light breeze cool my sweating body.

Dripping perspiration and visibly exhausted, the flight cadet now emerged from the forward cockpit.

Ronny, the cadet, knew that this flight with the commander of the basic training squadron was of great significance to his future flying career. He was also aware that in the preliminary course, several months earlier, his personal trainer had had doubts regarding his suitability. When he'd moved to the basic training squadron he'd hoped to start afresh with a clean slate. Ronny was likeable, smart, well-mannered and companionable. He'd even managed to strike up a comfortable mutual relationship with his trainer, a withdrawn individual who wasn't an easy man himself, without crossing the boundaries of distance subsisting between trainer and trainee.

After a month or so of flying in the basic course, Dooby,

Ronny's trainer, had come to me with doubts concerning his trainee.

'Ronny is undoubtedly first-class officer material and a fine individual, but in flight there's a recurrent pattern where occasionally his thinking becomes frozen, and he stops responding to events with the necessary speed and decisiveness,' he said.

'Maybe it's you who's putting too much pressure on him? Striking fear into him?' I ventured.

'I don't think that's the case, but I could be mistaken in my evaluation of my own attitude towards the trainee,' Dooby candidly replied.

I brought my deputy Amit, who was also the squadron's veteran trainer, into the discussion. The three of us looked through Ronny's files and tried to figure out what to do in this matter. After another two weeks I decided to break up the existing trainer-trainee arrangement and transferred Ronny to a different trainer – a more open, gentler man. In view of all of Ronny's good qualities, I dearly wished him to succeed. But now, when his new trainer also encountered the same phenomenon of a mental 'freeze' under the pressure of flying conditions, and after another month of constant training flights in a wide variety of topics, it was time for Ronny to perform a special test flight with the squadron commander.

From my own experience, I knew how stressed a flight cadet could get at having to fly with the squadron commander even on a routine flight, let alone something defined as a test. I therefore tried, to whatever extent possible, to project an easy atmosphere from the moment we met in the briefing room, speaking to him in a calm and affable tone of voice. During the course of the flight I hardly interfered in the performance of the exercises, sufficing with brief, quiet instructions to take him through the topics. In one of the exercises, which wasn't polished enough, I took hold of the controls, asked him to keep his own hands on the controls and stay with me, and got him to perform the manoeuvre independently, quite handsomely.

According to plan, we now descended to low altitude. As we neared the ground I notified Ronny that I was putting him into the procedure for an emergency landing with no engine, and I pulled the throttle back into idle. All at once the engine noise fell and the plane's speed began to drop rapidly. A situation of this kind demands a short and simple series of actions, which takes account of the limited time at the pilot's disposal and the stress under which he's necessarily functioning. The most immediate action, which must be taken without delay, is to maintain the plane in a state of full control – other words, to stabilise it at a safe gliding speed.

A worrying silence and lack of response were emanating from the forward cockpit. It took nerves of steel for me not to intervene immediately, neither at the controls nor in speech, but to wait patiently. The plane continued in the direction it had been flying, its speed rapidly diminishing. This disconcerting situation persisted for fifteen seconds – an eternity. 'Reopen engines thrust,' I instructed the cadet, stopping the exercise when it became clear that continuing with it would lead to a crash. The flight continued for another few minutes, until I asked Ronny to fly the plane back to base.

On the way back I had time to think things through and summarise the situation to myself. As a squadron commander at the flight academy, it was my job to train new pilots for the Air Force. In the almost perpetual argument regarding who was better – the 'hands' pilot, who was natural, quick to react, and had honed instincts and a fine sense of space and speed, or the 'head' pilot, who was cerebral, analytical, methodical, and took things one step at a time – I was inclined towards the latter. I believed that the 'head' pilot had a more promising future, and that all in all he'd be the one of greater benefit to the service. But I also knew there are situations in which the threshold of a pilot's instincts is tested. Those who are unable to pass the threshold, smart as they may be, aren't going to last long. After all, among my duties it was also my responsibility to weed out, well beforehand, those young men who might be dangerous to themselves and to others, and to block their prospective promotion to pilots.

'How would you yourself evaluate your flight today?' I asked Ronny after he'd cooled down a bit and joined me in the shady shed, sitting on the railing beside me.

'I thought it wasn't a bad flight at all,' replied Ronny. We discussed the course of the flight and the various exercises which had been performed. This debriefing removed any lingering doubt from my mind when I realised, with some surprise, that Ronny hadn't even noticed those episodes of 'freezing' that had turned up in today's flight, as in previous flights. Perhaps he had completely repressed them. He hadn't really noticed the emergency situations in which he'd found himself, and they hadn't roused him to take the necessary swift action.

Both of us returned on foot and took our leave of each other with a salute at the entrance to the squadron building. At noon, after I'd summoned my deputy and Ronny's two trainers to my office for a meeting, Ronny himself was called to my office.

'Ronny, I and all your trainers are convinced that you're a smart, talented and upstanding young man, but nevertheless you're not cut out to be an Air Force pilot. Due to your make-up you're liable to fall headlong with your plane into a death trap. We cannot, we have no right to let that happen. I wish you success in any post you shall be called to fill, but your flight training must come to an end,' I said to him. I was fully convinced of the justice of my case.

About two years had gone by since I'd been commissioned as the commander of the basic training squadron at the flight academy. At first I hadn't liked the idea at all and would have preferred to continue flying regularly in the Mirage squadron, even dreaming of the day I might get to command it. But as time went on I found great interest in my new job and took it as a personal challenge. I also discovered that there's no tool like flight training to broaden and deepen a trainer's aviatic knowledge and skill.

One day, after several months in my job at the flight academy, Yacov, the academy commander, came to see me on one of his visits to the unit. He proposed that I perform the aerobatic display at the upcoming 'wings' parade ceremony. I immediately accepted, with enthusiasm. From then on, for almost two years, this duty was entrusted to me on all ceremonial occasions, and I devoted a lot of time, thought and practice to it. For me this was the 'cherry on the cake', which sweetened the routine of flight training.

I always felt a sweet exhilaration accompanying my perfor-mances. I liked the feeling of the virtuoso performing for a wide audience, capturing their hearts and giving them a thrill, if only for a short while. Although I couldn't see the anonymous spectator's eyes grow wide with wonder, I always knew he was there. He, the spectator, was lifting his head to the sky and gazing in rapture at the metal bird rolling above him, as if it had freed itself from Newton's laws of physics. The ability to put on rare and exceptional performances, safely and at the highest level of proficiency, gave me great satisfaction.

One of the embarrassing and perhaps most dangerous, incidents in my life occurred while performing this duty. The 'wings' parade ceremony was due to be held in another week. It was to be the fourth ceremony at which I'd perform, and not an especially large one at that, and so seemingly quite routine. I'd been working for some time on preparing a new aerobatic programme, significantly more extreme and daring than its predecessors. I presented the programme in outline to the academy commander. After asking me to introduce a certain change, he confirmed it.

As was my habit, I began training for the performance at higher altitude, first above 3000 feet (914 metres), then 2000 feet (607 metres), then down to 1000 feet (305 metres). Only when I felt fully confident did I descend to the meagre altitude set for the performance itself – 200 feet (about 60 metres) for the vertical exercises and 100 feet (30 metres) for the horizontal exercises. At the end of my programme I was supposed to stabilise the plane in a direction directly facing the grandstand, at an altitude of 200 feet, for a final pass over the crowd of spectators. In order to draw a last gasp of amazement, however, I wasn't going to suffice with the 'ordinary' low pass. I planned to roll my plane over on its back directly in front of the grandstand and pass over it in that fashion, wagging my wings up and down in the gesture of goodbye that is familiar to every aviator. My rehearsals at high altitude and in remote flying zones had gone well and I was satisfied. Now it was time to rehearse the performance above the base, in the area where the grandstand was due to be erected.

'Tower, this is zero seven, requesting permission to go into my first run through the performance, minimal altitude 500,' I radioed the control-tower.

'Zero seven, you are clear to go,' came the reply.

I went into my run and performed the series of exercises in its entirety. I carefully noted the various heights that were 'seared' into my memory of the vertical exercises, finding a complete correspondence with my previous calculations and the data I'd accumulated in previous rehearsals. On the other hand, I discovered that when I let the plane's nose drop towards the ground after a certain corkscrew manoeuvre upwards, the plane wasn't orientated in the particular, precise direction I'd intended. I made a small correction, went on and finished the exercise according to plan, but I wasn't satisfied with the performance as a whole.

I left the runway area and climbed above the airbase, circling for a couple of minutes to think over my execution. I breathed deeply, wiped the sweat from my brow, and pressed the oxygen mask to my face once again.

'Tower from zero seven, request to repeat the same exercise.'

'Zero seven, clear to go,' the controller confirmed again.

I again performed the entire series of exercises, making my corrections wherever necessary, and now felt fully confident in my programme.

'Tower, this is zero seven. Request to repeat exercise third and last time, minimal altitude 200,' I said to the tower.

'Zero seven, clear to go,' came the reply again.

I checked my speed, altitude and engine readings; everything looked okay. I went into my third performance of the entire series of exercises, and everything was going smoothly. I could already precisely identify the picture of the base when I was upside down on my back, when I rolled the plane over on its axis, or as it would appear 'above' me when I came out of a loop. The time came for the last diagonal turn, at the conclusion of which I found myself, just as planned, flying at 200 feet (60 metres) directly towards the grandstand area. 'Everything's fine!' I thought to myself, and the feeling of a successfully completed performance began to creep into my heart.

I checked my altitude for the last time, raised the plane's nose slightly above the horizon, rolled the plane over on its back, pushed the stick forward hard and immediately felt the expected reaction – my body's entire weight hanging from the seat straps as if an unseen force were trying to hurl me to the canopy and out of the plane. I saw the grandstand area approaching from in front and 'above' me, and I wagged my wings in goodbye. Upside down, the plane passed precisely above the spot designated for the central tier of grandstand seats.

'A great performance,' I congratulated myself, with a sense of relief at having concluded the exercise. 'I'm done,' I thought, 'and now it's time to climb to higher altitude.' I began to perform the most instinctive movement of any pilot who intends to climb: I stopped pushing the stick and started pulling it instead!

On its back, the plane responded precisely according to the laws of physics. It 'raised' its nose directly towards . . . the ground, which was less than 330 feet (100 metres) away. In the few split seconds I had left, I came to my senses and realised what was happening.

I reversed my motion and pushed the stick hard ahead, pointing the nose of the plane 'down,' that is to say, up! The plane continued flying upside-down, passing very low and close to the roofs of the hangars and the gigantic workshops in the western section of the base, just clearing the tops of the eucalyptus trees behind them as it came out of the dangerous plunge. I now rolled the plane over into its 'natural' belly-down position and took it back up to higher altitude.

I broke into a cold sweat as I tried to relax and get a grip on myself.

'*Mazel tov* on being reborn, you idiot!' I said to myself aloud, repeating it again for good measure as I taxied the plane back to the line.

The joy of flying, the responsibility of commanding people, and the progress I felt in my own professional capacities – these were the factors drawing me ever deeper into my job. I loved what I was doing. I enjoyed investing in my job as I enjoyed the feedback I received for my performance. The cadets admired me; the flight trainers whom I commanded liked me and found ways to express it; and my commanders made no secret of their appreciation of my work.

It was my home, the family, and my life with Rachel, however, that began to pay the price for this personal development. I hadn't stopped loving Rachel, but when the needs of the job came into conflict with the needs of the home, the former almost always won. My ambition and indefatigable drive to achieve and be acknowledged, as well as the satisfaction I took in my successes, all combined to put other considerations, into second place. It wasn't hard to feel the slow subsidence of the relationship between Rachel and me. I knew it. And I knew she knew it. But the process appeared to be stronger than both of us.

CHAPTER TWENTY-FOUR

Fire – Mount Hermon Skies, 12 May 1970

Asher Snir was one of those people you come across once in a lifetime. He was a unique and exceptional character. He was 'just' one of the leaders in the squadron when I was given command of it, but his pre-eminence was evident everywhere, in everything. Diminutive, slender, not handsome by any means, with black hair, fair skin and a pair of steel-blue eyes that could bore through anybody – now there was a man! Both great and small would listen when Asher spoke, and it hardly mattered what about. He was an almost infuriating package of knowledge, logic, expressive ability, understanding and humour. As for me, Asher won my heart immediately.

It was a difficult time then during the War of Attrition for the military services in general, and for the squadron in particular. The activity and tension went on around the clock, while the pressing lack of commanders and leaders increased the burden on the shoulders of the regular senior pilots, making life difficult for them. On the outside, in prominent fashion verging on effrontery, civilians were celebrating the economic boom. The pilots who dared to leave the service came back to the squadron telling tales that quickly spread of the good life outside. The efforts by commanders to keep the best people enlisted in regular service were largely fruitless, and the ranks continued to dwindle.

Uri, Eitan, Avraham, and Ruvik – the pick of the squadron's leaders – came to me one after another and informed me of their intention to leave the service. I was counting on Asher; I'd put my trust in him and had him in mind to be my deputy. I knew great things were in store for Asher with the Air Force.

On a Monday evening the squadron was emptied of its occupants. At the squadron remained only Nir and I (who were on standby), Anat, who sat in the operations room downstairs and was handling various reports, and Asher, who was always doing something that turned out to be beneficial. I'd been serving at my post as squadron commander for a year. I was sitting in my room and reading the mail when Asher stood in the door and asked if he could come inside. I swept aside the ugly brown files and invited him to take a seat.

'I know you're counting on me for the position of deputy, and I appreciate it very much,' he said. 'I'd also like to mention my appreciation for the way you've come in and handled life and operational activity in the squadron.' 'Nevertheless,' he went on, 'after giving much thought to my future course in life, I've come to the conclusion that I want to leave the service and go on to a career on the outside, probably an academic career.'

I hadn't been expecting any such announcement, and perhaps I'd been putting it out of my mind to avoid dealing with it. But now I was facing it, like it or not. I knew for a certainty that Asher would be a success in the academic world. Furthermore, I thought the academic world should thank its lucky stars for the likes of him, when the time came. On the other hand, I knew his leaving the squadron would be a grave blow to the texture of this important fighting unit.

'As you well know, Asher, I have no way of stopping you,' I said. 'I do think, however, that your leaving here now would be a terrible blow to the squadron, especially after the spate of departures we've recently suffered. You mustn't leave now, you're too important here, and I strenuously object to this decision.' I didn't leave a crack or chink that might let him think that I was buying his arguments. For his part, Asher added several more explanations, formulated to the best of his ability, regarding his reasons and the advantages of the road he'd chosen. Our conversation ended without Asher having gone back on his decision. He bid me farewell, got into his car and drove away from the squadron building.

That Thursday an especially complex spy-photo operation was planned to take high-altitude pictures of three airfields along the Iraq-Syria border. The planning was in its advanced stages and everyone involved in the secret operation was already in a state of feverish excitement. I had designated Asher to be the leader of the pair of spyplanes that would carry out the mission.

After Asher left the office, I stayed seated and thought over this new situation. After several minutes I went downstairs to the operations room. I saw Anat sitting there working. She turned to me with her usual smile, but immediately felt that something was amiss with me and stayed put. I went over to the classified operations board and removed the dark green screen that covered it. On the board, two red plastic slats carried the names of the designated pilots for the mission, Asher and Ruvik. I removed the slat with Asher's name on it from the board and put it back in the drawer; in its place I took out the slat with my name on it and attached it to the board in the box for the designated mission leader. Having done this, I covered the board again and wordlessly returned to my room.

I was well aware that I was going for broke in everything concerned with Asher's release from the squadron, but I'd decided to take action.

On Tuesday, the squadron went into a state of 'radio silence', so to speak: everyone knew what was happening, but nobody was saying a word. Asher was seen pacing irritably about the balcony, but nothing happened. Early on Wednesday morning, before the morning briefings, Asher stepped into my office and sat down facing me.

'Amos, you clever bastard,' he said, 'you've really got me by the balls! You couldn't have made me change my decision in any other way. But I am unable to remain indifferent to being relieved of performing exceptional missions of quality. I've decided to reverse my position. I'm staying with the squadron, my resignation is cancelled.'

Having said as much, he left the office. I stepped out after him without betraying my feelings outwardly. I went straight down to the operations room and wordlessly put Asher's name back on the operations board.

The loud scramble alarm shook the standby cabin and the whole shed of interceptor planes next to it. Dror and I tossed aside whatever we were doing, burst through the door and rushed to

the standby planes. From the rooms next to us the standby
mechanics also came running, each rushing to his position and
post. The two of us scrambled quickly up the ladders, sat down
inside the cockpits, and strapped ourselves in with the assistance
of the mechanics. I dismissed my mechanic with a wave of my
hand, put on the helmet and heard the rustling of the radio over
the earphones.

'Red one, on air,' I notified the tower.

'Two, on air,' Dror chimed in immediately after me.

Out of the corner of my eye I caught sight of the standby jeep
as it arrived from the direction of the squadron and drove up to
the shed. Eitan and Asher got out of it and rushed over to the two
other planes at the site, which were ready to go. On both fronts it
had become common procedure at that time for the controller,
when the first pair of pilots had been put into 'immediate'
standby, to place another pair on standby automatically, just in
case additional forces should be required for combat.

In my capacity as squadron commander, I'd decided long
before that the second pair of pilots would join the first standby
pair and man their planes without waiting for a specific instruction from central control. The experience accumulated by the
fighter squadrons had taught us, the commanders, not to spare
any effort in maintaining standby readiness and not to wait for
strings to be pulled from above. We had to do as much
pushing, and as hard, as we could by ourselves. Our impulse to
make fighting contact with the enemy was intense and overwhelming.

'Red formation, scramble, direction north!' radioed the
control-tower.

Even before the message had reached its end and without
wasting precious time to confirm it, I hit the purple ignition
switch that activated the huge pressurised air tanks beneath the
plane's underbelly. As I was completing the ignition procedure,
I noticed that mechanics were hurrying over to Dror's plane, my
number two, with a spare pressure tank.

'Green one, on air.'

'Green two, on air.' Eitan and Asher's voices were heard on the
radio, reporting to the tower.

My plane was standing, engine running and ready to move,

when I noticed that Dror's plane had a problem and he couldn't start the engine.

'Green two, start your engine and join me. Red two, switch planes and join Green formation,' I announced, and received confirmation from all three pilots involved.

When the mechanic raised his arm to give me the go-ahead signal, I leapt ahead towards the runway. To my left I saw the canopy of Asher's plane drop shut, the mechanics back away from it, and the plane taxi speedily to join me. Without waiting to straighten out properly, I opened up the engine full-throttle and switched on the afterburner. The jet hurtled forwards with its huge, typical roar. I didn't even bother to look for Asher behind me. I knew he was there, and that he was doing exactly what was required. He'd be beside me to my left, exactly in place, when I straightened out in a northerly direction. If there was anyone I have preferred to have beside me in combat, Asher was the man.

'Red two, do you read me?' I asked, after I'd switched the formation over to the control channel.

'This is two. I read you loud and clear,' came Asher's hoarse voice in reply.

Asher's plane came up close and assumed a position to my left, slightly to the rear, at a distance of about 200 metres (220 yards).

The intermittent noise of battle could be heard over the secondary radio channel, to which our formation was merely listening. It was impossible to tell from the voices what was going on, except for the fact that fighting contact had been made between our planes and Syrian planes. The controller also passed on a bit of information. Anyway, it would take us ten minutes to arrive at the arena, and I knew that any battle that was now taking place would surely be over within two or three minutes.

With Asher beside me, I entered the sky above the northern Golan Heights 10,000 feet (3048 metres) above the surface of the terrain. From experience I knew that the radar coverage in this region, at the lower altitudes, was bad, and that I couldn't expect any real help from control. We drew near the border with Syria and turned back above the southern reaches of Mount Hermon.

'Red, drop fuel tanks! Eye contact with enemy target low at ten o'clock. Red two, come with me!' I barked over the radio, rolling the plane over on its back and plunging like a hawk after its prey.

In a bend in one of the wadis I'd identified a MiG-17 jet fighter, painted in dark green-brown camouflage colours. It was flying at very low altitude in a north-easterly direction, towards the border and Syrian territory. I found it hard to believe this MiG was out there alone, and I made a special effort to locate its wingmen in the formation. None could be seen in the area. Two Israeli Mirages, flown by experienced fighter pilots who'd already shot down several enemy planes in the past, against a lone MiG-17, inferior in speed – this certainly didn't seem like a fair or well-matched fight. This was going to be a quick and easy kill, I thought. The next four-and-a-half minutes would prove how wrong I was.

I tightened my turn a little, got the MiG in my sights, and rapidly closed the distance to him. The air-to-air missile was prevented from working properly by the heat being radiated from the scorching earth, so close to us, and it was of no use to launch it. I activated the cannon switch and drew back the trigger. 'You've got another five seconds,' I whispered, whether to myself or to my adversary I couldn't tell.

All at once, the MiG pulled sharply upwards and to the right. In the wink of an eye what had seemed to be a simple and lethal run immediately became impossible to execute. I also raised the nose of my plane, avoiding an almost certain collision with the MiG, and passing to his left with only a few metres to spare. From close up I even managed to see the helmet on the pilot's head, and then I took advantage of my speed to climb high above him.

'Red one, I'm going in after him,' cried Asher, who realised exactly what was going on.

'Alright, two, go in!' I replied, taking up my position above Asher, ready to go in again if his pass should fail as well. The pilot of the MiG, who'd seen the first Mirage break off its pursuit and climb, went directly back to his escape route, at extremely low altitude, in the direction of Damascus.

I saw Asher go into his run. The MiG performed the same trick again, successfully foiling Asher's run too.

'We're dealing with a real fighter pilot here: courageous, cool, and good at his craft,' was the thought that went through my mind at that moment. In light of the numerous previous encounters my comrades and I had had with Syrian pilots, I knew they were generally an unruly and not very professional lot. This made the present instance both a surprise and a challenge.

Three times I tried to force the issue and shoot down the MiG. Three times the MiG took decisive action to foil the attack, at exactly the right time and distance. On my third run I managed to get into shooting position and fire a long burst of shells at my target. They missed. Three times Asher went into a run after the MiG in my wake, and on two of them he too was unsuccessful. The pilot of the MiG, truly a valiant fighter, continued to steal away with every interlude in the fighting, trying to close the distance to home and safety. But this exhausting struggle was a lost cause, from the Syrian's point of view. All three pilots participating in the battle knew this to be a near certainty. But nevertheless it continued. There would be no capitulation.

It was the sixth run in total, and Asher's third. The slopes of Mount Hermon were levelling off to the east. From above I saw Asher settle onto the MiG's tail at too long a range for cannon-fire to be effective. I glanced ahead and realised what his plan was. The MiG, and Asher behind him, were flying above a plateau that was about to be intersected by a steep cliff directly ahead of them. All at once the Syrian pilot found himself flying at an altitude of several hundred feet instead of the extremely low altitude that until now had served as effective cover.

The Syrian pilot tried to push down the nose of his plane and get back to lower altitude, but Asher was too quick for him. Barely had his Mirage cleared the last promontory when he slipped down behind the MiG and slightly beneath it. In this sort of deployment, when the Mirage's wing-borne missile wasn't pointed at the ground, it became possible for it to sense the heat waves emanating from the MiG's engine. The missile that Asher launched was deadly. The Syrian fighter pilot, skilled warrior that he was, was blown to bits together with his plane, which exploded before the very eyes of the two Israeli pilots who'd been pursuing it.

I was glad at the outcome. True, my joy may have been more complete if the prey had fallen at my hands. After all, these victories in the air were the name of the game. The competition amongst the squadron pilots, in fact among all the fighter pilots in the service, for a place on the 'kill parade' was no secret. But I tried my best to avoid falling into the trap of jealousy, though this had never been one of my prominent traits. I generally took the trouble to look for, and find, a way to derive benefit to the unit and to myself from the strong and able people, like Asher Snir, whom I posted in my vicinity and promoted wholeheartedly.

One day Asher would write a wonderful essay entitled 'Ballad to an Adversary', in which he'd tell the tale of this battle and the brave Syrian's fight for his life.

Our way back south was marked by a tranquility that contrasted starkly with the tension of the battle. With the voices of the pilots and controllers over the radio in the background, I let my thoughts wander.

On a rational level, I knew, like any other fighter pilot, that beneath my gunsight, sits another pilot, a man just like myself. I knew that at the end of the battle only one of us would return home. The winner. It was a fight to the death.

The time for emotions was past, frozen, the moment I'd turned the nose of my plane towards the 'encounter'. Now there was no compassion, but no hatred either. There was only cold, calculated and professional grappling in a zero-sum game in which the winner takes all, literally everything. In this world, the world of three dimensions, the world of aviation, there is a fraternity amongst the fighter pilots. I 'know' him, my adversary, without ever having met him. He could have been a good friend of mine. We may have much more in common than I have in common with many of my actual friends. But here and now, he'll kill me if he's able to, and I him. There is an extreme simplicity to this situation, a simplicity that leaves no room for doubt. This battle is going to squeeze everything I've got out of me, every iota of my true ability. And that, my true ability, will not always suffice! The fight isn't always, in fact it's almost never, fair. In the rules of warfare this isn't a relevant factor.

This victory has to be sharp, clear, and . . . mine!

When the battle is over, when I return home, emotions will return to my body, to my mind. I may even be able to honour my defeated adversary; to confer titles upon him, sing his praises, or even heap scorn upon him.

It's a cruel place, the battlefield, where predators hunt their victims.

The two Mirages retraced their route and landed back at base in the south of Israel. Asher and I met in the jeep that drove us back to the squadron. In two or three brief sentences we summarised what we'd seen, still feeling the dogfight we had just experienced in our bodies. Differences, there were none between us. Not this time.

CHAPTER TWENTY-FIVE

Tel Nof Airbase, July 1968

Squadron commander. There isn't a pilot in the Air Force who doesn't aspire to, doesn't dream of being a squadron commander. Most will admit it, a minority will dissemble, but all of them, to the last man, share the dream. Throughout the history of military aviation, it has been a job that demands a combination of the fighter pilot's personal and professional skill with the capacity to command an operational unit that has a defined operational purpose. Only in this post does the aggregate of these two qualities reach its highest level, for which reason it usually marks the summit of a fighter pilot's life and career.

Waiting for me on the telephone line in my office at the flight academy was Major Orit, chief of staff to Motti Hod, Air Force commander.

'The commander would like to speak with you,' she said.

'I'm here,' I replied.

'Hello, Amos. How are you? Has Rachel had the baby yet?' asked Motti, immediately striking up an atmosphere of pleasant and personal conversation.

'I'm well, thanks. As for Rachel, she's just started the ninth month, and all's well with her, too.'

'Amos, a couple of hours ago the plans for the yearly personnel postings were finalised in my office. Your name also came up in this context, and I had to make a decision. I know you were hoping to receive the command of the first Mirage squadron, the senior squadron. However, I've decided that you'll take command of the third squadron, the youngest, which carries the load of recce missions in addition to the duties of a regular fighter squadron. You will have to contend with a new task, as well as with the problem of being "transplanted" from the outside into a tightly woven body of fighters and stepping into the shoes of Ran, an able and charismatic commander. Easy it isn't going to be, but I have the fullest confidence in you.'

'Sir, I gladly accept your decision, and I will do my utmost to perform the job well.'

'All the best, Amos. Goodbye.' The click of the line being disconnected echoed in my ears as I slowly replaced the receiver.

'Amit, please run the show here for the next two hours, I've got to go out. I'll perform the test flight I've got scheduled as soon as I come back,' I spoke over the intercom to my deputy and received his confirmation.

I stepped outside to the Willys pickup truck that was in the parking lot, started the engine, and drove slowly toward the rear gate of the airbase, which led to the Halutsa sands. I felt I had to get away by myself to a quiet spot and think about the new situation. It had been ten and a half years since I was awarded my wings – intensive, focused, exhausting years – and here I was, about to receive the most wonderful job in all of aviation.

I drove along the dirt track winding south between sand dunes, which were partly covered with green-brown desert shrubbery. After twenty minutes' driving I stopped the vehicle in the middle of nowhere and switched off the engine. The rustling of the dry desert breeze was interspersed with the distant dull roar of jet engines overhead.

Behind my courteous, cooperative and apparently sociable behaviour lurked a powerful ambition. Just as in my childhood I'd aspired to take the rudder of the heavy sailboat into my own hands, and just as in my youth I'd aspired to a leadership position within the youth movement and settlers group, so too over the course of my service in the past decade my ambition had been focused on obtaining the coveted command of a prime fighter squadron. These weren't the delusions of a naïve dreamer. They were clearly formulated ideas and plans that had been coursing through my veins for years, on a foundation of self-confidence and sober assessment of my own ability. I was thrilled by the offer of the post, but it didn't surprise me. Yes, I did derive satisfaction from an aim accomplished. I knew for a certainty, however, that it was in the nature of this path up the precipice of success that as soon as it arrives at the nearest summit, it reveals another, higher summit beyond. There, in the quiet of the Halutsa sands, for the second time in my Air Force career I dared to seriously contemplate my chances of making it all the way up the exhausting ascent to the post of Air Force commander itself. An idle dream? Not necessarily.

A cloud of dust rose behind the pickup when I drove back from the sands to the airfield.

From the office I telephoned home. Rachel was at an advanced stage of pregnancy; we were expecting our third child, a brother or sister to our two sons, aged eight and four. Life at home wasn't ideal, but we tried and managed to maintain an equable and rather pleasant atmosphere. I hoped to find her at home at this hour, and I wasn't wrong. With uncharacteristic excitement I told her about my conversation with the commander of the Air Force. I didn't elaborate on the difficulties stemming from the appointment. Rachel knew I'd been expecting to receive command of the first squadron, in which I'd served for years, the command of which also carried a special aura of respect and past heritage. Being familiar with the tone of my voice, she immediately sensed that the picture wasn't as shiny as it looked and that the appointment had its problems. She, who knew how important the command of a fighter squadron was to me, warmly congratulated me.

'Rachel, you've got to understand that accepting the appointment means a change in our lifestyle too. We have to get ready to move to another base.'

A minute of silence went by, then she replied: 'That's all-right, but on condition that we move only after the end of the children's school year.'

'Of course,' I assented.

As usual, we concluded our conversation in a businesslike manner. For my part, I knew that her devotion to me and my way of life eliminated almost any chance she had for a serious, consistent professional career of her own. I was aware of this injustice, but I didn't know of any acceptable alternative to this unbalanced arrangement, and in effect I struck the issue from my regular agenda.

This was a dark cloud in the life we shared, one we were fated to live with for as long as we stayed together.

At dawn on 4 July, 1968 – the Independence Day of the United States, which from now on I would remember with particular fondness all my life – Rachel woke me from my sleep.

'It's time to go to the hospital,' she said.

We quickly got organised. We woke up Hava, our neighbour in the pilots' residential neighbourhood, to take care of the children in the morning, and then we set out. The two cycles of labour contractions that Rachel felt on the way testified to the imminence of birth. After she'd been registered and examined in the maternity ward, she came back to me in the waiting room.

'Amos, in another three or four hours you're due at the ceremony to receive the command of your squadron. I suggest you go home now and don't postpone the occasion. Anyway, I plan to call my friend Osnat. I'm sure she'll come here later, and I'll manage. Go!' I hugged her in elation at her being so understanding, gave her a kiss and drove away.

Ran, the departing squadron commander, and I, who was about to assume the post in a few minutes, sat in the office and awaited the arrival of the airbase commander and Air Force commander. Outside, in the parade ground, Eitan, the deputy, was making final preparations for the change-of-command ceremony – small in extent and modest in character. Except for the two senior commanders who were due to arrive for the ceremony and the commanders of the other squadrons at the base, no outsiders had been invited. The Air Force commander's Plymouth Valiant slipped silently into the parking lot just as the telephone rang in the squadron commander's office.

'Somebody's looking for Amos,' the secretary said.

I picked up the receiver and put it to my ear. Ran and the two senior commanders, who had just entered the room, saw a broad smile spread across my face as I ended the brief conversation.

'Half an hour ago my wife gave birth to a daughter, a sister to my two sons,' I told the company, my face shining with joy. I immediately began to receive slaps of congratulation and '*mazel tov*' from everyone there.

A few minutes later the command of the Mirage squadron was transferred from Ran to me. This was the most wonderful day of my life. In all my dreams, I couldn't have expected anything better. Unless, perhaps, the day would come and I'd get my chance to compete for the post of Air Force commander. However, even in my enormous satisfaction at the coincidence of these two events, I couldn't forget, not even for a moment, the enormity of the responsibility I'd been entrusted with.

I didn't have blind confidence in my success, but I was certainly ready for the challenge, with all my heart and soul.

The next morning I asked to have a plane prepared for an ordinary flight, very early, before the start of the routine flying day, in order to 'scrape off the rust' after not having flown for quite some time. When I took off, a flat layer of clouds covered the sky throughout the south of Israel. When I passed through the upper edge of the clouds, I stopped climbing and stabilised the plane close to the cloud layer, almost touching it from above. It was a sort of low-altitude flying, with the roof of the clouds playing the role of the surface of the earth, but in much more forgiving fashion . . .

Below me to my right, a 'pilots' cross' was reflected from the surface of the clouds, dashing along together with the plane, attached to it like its shadow. It was a precise circle of light, a glowing aura, inside which lay a silhouette of the plane's fuselage and wings. This exquisite optical phenomenon is vouchsafed only to pilots. For a minute or so I gazed at the aura with pleasure. When I'd had my fill, I pulled the plane up and departed from the clouds into the wild blue yonder.

CHAPTER TWENTY-SIX

Fire – Iraqi Skies,
May 1970

Gathering intelligence for the benefit of forces fighting on land was the first military use of aircraft, as early as the First World War. Military commanders quickly realised that aerial photographs are the most reliable and up to date source of information for what's going on behind enemy lines; much more reliable than the information obtained from prisoner interrogations, from agents whose reports are of doubtful veracity, and even from intercepted enemy communications, which have sometimes served as a convenient medium for deceiving the eavesdropping intelligence service.

Over the years, and especially during the Second World War and in its aftermath, the means of aerial photoghraphy were developed. The planes that carried the cameras went faster and higher, dramatically increasing their ability to cover broad expanses of enemy territory. The means for deciphering the photographs advanced as well, and decipherment itself became an important and primary specialisation in the process of intelligence-gathering.

In the Israeli Air Force, and especially its intelligence departments, there was a high awareness of aerial photography from the initial days of the service during the War of Independence. For Israel, a small country surrounded by enemies, state security was based on the ability of intelligence at all times to provide a true and up-to-date picture of the situation behind the lines on all the fronts, deep in the heartland of the hostile countries. A great deal of money was also invested in obtaining the most advanced equipment in the field of aerial photography: cameras, decipherment facilities, and, of course – suitable planes.

Spying from the air has always been covered with a heavy mantle of secrecy. Naturally, many important espionage missions are carried out in the intervals between the wars, when the battlefields are relatively tranquil. No country, Israel included, wants activity of this type to be publicly disclosed. The discovery and repulse of an aerial spy mission is liable, in addition to the failure of the single mission itself, to hamper continued activity of this sort, which is so vital.

The sensitivity of these operations, their secrecy, indispensability and great complexity, made it necessary to entrust the task of aerial espionage to a small number of units. These units were awarded exceptional trust and attained the highest level of professional and operational ability.

My squadron was such a unit. In our squadron a serious, professional and rigorous approach to these espionage missions had been developed over many years. This long period and hundreds of such photographic sorties had augmented and broadened the experience gained in this field, but without breeding any insouciance in the unit. The intelligence units within the Air Force command and in the parallel technical branches, who assisted the squadron, also shared this serious attitude, and the results were impressive.

Faultless execution was demanded of the pilots who carried out the missions. Navigation to the target had to be absolutely precise, and the timetables were adhered to within an exactitude of seconds. In every operation, without exception, the execution and quality of the photography were examined and graded. Everything was registered in the pilots' special personal files and carefully supervised by the Force's photo-ops officer, the squadron commander and other higher echelons.

Quietly, with no publicity or braggadocio, the Force's espionage pilots flew hundreds of daring photographic missions behind the lines, passing swiftly through the skies of areas and places that the imagination may find difficult to conceive.

For many years, a lengthy oil pipeline has linked the oil fields in Iraq with the seaports of northern Syria and Lebanon. Part of the pipeline runs through the Golan Heights, for which reason the flow of oil was shut down during the Six-Day-War and never resumed. Five pumping and guard stations were built along the pipeline in the vast expanse of the Iraqi-Jordanian desert, designated by the letter H and numbered from H-1 to H-5. Over the years large military camps and installations were also constructed at these stations. Especially prominent in size and importance were camps H-3, belonging to Iraq, and H-5, belonging to Jordan. In these two places airfields were also established, which over the years grew to be of crucial military significance to the State of Israel.

The Iraqi airfield at H-3 was considered highly significant by the Air Force because of its size, the extent of the aerial forces based there, and its important strategic location as Iraq's forward position facing Israel. The airfield's distance from Israel was also problematical, making it especially difficult to penetrate its airspace at low altitude because of the range and high fuel requirement. Nevertheless, one of the Israeli Air Force's hardest battles took place over H-3 during the Six-Day-War, involving Vautours and Mirages from Ramat-David Airbase and Iraqi MiG-21s and Hunters. Two of the Israeli planes were shot down in that engagement.

I stepped into my office and laid my helmet down on the chair in the corner. The room was chilly, in refreshing contrast to the oppressive heat outside. It took me about three hours to get through all the debriefings following the large exercise that had ended that morning. Over the years a culture of veracious debriefing had become second nature among the Force's squadrons. We zealously saw every debriefing through to its end, without any obfuscation, without concealing mistakes. We drew the fullest conclusions from the good and the bad in every flying incident and disseminated them to the relevant personnel for study and rapid implementation. Asher, my sharp, clever and discerning deputy, was always of great assistance to me in this matter, which often involved stepping on the toes of somebody in the unit.

With a serious expression on her face, Anat knocked twice on the open door, scrupulously polite as usual. She approached, placing upon my desk the brown military file with the prominent red 'X' and an inscription on top that read, 'Recce-Ops – Top

Secret'. She was also carrying a double-layered sealed envelope, which had arrived at the squadron by special dispatch from Air Force command. She asked me to affix my signature to the voucher confirming receipt of the missive, bending forward to take the signed piece of paper from me. For a moment I felt the proximity of her face to mine and breathed in her pleasant fragrance. Then the moment was past; she stood upright again, took the voucher and left the room.

According to procedures in the squadron, documents of this sort were only for the eyes of five officers at most: the squadron commander and his deputy, the photo-ops officer, and the two pilots assigned to carry out the mission. In addition, only the same five officers were permitted to deal with the administrative handling of the file, records and necessary accessories. No deviation from this protocol was tolerated.

I opened the first and then the second, inner envelope, making sure that no stray piece of paper remained inside them, and tossed them into the waste bin whose contents would be burned at the end of the day. I held in my hands what looked like a routine operational command. The document contained the gist of the command, written on white paper, as well as most of its appendices (dealing with communication, control, intelligence and the like) written on pages of various colours, a different colour for each appendix. I knew that other, appendices to the command had also been written, which were not related to the operational force itself, and which would be kept confidential even from me and from the pilots carrying out the mission. All the espionage pilots knew there was a possibility that their missions would end in failure, which might mean ejecting deep behind enemy lines and being taken prisoner. Any detail they knew nothing about was something else they'd be unable to divulge to enemy interrogators in such a worst case scenario.

Under the heading of 'mission objective', the command read: 'high-altitude photography of the H-3 airfield and all the army camps in its vicinity.' The date of execution was set for five days' time. I carefully perused every word of the command and its appendices. When I'd finished, I reread the entire document and, using a sharpened pencil, marked those points that I thought required further elaboration. In the upper left margin of the first page I jotted down the names of the pilots who were to read the command and affix their signatures, adding underneath: 'Mission pilots of record: leader – Amos; number two – Avraham.'

The general briefing for all the forces participating in the operation was held two days later, in the briefing room at the base.

General Benny Peled, who was Head of Operations and deputy commander of the Air Force, arrived from Tel Aviv to conduct the briefing, together with the head of the photo-ops branch and other senior staff officers. When everybody had assembled inside the hall, it became apparent how complex the mission really was and how many forces were party to its execution: commanders of supporting units, intelligence officers, controllers, meteorologists, and many others.

The planes performing the mission were to reach a spot in the Iraqi desert south-east of the target, at low altitude; from there they would turn west and climb to an altitude of 35,000 ft (about 11 km), stabilise on their projected course and take pictures of the entire area to be covered, with the airfield in its centre.

It was clear to me, as it was to everyone else at the briefing, that the discovery of the planes by Iraqi control could be expected, with a certainty, from the moment they left low altitude and climbed preparatory to executing their photographic run. It was also clear that at this long distance from home, and with the high altitude of the photography, they would have to continue to fly home at high altitude, in full view of Iraqi, Syrian and Jordanian radar stations.

The calculations of time and distance showed, to an accuracy of only a few dozen seconds, that the pilots had a reasonable chance of returning home safely. However – and this was something everyone also knew – deviations and accidents are an inseparable part of operations. Any chance discovery of the planes during their low-altitude flight eastward, by a squad of lookouts or a military unit with a particularly alert commander, could give the enemy those few precious moments he would not otherwise have in order to intercept the spyplanes and shoot them down.

When two hours had elapsed, and after all questions had been answered and all ambiguities cleared away, the Head of Operations summarised the briefing in his clear manner. Everyone dispersed to their units: this complex machine stood ready and waiting for h-hour.

The evening before the operation, dressed casually, I set out in the direction of the photo-lab. The tension and unease prior to any serious operation filled my thoughts and heart. The guard at the entrance halted my vehicle, waving me through as soon as he recognised the squadron commander sitting in the driver's seat.

I got out of the car and entered the lab. Inside it I found, as though this went without saying, the senior personnel of the photo-ops branch. Even though they didn't know the precise location of the target, all the branch's officers and NCOs were in the grip of the typical suspense before any serious photographic operation behind the lines. After so many years in the 'business', they could almost smell the degree of seriousness and danger that distinguished one mission from the rest. This time, they knew, it was serious. I spent quite some time in the company of the photographic technicians, asking professional questions as was my wont, and receiving open answers in reply. I was satisfied with the answers I got. I exchanged a joke or two with the people around me, and left.

As I was walking towards my parked car, another vehicle drove up and stopped. Reuven, the squadron's photo-ops officer, had also come from his house in the pilots' residential neighbourhood to check that everything was proceeding smoothly.

Reuven was the paragon of an earnest and punctilious officer. He carried out his professional duties with a devotion bordering on the sacred. He learned the cameras inside and out, getting to know them as well as the best engineers of the group. These were among the most sophisticated cameras in the world, capable of pinpointing a football at a range of 10 km (6.2 miles). Someone like Reuven, I knew, could not remain indifferent before an important operation. I had no doubt that Reuven would pester the technicians and give them no rest until he was absolutely certain that everything was in order. We exchanged a few words and took leave of each other. My heart was filled with pride by the atmosphere of dedication and responsibility that marked all the officers and soldiers in the squadron. I had an exceptionally able group of people around me.

From the lab I went over to the spyplane hangar. There was a great deal of hubbub around the two planes set to perform the mission the next day. The procedures for this special inspection were nearing their end; there wasn't a system that hadn't been checked by at least one senior mechanic and an additional pair of eyes – and so double-checked and confirmed by signature, as required. I took the 'Chef', the squadron's technical officer, a few steps aside from the people busy at work

'What's the situation, Chef?' I asked.

'We had to take the "ninety-eight" out on a special engine run due to some suspicions that arose. There was an argument between us about the need for this run. I'm glad I decided to perform it, and indeed we did discover a fuel leak and solved the problem. Now all the work that's left is routine, and we'll be done in a couple of hours. Don't worry, Amos, the planes will be fine,' he concluded.

I turned around and went back to the small Citroen 2CV I was driving. The tension I felt hadn't dissipated, but it was accompanied now by a feeling of confidence that everything that could and should be done, had been done competently and professionally. I turned the car in the direction of my home in the pilots' neighbourhood. It was nearing midnight, and my body longed for the few hours' sleep that remained to me.

I raised the landing gear handle in a single, practised motion. The green lights immediately went out and the orange lights lit up instead, indicating that the wheels were unlocked and on their way up. Another three or four seconds passed, then a couple of dull thumps testified that the wheels had reached their docks and the three orange lights went out too, almost at the same time. The landing gear was now locked in 'raised' position. The fuel-laden plane began to climb and leave behind the black asphalt runway, wreathed in the vapour of hot air and burnt fuel spewed from the scorchingly hot exhaust pipe. I gently inclined the plane to the right, eastward, and then back to the left, north-eastward, thus allowing Avraham, my number two, to take his place in the formation.

The routine of radio silence was in force, as on all such missions involving penetration deep into enemy territory and requiring absolute stealth until the inevitable moment of discovery, when the planes climbed to high altitude on approaching their target. The stopwatch, which had started to run the moment the brakes were released on the runway, kept count of the seconds and minutes like the measured steps of a high-jumper, in perfect rhythmic control of his movement as he draws nearer to the bar for the critical leap.

Clock, map, terrain. Clock, map, terrain. This mantra – which is drummed into the head of every flight cadet and continues to echo inside the head of every pilot when guiding a plane from point to point – would inform my activity inside the cockpit for these forty minutes of low-altitude navigation to the point of the climb.

Clock. A quick glance at the stopwatch, hanging from the frame of the cockpit canopy directly in front of my eyes, made it possible to continue looking ahead and avoid the obstacles rushing by at a speed of 460 knots. The hands of the stopwatch now pointed to twenty-three minutes and forty seconds.

Map. Without looking, my left hand reached forwards instinctively and positioned the map where my gaze would be directed forthwith. The course of the flight path was pencilled in prominently with the time line beside it, a slender stroke for every minute, a fat stroke for every two. I dropped my gaze to the map for a brief instant. I already knew what I would see, I had no spare time at my disposal. I looked for and immediately found the thick stroke of the twenty-fourth minute. There it was: a tel (hill), apparently quite prominent, 500 metres (547 yards) to the right, and ten seconds later a bend to the north in the big wadi.

Terrain. My eyes left the map and returned to managing the flight outside. My mind processed what my eyes had seen. By instinct I knew that ten seconds had elapsed. On my right, ahead and very close to the flight path, the tel was rapidly approaching. Yes, that looked all right. Another ten seconds and the broad, flat channel of the wadi below me curved to the left. Okay. To this point I knew the navigation was going well.

I now had half-a-minute to concentrate on 'other' matters. I glanced to the right, a little behind me, and discovered the silhouette of my number two's Mirage. It was right where it should be. I glanced upwards and to both sides. Everything looked all-right. Far away to the left a small convoy, consisting of a pickup and two trucks, was wending its way from nowhere to nowhere. The drivers' cabins, brightly painted in red and green, snuffed out any suspicion it might be a military unit.

Clock, map, terrain. The routine repeated itself. In the twenty-seventh minute, as expected, almost all signs of civilisation disappeared. Except for the junction of two large wadis in the thirty-third minute, I could now rely only on my compass and my stopwatch. Now I put most of my effort into precision flying and looking around. I even had time to gain a personal impression of this vast, amazing wilderness.

Uh oh! My eyes locked onto the edge of a cloud of dust directly ahead of us at a distance of about 3 km (1.86 miles). The formation was now entering the most critical phase of the operation. Our premature discovery could spoil everything. I lowered and raised my right wing in a swift motion, signalling to number two my intention of turning right. I immediately lowered the right wing again, allowing the plane to swerve sharply away from its course. Out of the corner of my right eye I ascertained that number two had been following me. As expected, of course, I found that he'd seen and understood everything.

My eyes looked left again. Beneath the billowing dust, like tiny, dark bugs, appeared several armoured vehicles, apparently tanks.

The two Mirages passed about 2 km (1.2 miles) south of the Iraqi armoured force training out in the open. Both Avraham and I were aware of the problem and hoped that the force hadn't spotted us, or at least hadn't been suspicious enough to report our movements there.

The thought of cancelling the mission and returning flashed through my mind. After all, the postponement and rescheduling of the mission to a later date were preferable to the humiliating failure that might occur as a result of our being discovered. Here and now there was nobody with whom I could share the decision. It was my responsibility, and mine alone! I recalled my last visit to a training exercise by an IDF armoured regiment. I recalled how I felt and what I saw sitting inside the noisy APC (armoured personnel carrier), which was bouncing through the terrain and raising a cloud of dust around it, and I tried to calculate the odds of our being discovered. 'Carry on,' I muttered to myself, having made my decision, and filed away the event in a suitable compartment of my brain. I made a quick calculation as to how to correct our deviation from the planned course and guided my plane to the original flight path a minute before the scheduled pull-up and climb to higher altitude.

The fuel gauges indicated that the huge, detachable, external fuel tanks were empty. From now on they'd be nothing but excess weight and a drag on our speed, slowing us down and prolonging the duration of the climb to high altitude. The sole consideration in favour of continuing to carry them was economic. Taking into account the severe conditions that had now developed, I decided to get rid of them.

'Red formation, pull!' I announced, pressing on the broadcast button for the first time that day.

'Red, prepare to drop detachables!' I ordered.

'Red two, I read you,' came Avraham's immediate reply.

With both planes' noses pointing upward, at an altitude of 1000 ft (305 metres) above the surface of the terrain, I pressed the release switch. I felt the dull thud and the instantaneous 'lift' of the plane as it became lighter and more manoeuvrable. As I banked to the left, westward, I saw the detachable fuel tanks drop from Avraham's plane and spin off to the rear like two yellow pea pods.

The most crucial segment of the operation had begun. I utilised my left turn and the opening up of the horizon to dozens of kilometres on either side in order to identify my exact location and pinpoint the target zone. With my left wing inclined downwards, I had a good view of the area west of me and was able to identify the H-3 airfield and the large military bases around it. The entire target zone stood out due to its darker colour against the background of the bright desert surrounding it. I knew that this convenient state of affairs, wherein the target could be seen while the plane's wing was dipping downwards, was about to pass. Once I'd straightened out at the proper altitude and levelled my wings, any attempt to see the target with the naked eye would involve rolling over to the side and completely disrupting the conditions that were necessary for taking the pictures.

Number two assumed his parallel position to the right and north of my plane. The planes, now much lighter without their detachable fuel tanks, rose quickly to the set altitude for the photographic flypast – 35,000 ft (10.7 km).

'Red one, you're starting to paint,' came Avraham's voice over the radio.

Glancing to the right, I immediately saw that the exhaust pipe of number two's plane was emitting an unbroken white trail of condensed water vapour (I couldn't see my own jet stream). This 'painting', I knew, could betray our presence to anybody within dozens of kilometres and was therefore extremely dangerous. I lowered the plane's nose again and went back down to an altitude of 33,000 feet (10 km), where the vapour trail from number two's plane ceased. I knew that the now missing 2,000 feet (700 metres) relative to the planned altitude would cost us an additional 100 litres (22 gallons) in fuel consumption. Perhaps not much in ordinary situations, but quite a lot when the limits of the planes' performance were being pushed from the start.

'Red, this is Gold. Tomato,' came the voice of the chief controller of the northern control unit.

'Roger, Gold, I read you,' I confirmed. This code, I knew, carried a message with a twofold meaning. On one hand, it meant that the process of scrambling enemy planes to intercept us had begun, but on the other hand the situation at this stage could still allow the operation to continue.

I rolled the plane over on its right side and identified the approaching target. I straightened the plane on course and rolled over again, this time on my left side. This was to ensure that the target would be directly beneath my belly during the next two minutes, the second roll having cancelled out any deviation caused by the first. The plane was now back on its precise flight path, as planned.

'Red, activate!' I gave the command to run the cameras.

The two planes stabilised on course, both pilots knowing that now, for the entire span of the next two minutes, it was imperative not to move, not to turn, not to breathe! Everything was now dedicated to achieving the mission's goal: sharp, clear and consecutive aerial photos of the target and its vicinity – nothing more, nothing less. My squadron had gained an impressive reputation for the precise execution of its missions over the years, and I, of course, was unwilling to countenance any diminution of the high standards that had been set.

The flickering green light on the instrument panel told me that the camera was running as it should, its sophisticated shutter opening and shutting at the correct interval, adjusted to the speed of the plane's passage above the area to be covered.

'Chair, this is Gold. Assume azimuth zero, five, zero, and climb to 25,000,' I could hear the controller instructing the formation of interceptors that was patrolling in the north of Israel, ready to intervene in our operation if necessary.

I was listening to this conversation at low volume on the secondary radio channel. I didn't contribute anything to it, as it wasn't directed at me, but I could tell from what was being said that the duty officer in the 'Pit' at Air Force headquarters had decided to dispatch the patrolling force to the arena. Something was happening, I had no doubt of that. It was quiet inside the cockpit, quiet all around us. The two Mirages passed over H-3 airfield and its military bases in smooth and stable flight. Now there were forty seconds left . . . thirty . . . twenty . . . ten.

'Red, cease camera operation!' I gave the order to shut down the cameras, turning the square camera switch inside my own cockpit to the 'off' position. The green light went out; the reading on the film meter accorded with prior expectations.

Henceforth all my resources would be devoted to bringing that precious cargo, stored inside the film cartridge in the plane's nose, safely home.

'Red, this is Gold. Cucumber. Assume azimuth two, three, zero,' came the controller's voice over the radio.

'This is Red, I read you. Cucumber,' I confirmed the notification. In light of it I issued my command. 'Red formation, full dry.'

I opened full-throttle and then took it back down a notch, in order to leave some room to manoeuvre for my number two. The flight speed began to increase, stabilising at Mach 0.94, very close to the speed of sound, or approximately 600 knots relative to the ground below.

The code word 'cucumber' told me that the enemy's attempt at intercepting us had entered its effective stages. This required action on our part, such as increasing speed and changing direction to avoid contact with the interceptors. Both by nature and by training, fighter pilots aspire to come into fighting contact with the adversary. By contrast, the aim of espionage pilots is to get the sensitive and important material home – quickly, without damage, and at minimal risk.

Avraham and I, both fighter pilots in body and soul, were engaged now in an espionage mission of the first rank. We were well aware of it, and we almost always succeeded in adhering to both the letter and spirit of these priorities.

'Chair, this is Gold,' came the controller's voice, muted and low, over the secondary channel. 'Engage, azimuth zero, two, zero.' Now this was truly serious, I said to myself. The controller was throwing 'Chair' formation into battle with the MiGs – which appeared to be Syrian, judging by the direction our planes were being sent – to allow my formation to get away.

'Red, this is Gold. Bogies at your four o'clock, twenty-seven miles (43 km),' the controller notified me, and received my confirmation. The problem facing us now was our fuel supply. I knew that opening the afterburner would prevent the MiGs from closing the distance to us. Using the afterburner for more than fifty or sixty seconds, however, would lead to the depletion of our fuel and the shutdown of our engines before we could make it back to base. I weighed up the options and decided not to use the afterburner unless the range decreased to twelve miles. Meanwhile, I turned up the volume of the secondary channel in an attempt to ascertain whether the introduction of 'Chair' formation into the arena would force the MiGs to break off their pursuit of us.

'Chair, pepper go! Drop detachables!' I heard the leader command his formation to open afterburners and drop their detachable fuel tanks – steps that usually indicated imminent engagement in battle.

'Red, this is Gold. Bogies now at your five o'clock, range sixteen miles (26 km),' the controller notified me.

'The Syrians apparently haven't gone for the decoy put in their way by means of Chair formation,' I summarised the new situation to myself. They had designated my formation as their target of preference, and the time at my disposal for taking action was rapidly dwindling.

'Red, this is Gold. Assume azimuth two, two, zero.' I knew that this turn in a south-westerly direction would lengthen our journey home, with all the concomitant risks. I confirmed the announcement and turned in the direction indicated.

'Red this is Gold. Bogies still at your six o'clock, range twelve miles,' came another announcement from the controller. Now there was no choice left but to take immediate action!

'Red, pepper go!' I ordered the formation, opening my own afterburner to full power. The plane leapt ahead. My speed rose rapidly, within thirty seconds reaching Mach 1.2, well above the speed of sound, about 700 knots.

'Gold, what's the range now?' I posed this question of crucial importance to the controller.

'Fourteen miles and widening,' came the immediate reply.

'Red, pepper down,' I immediately instructed the formation to shut down afterburners in response. I was well aware that every additional second the afterburners were running could jeopardise our safe return home owing to a lack of fuel.

'Gold from Chair, eye contact with the bogies, engaging in combat with them in another fifteen seconds,' I once again heard the confident voice of Yehuda, leader of Chair formation and commander of the northern squadron of Mirages.

'Negative, Chair, negative! No authorisation for engagement! Turn right to azimuth two, six, zero. Please confirm!' intervened the controller at the last possible moment. I knew that Air Force command wasn't interested in taking the risk of a dogfight in this arena – at least not this time – but in getting the vital intelligence home with a minimum of bother.

'This is Chair, I read you. Turning right to azimuth two, six, zero. Chair, pepper down,' came Yehuda's voice, filled with frustration.

I heard the bitterness in his voice and couldn't help but smile to myself. It must have been such a disappointment for the leader of Chair formation, who had already seen his quarry in his path, but had been summoned to return without a fight . . .

'Red from Gold. Assume azimuth two, seven, zero. Bogies have changed direction to zero, two, zero, range twenty-five miles (40 km) from you and widening,' the controller clarified the new state of affairs.

So the Syrian interceptors had gone back on their tracks. The gauntlet that had been thrown down before them was too big for them, forcing them to break contact with their target. My formation swiftly approached Israel's eastern border on our way home. I knew that all the control and intelligence networks, both ours and our neighbours', were now intently following events in this arena. It was clear to everyone that my formation had no room left for manoeuvre, and that we would be landing with our last drops of fuel.

Over the radio I hear the controller dispatching a fresh pair of Mirages to the Jordan Valley area.

'They're not taking any unnecessary chances over there in the "Pit,"' I said to myself. The fuel gauge indicated there were 300 litres (66 gallons) left. Avraham reported that he had a similar amount left. The planes were about to cross the line of the Jordan River, heading west. I reduced engine power to idle, let my speed drop, and went on gliding toward the base in this fuel-efficient mode. I saw Avraham's plane approach to within 30 metres (33 yards) of me. I gave this fine number two of mine the thumbs-up; he gave me a thumbs-up in reply and nodded his head in satisfaction. Four minutes later both our planes' wheels touched down gently on the runway. Another complex mission had been brought to a successful conclusion.

As was our wont, at ten o'clock that evening Avraham and I set out in my car in the direction of Tel Aviv. We climbed the stairs and were swallowed up in the dark entrance of an old, nondescript building.

The duty officer at Air Force intelligence's photo-development lab came out to greet us and accompanied us inside. In the typical red light of the lab, we bent over the decipherment tables with the decipherers to gaze at the strips of celluloid moving underneath the magnifying glasses. The Force's head of intelligence was also there, beaming with pleasure.

'How much effort, strength, training, dedication, money and

risk has been invested in these strips of celluloid,' I marvelled, feeling pleased and proud myself.

The steaks we ordered at the 'Asa' roadhouse on the way back to base were even tastier and juicier than usual.

CHAPTER TWENTY-SEVEN

Tel Nof Airbase, June 1970

All the Force's base and squadron commanders participated
in the special conference summoned by the Air Force
commander at one of the centrally located airbases. Uri,
Oded and I, the commanders of the three Mirage squadrons,
took seats next to each other in the third row near the aisle. This
was a rather intimate gathering; everyone was personally
acquainted with everyone else, and the hubbub of people
greeting each other filled the room. The noise was abruptly
interrupted by a cry of 'Attention!' upon the commander's entry
into the room. The commander took his place in the front row,
and the head of intelligence was called to the podium. The
subject on the agenda concerned developments on the Suez
Canal front.

The survey by the head of intelligence was trenchant, precise
and troubling. With massive Soviet support, the Egyptian anti-
aircraft missile array had been rapidly expanding. The wide
spaces between the blocks of missile batteries in the northern,
central and southern sectors were being filled, and the array was
turning into a solid, extensive, and almost impregnable anti-
aircraft barrier. The types of missiles had also multiplied, and the
combination of different types led to better coverage of the
territory, from the defender's point of view, in all three dimensions of the protected space. Verily in front of the Air Force's
watching eyes, a space was being established wherein control by
the Force would be denied, despite the vital need for it. To make
things worse, the ability to obtain intelligence about what was
happening inside this space had also become limited, and the
photos that were being obtained were of inferior quality.

The next speaker was the head of operations. The Air Force

209

would attack the missile array in order to destroy it and regain control of this vital zone. The brunt of the effort would fall on the two Phantom squadrons, which were equipped with the most advanced early warning and electronic warfare systems. The rest of the Force's squadrons would assist in the effort, each in its own field of expertise. Several more speakers from staff head-quarters brought this first part of the conference to an end. Then the commanders who were present voiced their responses and asked questions.

To end the conference, a summary was delivered by Motti, commander of the Force. The situation, he said, was quite involved. The mission was particularly difficult, but the service would invest all its ability in getting the job done, including those innovative weapon systems. All of us sensed there was something wrong this time. The commander's appearance and remarks were unconvincing. They lacked the confidence and fluency that had characterised previous crisis situations. The group dispersed, each man to his own base, with a feeling of deep apprehension.

On the way home I was unable to compose my thoughts. The espionage mission – flying the camera-equipped planes on behalf of intelligence – was my squadron's primary task. The umbrella of surface-to-air missiles was preventing our planes from flying steady and true, without any turning or manoeuvring. It was distancing them from their targets, and in addition not allowing us to get good-quality photographs of the missile array itself. These thoughts gave me no rest. The matter had become especially crucial now that detailed knowledge about the missile array was absolutely vital to the success of the impending attack upon it.

The idea popped into my head while I was driving, somewhere in the vicinity of the Bilu junction.

Ten years earlier, when the first Mirages were received by the Force, my fellow pilots and I had been taught that a special rocket engine had been designed and constructed for these planes. This engine was to be located in the rear section of the underbelly, and was meant to endow the Mirage with the ability to accelerate with enormous rapidity and reach a speed double the speed of sound as well as previously unimaginable altitudes of over 60,000 feet (18.3 km). The designers at Marcel Dassault, makers of the Mirage, thought to counter the threat from the East in this way by enabling their aircraft to shoot down high-flying Soviet nuclear bombers before they could reach their targets. In order to perform this task, the Mirages were then provided with Matra-530 radar-guided air-to-air missiles, among the most technologically advanced in the world. The Israeli Air Force saw no operational need for the complex rocket engine, the maintenance of which was hazardous as well, and dropped it altogether. The space left inside the fuselage was utilised to install another fuel tank and add another 300 litres (66 gallons) of capacity to the plane's fuel supply.

This modification, which was undertaken in Israel, proved to be justified, and it was in effect adopted by the French and Mirage users around the world. I recalled, however, that among all the other items of equipment that had arrived in Israel, there had been articles intended for flying at altitudes of above 50,000 feet (15.2 km). I even remembered a blurred photograph of Joe Alon and Danny Shapira, the first pilots to take delivery of the Mirages in France, wearing a pair of 'space-suits', which had brought smiles to the faces of the young pilots who saw them.

When I arrived at the gate to the base at about 10 pm, I telephoned 'Chef' Alon, my technical officer, from the guardsmen's cabin and asked him to come down to the squadron.

'I'm looking for the high-altitude suits, "Chef". We may be needing them, and it's extremely urgent. I believe there should be two or three somewhere inside our warehouse, or in Squadron 101's warehouse,' I told him.

'Amos, if there are any such suits in Israel, anywhere at all, at 7.30 tomorrow morning they'll be at our safety and rescue equipment lab right here at the base,' said Alon. I knew there was nothing further I could do there and drove to my home in the pilots' neighbourhood.

At 7 am I arrived at the squadron and immediately went over to the safety and rescue equipment warehouse. Two white pressure suits, slightly wrinkled but intact, were lying there on the large parachute table. Prominently beside them lay the bulky, round helmets with screw-on attachments to the upper parts of the suits for creating a completely sealed space around the pilot's body. I wondered whether the suits would fit me or any other pilot, so that we might be able to make operational use of them. An officer and female sergeant who worked in the department awaited my verdict.

'Let's try to get me into one of these contraptions,' I said. Nobody there was really familiar with the suits or with the proper way of using them. Meanwhile, Reuven, the squadron's photo-ops officer, who'd also been summoned, arrived at the lab and added his keen intellect to the pool, without understanding at this point what exactly this was all about.

After about an hour or so I stood up and approached the large mirror in the corner. I laughed aloud when I saw the 'spaceman' reflected in the mirror, but my voice remained trapped inside the suit and those standing around me barely heard anything. The suit was a little too big for me, but I knew that only minor alterations were required to make it operational. I gave the necessary instructions and left together with Reuven and the 'Chef' to return to the squadron.

A handful of the recce pilots, Asher and Reuven at their head, joined me in the photo-ops room in the secure basement floor of the squadron building.

'We must get better photographs of the missile array, and fast,' I explained to the assembled company. 'As we all know, the expansion of the array has forced us to perform our passes at a great distance from the target areas, sharply bringing down the level of the photographs and intelligence. The idea is to make use of the pressure suits we have and to take the pictures at an altitude of 55–60,000 feet (16.8–18.3 km), instead of the less than 40,000 feet (12.2 km) customary till now. We'll be able to achieve a more perpendicular view of the targets without approaching the effective range of the missiles themselves or taking unreasonable risks. As you know, the problem in obtaining good intelligence isn't the distance from the camera lens to the target, but the angle of capture that has become far too flat. In a couple of hours I plan to perform a test flight here, in conditions similar to those at the Suez Canal, and after the photographic run we'll know whether we've hit on the solution,' I concluded my explanation. 'Meanwhile, I want Asher, Reuven and Nir to check to see who besides me fits the existing suits, or two others which are on their way here from Ramat-David Airbase.'

Anat was sitting in her usual place in the operations room when I stepped inside.

'What's happening?' I enquired.

'Four pairs are out on training flights, as planned. They're all in the air right now, and other than that everything's quiet, in my humble opinion,' she answered with a smile. 'So what's the story with the pressure suits? I'm dying of curiosity. Won't you tell me?'

'The pressure suits have to do with the need to eject from the plane in an emergency, or to hold out inside it when there's been a break in the canopy or the wall of the cockpit, resulting in a sudden drop of pressure to a level leading to immediate unconsciousness and the subsequent death of the pilot caused by lack of oxygen. If, let's assume, the plane is hit and has to be abandoned using the ejection seat, the suit creates a space around the pilot's body in which the oxygen supply is maintained out of a special, tiny emergency bottle, and lessens the traumatic effect of the pressure differential. As you can see, as long as everything's all-right, the suit is of no value at all. But if the pilot has to eject or if there's an air leak in the cockpit, it becomes essential for rescuing the pilot.'

'Now I understand, Amos. You explain things so well,' she responded with a warm smile. I smiled back at her and went up to my office to prepare my high-altitude spy-photo test flight.

'Hello, Yacov,' I spoke on the telephone in the office. I was speaking with the head of operations at Air Force command.

'What have you got, Amos?' he asked in reply.

'We've found a way to significantly improve the quality of our photos in the Canal area. I'm pretty sure you're going to like this,' I added, going on to explain the proposed innovation in our method of taking spy-photos. Yacov listened intently and immediately grasped what I was saying.

'Amos, this is extremely interesting. When can you perform a test flight to check out the method?' he asked.

'Yacov, the flight was performed two hours ago. Part of the film is here in my hands even as we speak,' I had my answer ready.

'Be at my office in the evening. I'll summon all concerned, and we'll see where we take it from here.'

'Whatever you say, Yacov. Goodbye,' I answered and hung up.

Half an hour before the time scheduled for the planes' take-off, I entered the safety and rescue equipment lab opposite the squadron building. The high-altitude flying suit, complete with all its accessories, was lying on the table, and the department officer and a lab assistant were waiting for me. After two successful test flights, and because of the operational urgency of the entire matter, the operational spy-photo flight to cover the Egyptian missile array along the Suez Canal had been brought forward to this day. At 14:15 hours I was due to pass above the target zone. Half an hour later I left the lab, waddling clumsily in the white spacesuit, which had been fitted to my body as required, after its air-tightness and the oxygen supply had been tested and found satisfactory.

The squadron's pickup took me to the recce plane hangar. 'Chef' Alon was waiting in the hangar and running the show. The hangar commander, a veteran mechanic with the rank of sergeant major, came up to me to get my signature on the plane's logbook. The handful of mechanics and photographic technicians who were there stood and stared at me, their eyes bulging in wonder. I must have looked like an alien from space as I climbed the ladder step by step and sat inside the cockpit. The safety and rescue equipment officer placed the bulky, largely transparent, helmet over my head and locked it into the slot in the suit's neck with a swivelling movement. Now the space around my body was completely sealed off from my surroundings, to protect me in case there were any hitches during the high-altitude flight or I had to eject from the plane.

Now I turned all my attention to the faultless execution of the flight. As usual, there was no place for cutting corners, making compromises, or disregarding procedures. Today as always, an operational flight demanded the full and unconditional commitment of all my resources. I switched on the plane's engine, activated its systems, and taxied to the end of the take-off runway.

'Orange, this is Red. Do you read me?' I called out over the primary radio channel.

'I read you loud and clear, Red. I'm above you, circling at 5000. I'll join you after take-off,' I heard the familiar voice of Aviem, a Phantom pilot from the northern squadron.

I could remember Aviem from the time I was a squadron commander at the flight academy. In that capacity I was occasionally invited to conduct the final tests for graduates of the course for flight trainers. This provided a splendid opportunity to get to know the younger generation of pilots, those with three, four and five years of flying experience behind them, who would soon be the heart of the service's fighting force. I was particularly impressed by the young cadet-trainer who sat in front of me in the forward compartment of the Fuga jet. This impression lasted throughout the test, starting with the clear, precise and well formulated briefing and ending with Aviem 's performance during the test and his ability to convey the flight material to others. I recalled that Aviem had received from me the second highest grade I'd ever awarded, in the course of conducting tests for hundreds of cadets at the flight academy.

I straightened out the plane on the runway, received authorisation to take off, and sped ahead. This time the Mirage's underbelly was 'smooth' for a change, without any detachable fuel tanks and air-to-air missiles. Everything was dedicated to enabling the plane to reach the peak of its ability in terms of speed and altitude. The plane accelerated rapidly and left the runway. I didn't wait long to shut the afterburner in order to save fuel. The time for the afterburner would soon come, I knew, and then I'd need every litre of jet fuel I could possibly save now.

As I banked left to the west, crossing the shoreline, I saw the Phantom's shadow pass over me, cross to my right, and take up position very close to me. I glanced in the direction of the Phantom and saw the pilot and the navigator in their picture-adorned helmets, gazing at me with interest. This reminded me that my appearance was by no means routine; my large, transparent helmet was not a familiar sight to our pilots. From his seat in the front cockpit, Aviem gestured with his left hand in greeting. I nodded my head in reply. The Phantom stood off now and took up position on my right, facing forward, about 300 metres (328 yards) away.

The Phantom crew had been assigned to the mission in the role of guard and watchdog. It was clear that during the picture-taking run, which would be executed at an altitude of 55,000 feet (about 17 km), when the pilot had to stabilise the plane in its orientation and altitude, he would be exposed as an easy target to the surface-to-air missiles. The pilot would not even be able to look down in the direction of the threat to know if and when he was in danger. The Phantom, which was equipped with electronic early warning systems for detecting missiles and radars, was supposed to fly several kilometres to the east of the 'photographer' and 10,000 feet (3 km) below him, and to warn him of any missile fire that appeared to endanger the plane and required aborting the mission.

Far out above the Mediterranean Sea, north of the central Sinai shoreline, at an altitude of 36,000 feet (11 km), I switched on the afterburner. The plane responded immediately. Within a few seconds the speedometer registered Mach 1.0 as the plane passed the speed of sound and continued accelerating. I banked moderately and at a flat trajectory in order not to impede my acceleration, turning the plane southwards in the direction of the northern entrance to the canal. When the speedometer indicated a reading of Mach 1.8, almost twice the speed of sound, I raised the aircraft's nose and began climbing to the picture-taking altitude.

When I looked up momentarily I saw the sky above me. Its colour was very dark, almost black, not the usual azure. I stabilised the plane at an altitude of 58,000 feet (17.7 km) and glanced at the stopwatch. I radioed notification to the controller and my escort, and turned the camera switch to 'on' position.

Both the controller and Aviem confirmed that they'd received my notification. Out of the corner of my eye I could see the dark Phantom far away below me to my left, in the east, against the background of the Sinai wilderness. I could see the long white vapour trail that was streaming from its exhaust pipe. I reckoned that my own plane was also 'painting' now. This was scarcely a comforting thought. I knew that in the entire Canal zone, for dozens of kilometres in every direction, anybody who raised his eyes was bound to see the two planes at high altitude without the slightest effort.

That day over fifteen missiles were launched at the insolent spyplane. Not one of them came close enough to pose a real threat and make it necessary to abort and run. The calculations we'd performed – I, Reuven and the specialists from intelligence – proved to be correct.

The Phantom crew also needed nerves of steel as they watched from afar and saw the missiles rising towards my plane. Aviem and his navigator could easily have called on me to abort the mission and break away left, to the east. At the preliminary briefing I'd already warned them not to take too large a margin of safety, lest they countermine the mission from the outset. Despite the danger to me, my own situation was simpler. Because of the horizontal and stabilised flight, I simply couldn't see what was happening beneath me . . . and perhaps it was for the best.

That night, inside the photo-labs of Air Force intelligence, the decipherers could finally be satisfied. After a long period of inferior photographic material, they again had the ability to provide the attack squadrons with intelligence of the first order. I sincerely hoped that the photographs would help the pilots in the operation, which was scheduled to take place two days later. After all, that was the primary and most important objective ahead of us.

CHAPTER TWENTY-EIGHT

Fire – 'Texas' Skies, 30 July 1970

S ince the beginning of the year there had been a burgeoning increase in the activities of the Russian 'advisers' in Egypt. They advised in all areas of the military, but in two of them in particular: the air force, and the air defence corps. For years the Russians had been equipping the Egyptians with weapon systems and teaching them how to use them, as well as combat tactics in general.

The squadrons of the Egyptian air force had been joined by Russian pilots, who didn't just provide training in the use of new aircraft whenever any arrived, but prolonged their stay in the squadrons for the purpose of consultation and supervision, to the point that they became permanent fixtures. The relations between the Egyptian and Russian pilots weren't particularly amicable. The Russians were arrogant towards the Egyptians and criticised their ability. The Egyptians' pride was offended, increasingly so as the War of Attrition went on and the number of Egyptian defeats in dogfights climbed into the dozens, with the Russians attributing them to the Egyptians' low level of flying expertise.

In spring of 1970 Russian pilots began to man operational flights in Egypt, limiting themselves at first only to flights deep inside Egyptian territory, taking care not to approach the Suez Canal front and avoiding any fighting contact with the Israelis there. Israeli Air Force intelligence attentively monitored this Russian activity and knew quite a lot about it. As the summer approached, and Egyptian losses in the air became very heavy, Russian pilots also began to show up in the vicinity of the Canal.

In early July it became known that a Russian pilot had been directly involved in opening fire on an Israeli Skyhawk jet, which had been attacking targets near the Canal, with the clear intention of shooting it down. He missed his mark.

Listening in to the enemy's communication networks was, and is, one of the important sources for obtaining intelligence. This is nothing new. To the contrary, it's almost as old as the networks themselves. It's no wonder, then, that Israeli intelligence had a pretty good idea when and where, and to what extent, there was direct Russian participation in operations.

Among other things, Israeli intelligence knew that formations of MiG-21s flown by Russian pilots were being scrambled from Egyptian air force bases in the Nile Valley (a few dozen kilometres south of Cairo), whenever Egyptian control discovered any movement of Israeli planes in the area south and east of the city of Suez. This was the area which we Air Force pilots dubbed 'Texas' – it was the Wild West of the Middle East.

Within the IDF general staff and at Air Force command in Tel Aviv, a decision was made that the Russians had to be dealt with; they could not enjoy any immunity when they intervened directly in battle with the Israelis. The five squadron commanders concerned with the matter were briefed by the Air Force commander in person.

I arrived first at the take-off position and parked my plane diagonally at the edge of the asphalt lot. The others arrived one after another – Avraham, number three; Asher, number two; and Gilad, number four – and parked in a staggered line beside me. In the few minutes that remained before take-off, I tried to calculate the number of enemy planes that the formation's four pilots could take credit for having shot down, arriving at twenty downed enemy planes altogether. 'It's hard, if not impossible,' I said to myself, 'to find such a group of fighter pilots anywhere in the world except for Israel. And it's probably even harder today to find a formation that will be able to contend successfully with such a side.'

Two minutes before take-off I eased the throttle forwards and slipped my plane into position on the left side of the start of the take-off runway. Numbers two, three and four immediately followed me and took up their positions. The process of testing the engines was swiftlly concluded. Radio silence was to be kept, as customary on long-range photo missions.

> Not for the first time, but with greater intensity than usual, I felt the sensation of approaching contention spreading in my blood and in my nerves. This was more than just a hunt; it was different from a panther's lethal pursuit of a terrified doe. This was a contest in which all the cards lay on the table, and the stakes were very high indeed. Here a clash of forces to the death could be expected. Everything was allowed. Sagacity, trickery, ingenuity, knowledge, personal ability, courage, strength – all of these would soon be put to the test.
>
> I knew exactly what was expected of me and my comrades, and despite not having any familiarity with the Russian pilot in battle, I was full of confidence and eager to engage in combat. I recalled how, as a maturing youth years earlier, I'd felt for the first time the power I had to act, influence, and make a difference. It was an almost intoxicating sensation, then as now.

When the second hand reached the scheduled take-off time precisely, first the engine and then the afterburner went to full-throttle, and my plane leapt forward. The other formation members followed me. I banked the plane westwards and climbed to an altitude of 35,000 feet (10.7 km), heading in the direction of central Sinai. Asher, number two, took up position very close to me, only a few metres away, almost in a tight formation. Avraham, number three, took up position to his left, about 700 metres (766 yards) away from me. Gilad, number four, took up position very close to number three, at the same distance as that between numbers one and two. Any radar station that might discover us would see only two blips on its screens rather than four and report a single pair of planes flying west in the direction of the Sinai Peninsula.

At this very moment, I knew, there were other formations assembling on the runways and preparing for take-off. At Ramat-David Airbase Avihu was leading a quartet of Phantoms, and he would be followed by Uri at the head of a quartet of Mirages.

Another formation of Mirages under Yiftach's command was straightening out and preparing for take-off at Hazor Airbase. Nobody would hear or see them until the critical moment. They'd be making their way to the Canal at treetop level.

Over central Sinai, approximately in the area of Jebel Libni, I descended to low altitude with my formation, disappearing from all the radar screens in the arena.

We crossed the Gulf of Suez and continued flying west into Egyptian territory. I momentarily recalled the first times I'd penetrated and flown behind the lines. The accumulated experience of dozens of sorties deep into Egypt had had its effect. The tension was there, always, but it wasn't any longer that inchoate, choking fear of the unknown.

At the scheduled time and place I gave the order, 'Red, pull!' Still in two pairs, each pair in close proximity and quite some distance from the other, we climbed to the customary altitude for taking photographs, 35,000 feet (10.7 km). But no, there were no cameras in any of our planes. All four of us were fully armed with missiles and cannon, ready to drop our spy-photo disguise at any moment and engage in aerial combat.

In the skies of the Middle East, the moment planes leave low altitude and climb, everyone can see and hear everyone else. I knew that we had to pull off this 'performance' without a hitch. This had been our briefing from the very start.

We were nearing the Nile Valley when we banked right in a north-easterly direction. Glancing to the left, I could see the dark, green-brown ribbon, wreathed in a haze of moisture or dust – this was the Nile Valley, traversing the desert from north to south.

'Red, cameras on!' I gave a simulated order to run the non-existent cameras, for the benefit of Egyptian intelligence's listening ears. The quartet continued flying in the direction of the city of Suez, above the wastes of 'Texas'.

'Red, this is Gold. Cucumber,' came notification from the controller.

'This is Red, I read you. Red, to the left, about face!' I had the formation turn back again, heading deep into Egyptian territory. This move, I knew, was too much of a temptation for the commanders at Egyptian air-control. They would simply have to send out interceptors to shoot down these 'two' insolent Israeli 'spyplanes'. It was to be hoped, of course, that the force scrambled against them would consist of Russian pilots. We had every reason to believe that this would be the case, but we wouldn't be able to know it for certain until several hours after the battle ended, if any were to take place at all.

'Red, this is Gold. Tomato,' the controller announced. The Egyptians had taken the bait! The code word meant that enemy planes were approaching our formation.

'Red, about face. Drop detachables!' I ordered. The formation turned east again to ensure that the battle, when it erupted, would be closer to our territory. The underbellies of our planes now free of the heavy detachable fuel tanks, our speed rapidly mounted. At my command all four pilots checked their weapon system switches one last time. In a few seconds this masquerade would come to an end; the gloves would come off, and the skies would light up.

'Red, this is Gold. To engage, assume azimuth two, five, zero. Quartet of bogies ahead, twenty miles, and another behind it, at range thirty-five miles,' the controller announced.

'I read you. Pepper go!' I gave the formation the command to open their afterburners. The voices of the leaders of two other Israeli formations began to come in over the secondary radio channel. I easily recognised them as belonging to Avihu and Yiftach.

'Red, high at eleven o'clock,' called out Avraham. At that moment my eyes caught sight of a pair of MiGs passing above us in the opposite direction.

'Three, go for the southern pair, we'll take the northern, high pair,' I announced, immediately receiving confirmation of the move from Avraham, number three.

'This is Gold. Attention, the second quartet is approaching the area, and a third quartet will be joining the battle in another two and a half minutes,' the controller notified all the formations.

In a sharp vertical manoeuvre, I raised my plane's nose towards the two MiGs, which could be seen high above us, diving in our direction. The blinding sunlight prevented me from following the MiGs when I suddenly heard Asher, number two, announce:

'One MiG passed me on the left, I'm going after him!'

I didn't like this one bit. The immediate significance of Asher's decision was that my pair, numbers one and two, was about to split up and lose its mutual defense capability. I turned my head as far as I could to the left in order to catch a glimpse of number two and 'his' MiG, but with no success.

'Three, I've shot down one of them!' came the announcement, with rather surprising speed, from Avraham's. Over the secondary channel could be heard the loud voices of our 'partners', flying Phantoms and Mirages, who were also in the thick of battle.

The large dark shadow of a MiG passed over the right side of my canopy. In a very rapid manoeuvre, I flipped my wings from left to right, in the direction of the diving MiG. Not far away from me to the south, I made out two mushroom clouds of smoke, memorials to two MiGs that were burning in flames.

'Two, I got one of them!' came the announcement from Asher. 'The devil knows where he is now,' I thought to myself.

'Red one in pursuit of MiG, azimuth two, seven, zero, altitude 14,000 and dropping,' I announced on the radio, in the hope that someone would be able to join me, or that the controller at least would be able to locate me in the general mayhem.

'This is Red two, I've apparently been hit. I'm heading home, plane under control,' Asher announced. I was alarmed for a moment. In the depths of my mind I knew this could have been expected from the moment my pair split up.

'Hang in there, Asher,' I prayed.

'My' MiG levelled its wings and fled west at high speed. I exploited my advantage in altitude and accelerated after him. Very slowly, at truly an annoying pace, the distance began to close. At a range of one kilometre (0.6 mile) I placed the threads of the sights on the MiG's tail. The missile was emitting a weak and intermittent buzz, indicating that it couldn't yet be launched.

'Just another three or four hundred metres,' I thought, 'and we'll finish this off. Fuel? There's enough to get safely back home.'

Suddenly, to my complete surprise, the 'MiG' began to bank to the left and climb.

'Damn it, that's not a MiG, it's a Phantom!' I screamed at

myself. Now I could see, out of the corner of my eye, that far away ahead of the Phantom to the west another MiG, a real one, was disappearing. Now the picture became clear. This Phantom had been pursuing the MiG and I'd been pursuing the Phantom, and I had to say I'd come too close for comfort to shooting it down.

'Who's that at 6000, turning left to the east?' I asked in an attempt to identify the Phantom ahead of me.

'This is Rabbit three. Who's asking?' came the reply.

'This is Red one, I'm now on your left. Join me in formation and let's return together,' I told the Phantom pilot. As we were covering each other on our way back east, we saw the parachute canopies of two of the Russian pilots who'd been downed and were still slowly descending. Columns of black smoke billowed up from the spots where the planes had hit the ground in this parched landscape.

Twenty MiGs and sixteen Mirages and Phantoms participated in that great battle. Five Egyptian MiGs, all flown by Russian pilots, were shot down. My formation was credited with two and a 'half' kills; credit for another 'half' of a MiG was divided between Avraham and Yiftach. The Phantoms shot down two more MiGs, one being accounted for by the crew of Avihu and Shaul, the other by Aviem and Fisher. A Russian 'Atol' air-to-air missile managed to get into the exhaust pipe of Asher's plane. Miraculously it failed to explode! Asher returned safely and landed at Refidim Airbase.

The Phantom, which I had been pursuing and had almost brought down, was piloted by Ehud Hankin – one of the original members of the northern squadron, an upstanding individual and a fine pilot. Ehud was killed three years later while attacking a missile battery in the Golan Heights during the Yom Kippur War.

In time it emerged that two parties were held that night: one in Tel Nof Airbase, where the Israeli pilots celebrated their victory; the other at one of the Egyptian air force bases, where the Egyptian pilots celebrated the debacle of those arrogant Russian pilots . . .

Chapter Twenty-Nine

Tel Nof Airbase, August 1970

Two weeks had passed since the ceasefire on both sides of the Suez Canal. The battles on land, sea and air had ceased.

The numerous victories during this long and complicated War of Attrition couldn't disguise the defeats that the IDF had suffered in a considerable portion of the engagements; in particular they couldn't disguise the surfeit of casualties and our inability to achieve a clear and unambiguous victory in the battlefield, as we had in June 1967.

In the air, our Air Force pilots won dozens of dogfights and gave the Egyptian air force, together with its Soviet trainers, a trouncing. The Air Force nevertheless failed to destroy the immense surface-to-air missile array that was being built west of the Canal, at massive investment by both the Egyptians and the Soviets. Several Israeli Phantoms were shot down in these attempts, and their crews killed or taken prisoner. Among those killed was Shmulik Hetz, commander of the first southern Phantom squadron and a much esteemed pilot. The hope that the newfangled electronic equipment would solve the problem and create a sort of 'protective bubble' of immunity to missiles around our planes, was dashed. 'The missile bent the plane's wing,' was a phrase making the rounds in those days.

The jangling last chord of this ceasefire came exactly twenty-four hours *after* it went into effect. During the night, in a logistical operation impressive in its own right, the entire Egyptian missile array was advanced in a single coordinated manoeuvre about 25 km (15.5 miles) east, in such a way that the missile range could

now effectively cover all the eastern, that is Israeli, side of the
Canal.

This move seemed to symbolise most clearly the Israeli failure
to achieve a decisive victory. It also gave rise to a new situation,
in which control of the air down the entire length of the Suez
Canal belonged to the Egyptians for the first time since the end
of the Six-Day-War. Or was this perhaps the harbinger of the
Yom Kippur War?

My squadron emerged from the War of Attrition with an
impressive record of victories. In dogfights its pilots had shot
down forty enemy planes, Syrian and Egyptian. Two of the five
Egyptian planes had been flown by Soviet pilots. The squadron's
spyplanes had provided photographic coverage of the entire
Middle East, making their crucial contribution to the success of
IDF operations in every theatre of war.

This squadron too, however, had suffered one prominent
fiasco, which cast a dark shadow over my thoughts. In one of the
battles in the northern Delta area one of the squadron's planes
had been shot down after it was caught without any mutual
coverage in formation. Luckily the pilot, Giora, managed to eject
from the plane and stay alive. He was taken prisoner by the
Egyptians and repatriated a year later.

Despite being pleased with the squadron's impressive
achievements and those of the entire company of fighter pilots, I
and all my comrades knew that the true heroes of this campaign
were the pilots of the attack squadrons. Those unsung warriors
had been exposed to the fire of the anti-aircraft guns and missiles,
and had set out day after day to perform the grey and onerous
tasks of grinding warfare. I felt this way with particular intensity
towards the Phantom pilots and navigators. They bore the brunt
of the most difficult tasks, and indeed they left many fallen
planes and comrades behind in the field.

An eerie and unusual quiet had descended on the squadron since
the start of the ceasefire two weeks earlier. Combat activities had
been abruptly curtailed. No planes were being scrambled, there
were no patrols, no imminent espionage missions, and I felt a sort
of peculiar emptiness. Training flights continued according to
schedule, but the absence of the 'daily' dose of adrenaline –

which came with operational activity, was evident everywhere.

'The commander of the Force wants to see you in his office tomorrow morning for a personal meeting,' Anat said to me over the intercom from the operations room, where she was sitting as usual.

'Confirm to his office that I'll arrive as requested. And for the sake of protocol, please notify the base commander of the summons,' I said to her in reply.

Asher knocked on the open door and stepped inside my office. He sat down comfortably in the chair facing me and gave me a look with his inquisitive blue eyes.

'What's going on?' he asked.

It dawned on me that my invitation to see the commander of the service was already known to the always curious Asher. After all, there was nothing routine about a squadron commander being invited to a personal meeting of this sort

'Asher, I haven't the slightest idea what it's about,' I replied. 'Let's wait and see.'

The subject was closed, and we went on to discuss the course for three young pilots that had commenced in the squadron. Asher reported to me on their initial flying performances and his personal impressions of the cadets.

'Two of the three are undoubtedly of the highest calibre. There won't be any problem integrating them into the squadron. The third is a slightly peculiar man. He's very introverted and doesn't always respond to things very intelligently. We'll have to keep an eye on him as the course progresses.'

'Keep me posted about him, and be especially alert to the aspect of safety in his regard,' I concluded, with composure and no enthusiasm. Asher went on his way.

I made a round of the technical department and visited the mechanics. I was worried that the drop in operational tension might precipitate a drop in the level of discipline and profession-alism. I'd decided to share my worries with the senior personnel of the technical department, and I was glad to find on their part the fullest understanding of my concern.

'Hello, Amos. Please take a seat. The commander's on the phone right now and he'll see you in a minute,' I received a very warm reception from Orit, the commander's adjutant, a cheerful officer with the rank of major. I made myself a cup of coffee and sank into the wide leather armchair in the corner of the elegant waiting room. On the wall opposite me two large and impressive pictures were hanging. One was a magnificent photograph of the Temple Mount in the distinctive early light of dawn; the other was a photograph taken through the gunsight of a Mirage, the threads of the sights superimposed on the fuselage of a MiG-21 in flames. A familiar sight . . .

'You can go in now,' Orit said to me.

'How are you, Amos?' asked Motti, the Air Force commander.

'I'm fine, thank you,' I replied.

The commander took an interest in what was happening in the squadron and among the pilots. He too, I realised, was worried that a decline in tension would be detrimental to the operational performance of the Force's squadrons. I didn't hide from the commander my opinion that the bitter contest between the plane and the anti-aircraft missile hadn't ended with the plane holding the advantage, and it was sure to be resumed with greater fury in the future.

'But this isn't why he's invited me here,' the thought flashed through my mind.

'Amos, yesterday we made a decision here at headquarters to close down one of the three Mirage squadrons and turn it into a Phantom squadron, which will also be the third,' he said. I listened carefully but made no response. The punchline hadn't arrived yet . . .

'I've decided that your squadron will be terminated. Its planes will be divided among the two sister squadrons at Ramat-David and Hazor Airbases,' he went on to add.

The blood froze in my veins. This decision certainly wasn't what I'd been expecting. The strength and proven successes of the squadron, which were known to everyone, had instilled the confidence in me that its existence was assured. I nevertheless maintained my composure and allowed him to finish what he was saying. The commander stopped for a moment, looked at me and went on.

'I want you to build the new Phantom squadron on the foundation of your squadron,' he declared.

The blood that had frozen in my veins renewed its flow, and now at an accelerated rate. All the cogs inside my brain were turning. I knew that I had to take a stand on the issue, here and now. 'Sir, I consider it an honour. I accept the assignment and will perform it to the best of my ability,' I replied, after two or three seconds of hesitation.

'I'm very pleased, Amos. I'm sure you'll perform it well, as you always do,' said the commander.

'Sir, I have two requests regarding the matter,' I added.

'Speak,' said Motti.

'The first request is that you allow me to choose which of the current team of pilots and technicians will get to carry on with me to the Phantoms.' I knew exactly who I wanted with me: Asher, Shmulik, Shlomo, Arnon. I wouldn't dream of not taking Anat with me either. Nor 'Chef' Alon.

'Agreed. What else?' asked Motti.

'The second request is personal. I'm asking you to support my dispatch to the American naval academy in the United States for a period of study, after I finish my assignment as commander of the squadron,' I said.

'Amos, you'll have my support,' said Motti, rising from his chair to walk me to the door. He clapped my shoulder, turned around, and shut himself back inside his office.

'Orit, is there any cold water?' I asked, and sat down for a couple of minutes in the 'recovery' room. I reflected awhile before bidding everyone goodbye and going on my way.

It's hard to explain the bond between a man and a machine. Such a bond is formed when man and machine become closely united through their mutual dependence on each other and long, unbroken physical intimacy. I, like most of my fellow fighter pilots, had developed such a bond with the Mirage jet over the years. I knew how to bring out the full potential of this elegant, sometimes untamable machine. Many times I'd felt that the plane – this conglomeration of steel and cables – was almost becoming a living creature under my hands. It moved, it vibrated, it kicked, it committed itself and took it easy, and it served you with dedication, but with limited liability.

The thousands of flying hours I'd logged inside this small and crowded cockpit had resulted in an intimate physical familiarity. I knew which foot would step on the last rung of the ladder upon entering the cockpit; which movement would connect the emergency oxygen pipe to its harness; how the cavity of the ignition switch would feel when I pressed it with my left index finger; the smell after an ignition failure; and exactly how the plane would respond to the pressure of my foot on one of the brake pedals. I recalled the intensity of my desire those many years ago to be among the chosen who would fly these beautiful planes. Flooding my memory came the thousands of times I'd shifted the steering stick, thereby performing thousands of rolls, loops, dives, escapes and all the other dance moves of the pilot in space.

All this was going through my head as I was getting down from Mirage number 58 inside the hangar at Ramat-David Airbase. I handed my flight helmet to the mechanic, waited while the security pins were locked in place, and remained seated inside the plane for another three or four minutes. The mechanic, whose face I was unfamiliar with, walked away from the plane. My gaze passed over the interior of the cockpit, the dials, switches, handles . . . Suddenly I noticed that many spots were worn and faded from years of being touched, like the corners of a child's room in an old, familiar and pleasant house.

This was the final curtain. I got up, placed my left foot on the ladder, set down my right foot after it, and briskly stepped down from the plane. I tapped the left side of the nose, decorated with emblems of the Egyptian and Syrian air forces to mark the enemy planes this plane had shot down. I continued to caress the side of the plane as I was walking. 'I'm glad nobody can see me now,' I thought to myself, wiping away a tear from the corner of my eye as I finally tore my hand away from the hard aluminium skin. I got into the vehicle that was waiting for me. Inside one of the eight small, round emblems of the Egyptian air force was a tiny red star, borrowed from the Soviet emblem – it was an enduring testimony to that battle against the Russian pilots in Egypt.

That morning all the squadron's planes were drawn up in one long line along the edge of old runway 27 at the base.

The families of the squadron's career servicemen, pilots and ground crew were seated on benches facing the planes. Also invited to the ceremony were several commanders and friends from the base and Air Force staff headquarters. In the lot opposite the audience of spectators stood two groups drawn up in parade order – the pilots in one of them, the mechanics in the other. I mounted a low podium erected there and delivered a speech of 'farewell to the Mirages':

> Go and ask the pilots of Cairo and Damascus what the Mirage is like. Hundreds of times our Mirages have dived at the enemy's airfields and installations; they dived and returned victorious in the Six-Day-War. Sixty-eight times the squadron's Mirages have returned after shooting down MiGs, Sukhois, Hunters and Ilyushins, opening wide the skies to the IDF.
>
> With your permission, I'll say goodbye to 03, oldest of our planes and first in the squadron to shoot down a MiG, with a total of five kills. And to 68, the ubiquitous Air Force champion, which shot down a grand total of eleven enemy planes, a few Russians among them. And to 58, the master sniper, which shot down a MiG with only fourteen cannon shells, and with eight kills to its credit altogether.
>
> . . . And there are another two magnificent jets, 98 and 99, which spent more time behind the lines than any other planes in the Air Force. What tremendous performances! What amazing suspense! What fine results this pair of spyplanes achieved! The Mirage squadron is being shut down today. But only temporarily. The squadron will soon return to new life, and in our Phantoms we shall strike the enemy wherever he stands!

'Ground and air crews, take to the planes,' I ordered my men.

The two groups of men standing in parade order broke up and scattered at a run in the direction of the planes. A few minutes later the entire area shook as our twenty-four Mirages stood with their engines running and canopies shut, awaiting the order to take off. I glanced aside and recognised Asher Snir, the squadron's senior pilot, in the plane to my right. Asher gave a nod of his head in my direction, suppressing his excitement. Plane after plane in turn, the six quartets left their positions and taxied past the guests gathered by the side of the runway. Leading the pack, I caught sight among the spectators of Rachel and our two sons, Noam and Ram, beside her. Or, our two-and-a-half year old daughter, had been left at the nursery in the residential neighbourhood. Our eyes met, and I raised my left hand in greeting to them.

Immediately after take-off all the planes assembled to fly in formation. Two arrowheads, of three quartets each, passed in perfect coordination over the base and above the heads of the crowd, disappearing to the west.

'Grey, this is Red. You're on your own!' I notified Asher, who was leading the rearmost formation of twelve planes.

'This is Grey. Roger. *Bon voyage*,' Asher replied, banking south with the half of the force under his command to land at Hazor Airbase.

I led 'Red' formation, which was under my command, to Ramat-David Airbase. As I was landing, I saw two Phantoms waiting in the lot beside the runway. I knew that in another three months I'd be taking command of the first new Phantoms.

The very next day, 5 October, I had my first solo flight in my new plane, the Phantom.

'Chef' Alon, Arnon and I met the commander of the construction unit of Tel Nof Airbase and the engineer who came with him in the entrance to the squadron building, the new home of the third Phantom squadron. A smell of fresh paint wafted from the gleaming walls. Every noise or sound made inside the empty rooms gave rise to multiple echoes. In a month and a half the rooms would be filled with people and the squadron would spring back into action. The group consisting of 'my' officers, the people I'd chosen to build the rejuvenated squadron, was filled with a motivation to do everything better. They were driven by a shared heritage, by the high expectations of everybody around them, and simply because that's what they were like.

The tour of the renovated building went from room to room. We stopped everywhere, drew out our plans, compared them, compiled and added data, made our summaries, and moved on. All the experience we'd accumulated in the old squadron, every-thing we'd learned from the existing Phantom squadrons – all this we now wanted to apply in the new building. When we had finished we stepped out onto the front balcony. In the lot in front of the building a tall crane was lifting an old Meteor jet into place atop a large concrete column. Nocturnal Meteor jet fighters had been the first to see service in this squadron, under the command of Yoash 'Chato' Tsidon, even before the Sinai campaign. Later they'd been joined by French Vautour jets, also specially equipped for nocturnal combat. It was only in the next round that the squadron had received its Mirages, and now – the Phantoms were coming. It was no wonder, then, that we'd made every effort to locate a wholly intact Meteor jet to put on display in front of the new squadron building's façade.

I divided the first crews of pilots and navigators, who were going to establish the third Phantom squadron, into two groups that split up between the two veteran squadrons at Ramat-David and Hazor Airbases. I wanted us to pick up every scrap of information we could from them.

Autumn was already in the air; the days were getting shorter, the skies filled with clouds, and the bustle of the holiday season was over. It was nearing the end of October, 1970. A brief and hearty leave-taking ceremony was conducted at the northern Phantom squadron. Glasses of wine were set out on the table and toasts exchanged between Avihu, commander of the veteran squadron, and myself, when my crews finished their short period of training and prepared to set off for their old-new home.

Four almost-new Phantom jets, acquired in the most recent procurement, were scattered in four different hangars, gleaming and ready to fly. Berko, one of the few relatively seasoned navigators who'd been attached to the founding team of the third squadron, was listed as my crewman and navigator. We both shook hands with our northern colleagues in farewell, put on the flight suits with their numerous pockets and buckles, and boarded the bus. The other three crews were already sitting there waiting for us.

During twelve years of flying jet fighters, ever since I'd been awarded my wings, I'd been accustomed to getting into the plane alone. I'd always felt there was something very special about the solitude that fell upon me the instant the canopy was shut, the cockpit sealed, and only I remained to be my own king, or slave. Twelve years, thousands of flying hours, hundreds of operations and dozens of dogfights had transpired while I was alone in that narrow cockpit, which fitted me like a glove. Not any longer.

Berko stepped right up to the plane and began the usual turn of inspection around it. I went over to the mechanics' room to sign the plane's logbook. The commander of the hangar, a sergeant-major, greeted me there. Another mechanic showed initiative and took the trouble to bring me a cup of sweet Turkish coffee and a pair of red roses as a token of farewell. I went over to the plane and performed my own quick inspection. The two of us clambered up the ladders to our cockpits, accompanied by two mechanics.

The peculiar feeling hadn't left me yet – a feeling shared by every veteran Mirage pilot – of finding the Phantom's cockpit to be extremely spacious: too spacious, in fact. To reach the switches which I'd formerly accessed by extending a finger, I now had to extend my arm full length. I had the feeling of someone who's traded in a powerful, speedy motorcycle for a sophisticated car – fast it might be, but big and cumbersome as well. In the previous jets I'd flown, I'd learned how beneficial it was to be small in the space of aerial combat. Small meant swift. It meant being less visible, less of a target to the enemy. Now I had to change my entire way of thinking. Into my hands, and into those of the soldiers under my command, had been delivered these new war machines, the latest development in aviation. From these machines, I knew, we would have to extract everything they could deliver; we would have to minimise their disadvantages and make the most of their advantages. Study, training and hard work were the name of the game from now on.

Berko and I exchanged a look between us – this was another 'historic' moment in my life. Then we climbed into our cockpits, I into the forward pilot's cockpit and Berko into the rear one. A minute and a half later the navigator's voice came over the intercom system. We checked the communication between us and Berko gave notice that the process of zeroing the plane's inertial navigation system had been concluded. With a twirl of my finger I gave the signal to start the left engine, followed by the right. The noise of the running engines was deafening both inside and outside the hangar. The helmets over our heads somewhat reduced the noise, making it bearable. When we shut the two canopies the noise was almost completely suppressed, and a businesslike atmosphere descended on the two-seat cockpit.

The four planes, all of them painted in brown-green camouflage colours and bearing the old-new squadron emblem on their tails, left the different hangars in which they'd been readied and arrived at the parking lot beside the runway.

'Red, permission to straighten out,' I requested the control-tower, after the communications among the members of the formation had been checked. Out of the corner of my eye I saw two photographers standing at the side of the runway, apparently recording the event for posterity.

'Permission granted, Red,' came the reply.

Ramat-David is an attractive airbase. The fields and settlements of the Jezreel Valley surround it. The ridge of Mount Carmel is opposite, the bluffs of Tivon are to the right, the bluffs of Nazareth are behind it, and the base itself is dappled with trees and greenery. All of this was a heartwarming sight to my eyes. The atmosphere of the Valley and the pioneer tradition of the north had always been among the hallmarks of this Air Force base. As I was taxiing my plane to the end of the runway, I recalled the period during which I'd been posted with the Meteor squadron here at the end of my flight training course; I was reminded of Aharoni, the squadron commander who wore his wristwatch on his right hand, and of Harry, the great, moustachioed Australian trainer.

'Red, take-off.'

'Red, permission to take off, and good luck to you!' came the reply from the commander in the control-tower.

Inside the eight tremendous jet engines the revolutions rose to full power. I removed my feet from the brakes and the plane leapt forward. I pushed both throttles all the way to the stop and shifted them left into the slot that allowed them continued forward motion. I continued to press them forwards. In both engines the afterburners were ignited. Now the plane shot forward at full power. At ten-second intervals all four planes left their spots at the end of the runway and, with a thundering roar

that shook the entire vicinity, accelerated down the runway and
rose into the air.

After take-off I cut back engine power to allow the other
planes to join me in tight formation, staggered to the right, in a
wide left turn. In this formation we performed a pass at low altitude over the building of the 'Hammers' squadron, the northern
Phantom squadron, which had been so much help to us in our
drive to achieve independence quickly.

After half an hour, during which we exploited the fuel in our
tanks to practise aerial combat in pairs among ourselves, the four
Phantoms reassembled in tight formation to make another pass,
this time over their new squadron building in their home at Tel
Nof Airbase.

A small party awaited us inside the hangar that had been
prepared to receive the Phantoms. Three or four tables had
been set up in the open area. All the squadron's personnel were
excitedly waiting there. A few guests and intimates had also
arrived. The place fell silent when the pilots switched off their
engines. We descended from our planes and were greeted with
hugs and claps on the back.

> I was aware of the fact that the eyes of all the servicemen
> under my command were upon me. Unlike two-and-a-half
> years previously, I was now a seasoned, battle-scarred,
> successful and authoritative commander. I was already very
> adept at determining objectives, hatching a plan and leading
> my men in its execution. I was in control of the people and I
> knew what I was doing. I was proud of my ability, though
> not inordinately arrogant or power hungry; I was a
> squadron commander through and through.
>
> They stood there, in the yard of the gleaming hangar, all
> of them: Asher, Shmulik, Shlomo, Arnon, Omri, Zvi, Fisher,
> Berko, Moshe, Ofer, Sagi, and 'Chef' Alon of course, and
> Aharon and Tal, and many other fine individuals. They
> trusted me, and I loved them!

With unprecedented speed – it had been exactly four weeks since
Asher and I had taken off at the head of that formation of
Mirages, split up the planes and closed that fascinating chapter in

our lives – I landed the formation of new Phantoms at the airbase. Three months later, in the spring of 1971, I led a formation of Phantoms on an operational flight beyond the border for the first time in the present configuration.

A brown-skinned and handsome young navigator arrived at the squadron, together with two of his buddies, and immediately commenced the process of training to fly operationally. This small group of newcomers stood out because of its youth, and the veterans made every effort to let them feel at home as quickly as possible.

I, thirty-five years old, a squadron commander and a lieutenant-colonel, and Amram, the navigator, a twenty-year-old second lieutenant, opened the canopies of our cockpits, still sweating from our exertions. We rose from our seats to descend from the plane, whose engines had fallen silent. We finished the process of signing our names in the plane's logbook, and sat down on the edge of a low concrete barrier waiting to be picked up.

'Amos, can I ask you something?' said Amram.

'Of course,' I answered immediately.

'Do you remember having a housekeeper by the name of Sarah, when you were just a little boy?'

'I remember her perfectly! She was almost as close to me as my mother, and I loved her very much. I also used to spend a lot of time at her house in Kerem Ha-Teymanim.' ['The Yemenites' Vineyard' – an early neighbourhood of Tel Aviv populated by Yemenite Jews.] I wondered where this peculiar question was leading to.

'Amos, I'm Sarah's son,' said Amram.

My breath was taken away for a minute. Amram's identity was a stunning revelation. The image of boundlessly faithful Sarah, such a simple and warm woman, came rising to the surface from my childhood memories, wonderfully sharp and clear.

'How wonderful are the ways of this country and this people,' I thought, as I embraced the shoulder of the young navigator, my own crewman, Second Lieutenant Amram.

From a faded wooden chest, which I'd found in my father's desk after he died, I poured out a pile of old photographs on my desk. After rummaging for a few minutes, I found the picture I was looking for. Between the two rows of fig trees along Tel Aviv's Rothschild Boulevard stood a smiling Yemenite woman, holding the hand of a curly, four-year-old boy with a high-brimmed white cap over his locks. Sarah.

CHAPTER THIRTY

Yom Kippur Day, Tel Aviv, 1973

A warm breeze greeted us when we alighted from the El-Al plane that had brought us back from the United States for Rosh Hashana (the Jewish New Year). Rachel, the three children and I had been there for a year and a half. I'd been studying towards my master's degree at the American Naval Postgraduate School and enjoying this opportunity to open a window onto the wider world. This experience of American life, a first for me, had a great impact. For the first time I was exposed to a culture of system and order, the complete opposite of Israeli improvisation and laxity. It was a good time for both me and the family.

It took two or three days to get organised, and then I reported for duty to perform an overlapping period with my predecessor before assuming the post of Air Force head of operations. I'd been assigned to this post by Benny Peled, the Air Force commander, who had informed me of the posting just a few weeks before our return to Israel. I was bursting with enthusiasm and plans for the job, which I'd coveted for some time.

At 12.30 pm on the eve of Yom Kippur, in the parking lot outside Air Force headquarters, there was a gathering of senior officers who'd left their offices and were on their way home. Almost all the offices were empty already, and the traffic in the street was thinning too, on its way to lapsing entirely, as it always does on this day. In the morning there had been a conference of senior commanders with the commander of the Force himself, at which warning was given of the imminent outbreak of war as early as the next day. A rather detailed intelligence survey was delivered, and in its wake the head of operations gave notice of the special standby arrangements for the holiday. Two Fuga jets from the flight academy would be placed on special standby, and they'd circle the big city centres if there was any need to summon the career servicemen back to the wings and squadrons. The Air Force commander summarised the discussion, determining that initial efforts would be directed towards defending the country's skies and the expanses of Sinai. Then – if things were to get more complicated – the Force would set about as quickly as possible to attack the missile arrays and wrest for itself freedom of action in the combat arena.

'Will a war break out tomorrow or not?' This was the question preoccupying the group of officers in the parking lot. Opinions were divided. But it was only natural that the Head of Intelligence's opinion should be the focus of greatest attention, for who should know better. With a disdainful and unequivocal gesture of his hand, this worthy pontificated: 'Lay off it, boys – nothing's going to happen!' He tugged at the collar of his shirt, turned on his heel, and walked off arrogantly to his car.

I heard his remarks with the greatest clarity and inscribed them deep in my memory. It was the informal nature of the occasion that gave them that much more weight. We separated and left for our homes, against the background of the warning of imminent war and the briefing delivered by the Air Force commander. There was a feeling that even if a war were to break out, we'd be able to put up a defence and turn it into an impressive and rapid victory.

On Yom Kippur Day, 6 October 1973, at about 9 am, the telephone rang in our house, which was still cluttered with packing cases and trunks.

'For you,' said Rachel, handing me the receiver.

'Come to headquarters immediately,' I was told.

On my way to the defence ministry complex in Tel Aviv, I saw a Fuga flying low above the city's buildings through my car window.

'Hostilities are expected to commence at 6 pm,' I was informed when I arrived at the 'Pit'.

'Most of the effort is to be devoted to preparing our assault on the missile arrays tomorrow morning,' the staff officers were told by Giora, head of operations, immediately after he emerged from a consultation with the Air Force commander.

At 1.45 pm on Yom Kippur Day, the blips of the enemy planes attacking Sinai filled the radar screens. Now there was no longer any time to organise an aerial force for an assault, and all our forces were diverted to repulse the aerial assault. Planes that had been standing ready, armed for assault and bombing missions, now had to be 'stripped' of this excess weaponry and scrambled to the northern and southern theatres of battle. Some of them would take off with their bombs and drop them at sea, unarmed, before joining the effort to repulse the enemy.

The outbreak of hostilities at that hour was in itself a surprise, for all the intelligence had been predicting 6 pm. Really, it was so unfair . . .

A flood of information, some of it contradictory, began arriving at Headquarters as evening fell. Many enemy planes had been shot down in dogfights, but from the fronts came reports of the intense pressure on the line of Suez Canal outposts and along the Golan Heights front, and of an extensive, surprisingly bold and fierce, ground campaign. In the offices of the 'Pit' at Air Force headquarters the chaos was extraordinary. Dozens of officers and NCOs were rushing about from room to room: some of them reservists whose presence was uncalled for; some of them good people who really wanted to help but didn't know how and in what way.

The venue was narrow, the information confused, and getting organised a difficult and slow process. Things settled down a little after clearer instructions arrived from the High Command and the commander of the Force. Our orders were to assist the forces under pressure along the Suez Canal during the night using 'Kela' pull-up toss bombing. This would not be very accurate but would allow us to operate in the margins of enemy areas protected by batteries of surface-to-air missiles, without paying too high a price through dangerous exposure to them.

I took aside Oded, my longtime friend and a former squadron commander himself. The two of us sat down in a corner of the room, spread out a 1:100,000 scale map of the Canal area, and plotted out rectangles, representing 500 metres (550 yards) wide and 1000 metres (1100 yards) long. These would be distributed among the squadrons as targets for the 'Kela' attacks. There was no time or cause to wait for better organised targets from Intelligence. The chaos and the dearth of information there were no less extraordinary.

The Egyptian and Syrian initiative and surprising timetable didn't change the policy line at Air Force headquarters. The brunt of the effort still needed to be devoted to preparing the assault on the Egyptian missile array the next day.

By personal order of the Force commander, I was 'leashed' to the head of operations. My request to leave the 'Pit' and rejoin my former Phantom squadron was flatly refused.

Thousands of hours of training flights, at the individual and system levels, exercises performed on models, studies, briefings and theories of combat had been devoted by the Air Force for three years. The aim had been to put together an efficient operational plan for the destruction of our Syrian and Egyptian enemies' anti-aircraft defence systems.

The scars of our defeat in battle against the missiles, which had been in effect concealed from the outside world when the cease-fire agreement with Egypt was signed in August 1970, hadn't healed within the Force's ranks, neither at the higher and mid-level echelons of command, nor in the squadrons that had been involved in the fighting at the time. While some of the commanders continued to dream of smashing victories à la the Six-Day-War, others – the more knowledgeable among them – understood that the aerial war would be decided by the contest between the Air Force's assault squadrons and the massive missile arrays facing them.

There was a disturbing delay in the development, and even more so in the production, of innovative, stand-off weapon systems to facilitate the execution of this complex mission. In the absence of such systems, the brunt of the effort, and most of the risk, fell upon the service's assault units, namely the Phantom and Skyhawk squadrons,which were armed mainly with heavy 'ordinary' bombs. The various types of rockets were in effect justifiably abandoned because of their low efficiency, and left in the stockpiles. The planes' cannon also ceased to be a vital weapon system in assaulting ground targets because they could be used only at short ranges and low altitudes, conditions which had become deadly as a result of effective anti-aircraft fire. On the other hand, there were hopes that the Phantoms' modern and advanced weapon guidance systems would, in time of need, make the difference and contribute crucially to the accuracy of the bombs.

The doctrine of warfare that was developed called for a full, concentrated and undisturbed effort to destroy the missile arrays during a twenty-four-hour period, and perhaps twice that, in order to gain the freedom of action so vital to ultimate victory in the campaign. Dozens of times in conferences and in compilations of standing orders, the commanders of the Air Force repeatedly demanded of the High Command the freedom to mount such a concentrated effort during the first two full days of war, whenever it should break out. Their explanations and demands were accorded the fullest understanding, as evidenced by all of the summaries and all the army's war plans, both in attack and defence.

The next day this sweeping commitment was to be put to the test along the Egyptian front.

Operation *Tagar* (Challenge) began at first light. On the morning of Sunday 7 October, the second day of the Yom Kippur War, our Air Force's Phantoms and Skyhawks set out on their first assault sortie against the batteries of surface-to-air missiles along the Egyptian front. The objective was to batter and suppress the anti-aircraft concentrations around the batteries with salvoes of cluster bombs, in order ultimately to reduce the number of casualties that could be expected later in the campaign. The bombing and destruction of the batteries and missiles themselves was meant to be undertaken in the following sorties, later that same day.

At dawn that Sunday morning, the Air Force commander was summoned to see the Chief of Staff for an urgent conference. As soon as he returned, he called together the service's senior staff officers. He was visibly upset and distraught. The atmosphere inside the commander's room was oppressive, especially in view of the bad news that continued to come streaming in from both the northern and southern fronts. We, however, the veterans of the wars, were sure that our assault, costly in lives as it may be, would generate the hoped-for turnaround in the battles along the front. The commander's orders were trenchant and decisive:

'All available aerial forces are to be diverted from the south to the northern front, where the situation is critical. These instructions are not open to further discussion. The dawn sortie, which has begun taking off already, will complete its mission, but the operation will then cease and all the planes returning from the south will be diverted to assaults along the northern front,' the commander announced in no uncertain terms. The atmosphere, which had been oppressive already, now verged on the calamitous.

My breath was taken away and my guts were churning. I knew that the true meaning of this order was the clear and predictable failure of the mission in the south, and the sacrifice of the effort in the south on behalf of another failure along the northern front. The efforts by some officers on the fringes of this debate, to ameliorate the decision so that the effort in the south might not be entirely abandoned, were dismissed outright. The most senior officers with the greatest authority and most operational experience, such as the deputy commander of the Force and the head of intelligence, either laid low or kept their silence, while the next in line down the hierarchy, the head of operations, lacked the personal charisma and the support necessary to change the situation.

I personally felt that the most basic rule of warfare, sticking to the planned objective, had been violated. This rule ran like a thread through the victories of all the great generals from Alexander the Great and Napoleon to Patton and Rommel. It was hard for us to understand who had chosen, and why, to make this horrendous decision, and in such a sweeping and extreme manner. Peled? Dado (Chief of Staff David Elazar)? (Defence Minister) Dayan?

My own feeling was that the Air Force, and the army in general, paid the price for the stand of a commander who may have been a prodigy in the fields of technology and organisation, but who lacked experience in the field of operational planning.

He did not properly appreciate, so it would seem, the extent of the damage that would be caused by his intractable decision.

The contention, that the diversion of the entire aerial effort from the south to the northern front would prevent its collapse was totally unfounded. What later proved to be the case was clear to me and others beforehand, namely, that our support of ground forces defending themselves against the invading Syrian armour would not be effective in areas protected by surface-to-air missiles. Our pilots would have to fly at very low altitude, on the one hand making it difficult for them to visually identify their targets, on the other hand bringing them within range of all types of ballistic anti-aircraft munitions: cannon, machine-guns and even rifles.

Furthermore, the Syrian armoured units, which had breached the Golan Heights and were threatening to descend towards the Jordan River and the Sea of Galilee, could have been stopped using only a small number of planes outside the Syrian missiles' effective sphere of action. This would not have diminished the primary effort in the south to any great extent.

The attempt to destroy the surface-to-air missile array in the north – in haste and without the proper disposition of forces, updated targets and tight control – was also a formula for disaster. Having rushed through procedures, the planes arrived at the Syrian front late in the morning, without the proper preparation and without the organisation of forces and timetables essential to the success of any complex assault. Many of the missile batteries had also changed location and moved to new, unknown sites. The effort in the north came to grief as well. Indeed, out of the thirty-odd batteries that were supposed to be attacked in the operation, only a few were hit and not even one was destroyed.

No fewer than twenty-two jet fighters were shot down on that first day of fighting, twenty-one of them by anti-aircraft fire from the ground. But worst of all was the fact that on that bitter day our planes' achievements and their true impact on the course of the war were almost negligible.

In the next two days, 8 and 9 October no new initiative was taken for an 'organised' assault on the surface-to-air missile array, and there was no substantial change in the picture. During the first four days of the war, the Air Force lost sixteen Phantoms and twenty-six Skyhawks – a devastating result, especially in light of its meagre accomplishments.

The ratio of losses to accomplishments in Air Force activity at the start of the war was dreadful, and unprecedented in the annals of the service. In the first four days of fighting no fewer than fifty Israeli jet fighters were shot down on both fronts – one out of every eight planes. Did the aerial force make a crucial contribution to halting the Syrian attack in the Golan Heights? This is doubtful. Would it have been possible to suffice with a smaller task force to make the same contribution, without irreparably derailing the effort in the south? Quite probably. I thought a mistake had been made, and it was critical to the overall effort and the failure of that entire first week. This was a thought that continued to prey on my mind for years.

> I admired General Peled, the commander of the Air Force. I loved listening to his analyses, opinions and plans. He was an illustrious figure in the higher echelons of the service, and of the army in general. With his learning and knowledge, and the acuteness of his intelligence, he was able quickly to identify the essential problems, break them down into their components, and define the required solutions with stunning clarity. He scorned convention and excelled at tackling the topics on the agenda from viewpoints nobody had thought of before. Peled himself was a courageous individual as well. His personal courage may even have led him into the trap of attributing his own abilities to other soldiers and expecting them to measure up to standards of fighting that weren't always realistic. He was a great reformer, and he left a better organised, more sophisticated, advanced and technological air force, to a degree that overshadowed all his predecessors, and all the commanders who followed him.
>
> But everything I had thought, and would think in the future, of this fine man couldn't change my opinion regarding that fateful decision on the morning of the second day of the war. In my opinion, Benny Peled made a mistake.

From the Air Force's viewpoint, the fighting developed into an arduous contest between plane and missile. After the stinging failure of the operations on both fronts, the Force by necessity was dragged into a grinding battle in which assaults were performed by smaller formations of forces, and were meant to achieve limited gains over a prolonged period of time. The plan to win control of the skies in a single, continuous operation became unrealistic and was totally abandoned.

Only when units of Israeli armour under General Sharon's command crossed to the western side of the Suez Canal did it become possible to encircle the Egyptian missile array, break it up into several pockets, and deal with each of them separately. Thus arose the embarrassing situation in which the armoured corps helped the Air Force win control of the skies in the battlefield. In contrast, the Air Force was unable to efficiently sweep the roads, outposts and concentrations of enemy ground forces and open the way for our own ground forces to attack, as happened in the Six-Day-War. The entire army paid dearly for this failure.

Beyond the humiliating operational failure, a grave credibility gap opened up between the Force's wings and squadrons on one hand and headquarters on the other. The units in the field held Air Force command responsible for the failures. Criticism was repeatedly levelled at the intricate plans, which depended on the complex coordination of forces, timetables and methods, but hadn't yielded the hoped-for results and involved numerous casualties.

'Now try to explain to the commanders in the field,' I reflected, 'that it wasn't the system that failed but its application, caused by a lack of adherence to the basic principles of warfare.' There was also an unwillingness among the squadrons to accept the fact they they were sent out on missions with faulty, shabby, some-times actually mistaken, intelligence. In the airbases local initiatives were undertaken to mount attacks in small, 'flexible' formations. These led to certain limited successes but to casual-ties as well, without having any significant impact on the course of the aerial war. With great concern I followed this worrying trend, which was unprecedented. I empathised with the forma-tion leaders and squadron commanders, but I knew that a complex aerial war could not be resolved using outdated methods in the tradition of the Palmach, with small forces and commando-like 'point' operations. This wasn't how you won an all-out war.

Ultimately, it was only after two bloody weeks, when most of the war was already behind us, that the Air Force achieved control of the skies on both the northern and southern fronts. In a series of operations, none very large, the missile batteries were destroyed or dispersed and ceased to function as a single efficient array.

The break-up of the missile array and the advance of IDF armoured divisions into Egypt forced the Egyptians to send out their fighter squadrons to the front in an attempt to halt the Israeli forces. The Egyptian MiG pilots took on the Air Force's Mirage squadrons, and it was like smashing into a wall. They fell in their dozens, leaving behind on the Israeli side new fighter aces, the likes of which there had been but few in the history of aerial warfare. About 300 Egyptian and Syrian planes were shot down in the air. Only eight Israeli Air Force planes were downed in aerial combat. About ninety Israeli planes, however, were downed by surface-to-air missiles and anti-aircraft fire. Fifty pilots and navigators were killed, and another fifty were taken prisoner in that brutal war.

During the third week of fighting, I was summoned to see the commander, who assigned me the post of acting head of operations. I received my full, official appointment two weeks after the fighting ended.

On 22 October the battle was launched to retake the outposts on Mount Hermon, which the Syrians had overrun at the start of the war. The Air Force was given the task of softening up the outposts with preliminary bombings before the ground attack began.

In the command room at Air Force headquarters, I relinquished my seat to Benny, the commander, who'd arrived to take charge of the Force's planes in battle. Benny sat in his chair and I, the head of operations, sat close behind him. On the screens in front of us and on the gigantic table behind the thick glass window, we could see all the data pertaining to the theatre, markers designating the forces in the air and their locations, and all the tables of relevant information required for the operation.

Three formations of Phantoms and Skyhawks were supposed to attack the outposts and surrounding gun emplacements, as a preliminary to the impending ground assault. The pilots had received all the required information and been briefed. Everything in the field was in readiness for h-hour. There was no report of any surface-to-air missile batteries in the area, and the operation seemed relatively simple.

A few minutes before h-hour, Defence Minister Moshe Dayan entered the 'Pit'. With little ceremony he shook Benny's hand, said hello to the others, and took the other chair behind the commander, next to me.

The first Skyhawk formation radioed its notification, 'Three minutes to entry'. A silence fell on the room, and from the other rooms could be heard the muted voices of conversations over the radio and of officers receiving and transmitting information over the telephone lines. Behind the window a control-monitor moved the small, tower-shaped marker, which lay on the big table and bore the call signal of the attacking Skyhawk formation, and placed it in the target zone. From where I was sitting I could see some unusual commotion among the intelligence officers in the adjacent cubicle. A note was thrust into the hands of the head of intelligence, who read it and passed it across to the commander. Benny perused the note and gave it to me. Electronic activity that indicated a missile battery preparing to fire had been detected in the sector relevant to the operation, the note said. I informed the Minister of this development in a whisper.

Benny appeared to be focused on the task at hand, but he gave no order to respond to the newly arrived information. The chief controller reported that the Skyhawks were going into their run. Sitting in the back, I was gripped with excruciating tension. I was very much afraid of such a missile ambush, and of additional casualties to the Skyhawk squadron, which had already suffered so many.

'There seems to be missile fire in the arena,' the head of control quietly announced to those sitting in the room.

'Number three's hit,' the chief controller announced at almost the same moment.

'Sir,' I said, 'I suggest that you consider aborting the attack. We seem to have a missile ambush that should be dealt with first.'

'Continue,' said Benny quietly, but with conviction.

'Don't stop the attack,' the chief controller passed on the instruction.

The attack continued for another twenty minutes. The plane that had been hit fell, and what had become of its pilot was unclear. Another missile was reported to have been fired, but didn't hit anything. The three formations hit their targets, and the Mount Hermon outposts were recaptured with relative ease, after the bitter failure of previous attempts.

At the end of the operation, when the Defence Minister got up to leave the room, everyone rose from their seats with him. Before stepping out the door, Dayan stuck his head back inside and said: 'Amos, I think you owe Benny an apology. Your advice was mistaken, and Benny was right.'

Without waiting for an answer, he left the room and went on his way.

I swallowed hard and kept my silence. I knew that Benny had been right, and that this comment by the Defence Minister, himself an old and experienced warhorse, was warranted. In a compartment of my mind I filed away this important lesson for the future.

When the war ended I was left with the distinct feeling that the contest between plane and missile hadn't been decided yet, and that the scale of the balance was still tilting in favour of the missile arrays. Once again the score dating back to the War of Attrition hadn't been settled. I took note of this matter as my primary, most essential task during my tenure as the new head of operations. I vowed to stick to it like a leech until there was a more realistic solution to this grave strategic problem.

At my summons – as I was now their commander – Shimon, head of control department, and Aviem, head of assault department, came into my room. I didn't invite them to sit down. I got up myself, and invited them to come down with me to the 'Pit'. The three of us identified ourselves to the guard at the gate and went downstairs. I didn't stop at the central control room but continued down to a lower level. We stepped into the narrow space fronted by the glass window looking out on the central tracking table. I shut the curtain and asked the duty-sergeant who was sitting there to excuse us and leave the spot.

We sat inside the cubicle for two and a half hours, without taking a break. I presented to them my opinion that we needed to prepare for an assault on the surface-to-air missile arrays in the future.

'Nobody is going to do the job for us. This is the most important mission the Air Force faces in the foreseeable future! It demands a sweeping, comprehensive and incisive solution. In the entire world you won't find another group of officers with as much combined talent and experience as the three of us and the ring of our subordinate officers. Another failure would be unacceptable to the Force, and so it should be. At a rough estimate we've got two years to complete the first stage. Progress should continue afterwards as well, and the more time we have at our disposal, the closer we'll be able to get to a more perfect solution,' I outlined my position to them.

I was very familiar with the two fine, dedicated officers who were with me, and I meant every word I said to them. The responses I received from them were encouraging. I didn't want them to accept my plan as some kind of 'holy writ'. I expected a critical and creative approach, and I thought such an approach was crucial to the success of the entire operation. When we left the 'Pit' and went back upstairs, I knew that my message had been taken to heart. With these two at my right hand, and with lots of hard work, it could be done. The goal was clear, and it would be accomplished!

CHAPTER THIRTY-ONE

California, 1975

In November 1974, a letter addressed to Colonel Amos, the Air Force's head of operations, arrived from Captain John Tallman. The upper edge of the page bore the large letterhead of the USS *Kitty Hawk*, the US Navy's huge aircraft carrier.

I met John in 1972 while studying for my master's degree at the Naval Postgraduate School in Monterey, California. As his name would suggest, 'Long' John Tallman was a rangy fellow about six-and-a-half feet tall. He was the commander of a Phantom squadron in the US Navy. He'd come to study at the academy and his family was also with him. It was only natural that the two of us and our families should get together, and a true friendship developed between us.

The stories I heard from John and my other classmates, all of them Navy pilots, sparked my longtime curiosity in regard to flying and living aboard an aircraft carrier. It was a topic of interest to me as a pilot on the professional level. As a commander, I was also interested in the arcane details of running a hugely powerful aerial force, with the widest range of capabilities, out of such a tiny, crowded and mobile base of operations. My curiosity was also piqued by the human aspect: how such a crowded 'colony' of thousands of military men, far away from their homes for extended periods of time, was able to maintain an organised, focused and marvellously efficient regimen. Towards the end of my studies and our departure from California, I made John swear that he'd do his utmost to wangle me a flight on a Phantom from an aircraft carrier.

'Amos, my friend,' wrote John in his letter. 'First I'd like to congratulate you on your promotion in rank and your posting as head of operations. As for me, about a year ago I was assigned to the *Kitty Hawk* and given the post of deputy commander, with responsibility for all the aerial forces aboard the ship – what we call an Air Boss. Now that I've settled into my new job, I've been able to process your request and arrange a flight for you with us. You'll have to obtain all the required authorisations on the Israeli side, and the rest will be taken care of by us. The *Kitty Hawk* will be arriving in San Diego in February and staying in the vicinity for a month for training exercises along the California coast. That'll be a perfect time to visit. Regards to Rachel and the kids from me, Mary and the kids. Hope to see you soon. Sincerely yours, John.'

The clumsy-looking, twin-engined propeller aircraft bearing the emblems of the US Navy was waiting for the small group of officers at the military airfield on the outskirts of San Diego. The other four passengers and I boarded the plane and took our seats. Within a few minutes the plane crossed the shoreline and continued westwards, into the depths of the Pacific Ocean. After about an hour's flying, one of the crewmen passed among the passengers and checked that everyone's seat belts were tightly buckled for the impending landing on the deck. Through the small window on my left I could see the floating airfield beneath us. The plane performed a circuit and landed on the deck of the huge carrier. When the arrester hook was released from the cable on the deck, the plane was moved to its parking slot and the passengers were allowed to alight. A bitterly cold wind struck our faces when we stepped outside. I took my small bag and, with my head bent against the wind, followed the group to a metal door that opened wide to let us in. John was waiting for me there and greeted me with a broad smile. We shook hands and exchanged claps on the back, and then John invited me to follow him to the cabin I'd been allotted. Over the next two days and nights this was to be my home. John promised he'd come back later and disappeared down the ship's endless gangways.

An officer had been specially assigned to be my escort during the visit. Peter, a navigator, was the commander of Phantom Squadron 114. This to me was intriguing, that a navigator should be serving as squadron commander. For some time I'd had the intention of implementing a similar promotion in my own Air

Force. I even had a suitable candidate in mind for the job – a gifted navigator and able commander by the name of Aharon Katz. (Aharon would be killed by a missile strike in the Lebanese War during an operational sortie in the Bekaa Valley.) To my surprise, I thus discovered that the Americans, whom we considered 'squares', actually had the lead on us.

Peter came into the cabin to introduce himself and we went off in the direction of the dining hall. We sat down at the table in the company of pilots and navigators from the two Phantom squadrons that were training aboard the carrier. A lively conversation sprang up among those seated around the table. Naturally my presence aroused the curiosity of the Navy aviators, and their questions regarding the Israeli Air Force and its numerous exploits rained down upon me in an unstoppable flow. As we were sitting there, a terrible blow struck the roof of the dining hall. I instinctively bent down and threw my arms over my head in alarm. To my amazement, I looked around me and saw that nobody showed any signs of being perturbed at all. To the contrary, they were smiling among themselves at my 'normal' response.

'Relax, man,' Peter said to me. 'We're sitting directly beneath the flight deck, and the noise you heard was the landing of a heavy Vigilant that is just now performing experimental landings.' I did relax, but I still couldn't help ducking my head every time another tremendous blow struck the deck above our heads as planes continued to land on the deck.

After dinner Peter led me up a winding stairway to the ship's bridge where the control room was located. It was dark outside, and the lights of the different instruments and green radar screens flickered all around us, without disturbing our view of the outside. When my eyes grew accustomed to the dark, I noticed John's familiar figure, seated in a high chair and purposefully running the show. John handed over command to another officer and placed himself at my disposal. We spent an hour or so in that fascinating venue while John explained what was going on around us. I kept trying to extract more and more answers to the countless questions I had, until I was momentarily satisfied.

When I lay down to sleep in my cabin, I still heard the thuds of one or two planes landing as they continued to train. But now the blows were weaker and farther away, until finally I fell asleep.

Jeff, the deputy squadron commander, accompanied me to my seat in the rear cockpit of the Phantom. I felt at home as soon as I was sitting inside it.

'Take heed, Amos,' Jeff explained to me. 'Before take-off press your back and head against the seat behind you, and keep your hands in place and don't let go until after take-off! Except for that, everything's as usual.'

The short briefing was over, and Jeff went over to the front seat. The mechanics finished harnessing us to our seats, then we checked our internal communication link and set out.

Jeff taxied the plane, under the guidance of the dispatch officer who stood beside us on the deck, signalling to us with his arms and barking rapid orders over the radio, which I found difficult to follow. I noticed how the plane was harnessed to the catapult, the powerful launching device, and the dispatch officer retreated a little. The function of the catapult was to launch the heavy Phantom from a standing position to being in flight at 220 knots, about 400 kph, on a short runway only 200 metres (220 yards) in length. Enormous energy was released in this fascinating process, and in order to avoid mishaps and accidents the strictest order and discipline needed to be maintained on the entire deck. Each man had his place, and each had his own specific attire, job and responsibility.

With my hands holding the throttle and stick in parallel with Jeff's hands, but without interfering in the manipulation of the controls, I felt the engine open to full power. I pressed my head back against the seat. The dispatch officer on the deck pointed his finger ahead!

An amazing feeling spread through my body and consciousness. I felt a tremendous force take hold of us, and hurl us forwards at a virtually incomprehensible acceleration rate. The short flight deck simply disappeared behind us in the wink of an eye. The plane dipped a little and righted itself in flying position. That part of the flight was a rare and exceptional experience for me.

At higher altitude we joined up in formation with another

Phantom above the ocean's endless watery expanses. We performed an interception exercise in which two pairs of planes participated – 'our' pair, and another which had flown out from an airbase on the California coast. The exercise was a simple and uninteresting one to me, and I waited in curiosity for the landing.

From afar the aircraft carrier looked tiny, just a dot against the background of the ocean. Still in formation, the two Phantoms descended towards the ship. As we circled the ship I caught sight of the helicopter flying beside it, in its regular position, on standby for rescue. This was standard procedure for the period planes would be taking off or landing on the carrier, only after which the helicopter would land itself.

Jeff straightened the plane in the direction of the short runway, which looked even shorter and narrower against the background of the surrounding water. As the plane was in its turn, with the left wing lowered, I managed to see the aircraft carrier's deck and the short surface that was meant to accommodate the plane. Despite all my experience flying jet fighters in difficult conditions, I found it hard to imagine how the plane's wheels were going to touch down exactly on the few metres allotted for the purpose, not to mention how the hurtling plane would be brought to a halt along this short runway. When the plane straightened out on course for the runway, the entire ship disappeared from my view, hidden beneath the plane's uplifted nose. Only the broad surface of the ocean appeared to be approaching us. I followed the deployment of the landing gear, and I saw the arrester hook handle move downwards after the wheels. The large metal hook was anchored to the plane's belly. When lowered, its function was to catch hold of one of the steel cables lying across the runway, by this means stopping the plane before it had a chance to hurtle off the other side of the ship and fall into the water.

In the final seconds the deck came back into view on either side of the nose. Now it was aproaching swiftly, and the Phantom dropped towards it at a much steeper rate of descent than I was familiar with in ordinary landings on land. The plane's landing gear struck the runway with great force. Again, I had the feeling of an unseen but immensely powerful force. The plane was brought to a stop at an astounding rate of deceleration.

Before I had time to digest what was happening, the hook was released from the cable and the plane was quickly wheeled away, in order to make room for those after it.

I stopped to watch the next plane strike the runway, its heavy arrester hook catching hold of the second of the four cables stretched across the width of the runway. It was a textbook landing. The orderliness, organisation, swiftness of action and response of the dispatch personnel on deck and of the pilots – left a powerful impression on me.

When I left the deck to board the small cargo plane on my way back to San Diego, I was wearing the black cap of Phantom Squadron 114. I bid goodbye to my friend John and to Peter, my wonderful host, and thanked them for the rare flying experience they'd afforded me. I especially exhorted John to return my visit and come to Israel.

The gigantic aircraft carrier *Kitty Hawk* grew smaller behind us, the vast ocean surrounding her, until she finally disappeared.

CHAPTER THIRTY-TWO

Tel Nof Airbase, 1977–1978

Twenty years after being awarded my pilot's wings and the rank of second lieutenant by Chief of Staff Laskov in the small parade ground at Tel Nof Airbase, I returned with the rank of brigadier-general to the same spot to take command of the Air Force's largest base.

No fewer than eight operational squadrons were placed under my command there: four helicopter squadrons – two of CH-53s, one of Bell 212s, and the young Cobra assault-helos squadron; and four fighter squadrons – one of F-15s, one of F-4 Phantoms, and two of A-4 Skyhawks. In addition, there were the Air Force's flight test unit; the 669 flying rescue unit; the airborne medical unit; the central aeronautic maintenance unit; the regional construction brigade; and a regiment each of anti-aircraft and infantry for ground defence. The airbase commander also had at his disposal three 'staff' squadrons – aviation, maintenance and administration – to help him conduct the widespread activity of this gigantic and diverse airbase.

The task of learning to control this huge organisational structure seemed a rather difficult one to me. The difficulty was exacerbated when I found out that there was to be no overlap period with the previous base commander, who'd concluded his posting a month earlier and gone abroad. Shmulik, the commander of the aviation squadron, a wonderful man from every aspect and my deputy in my former fighter squadron, was serving as his replacement in the interim period, and he welcomed me to the base when I arrived.

I was especially uneasy about the helicopter squadrons. I had no familiarity with the men and their machines. I recognised that

I would have to make a special effort and devote close study to what was happening in these squadrons.

It was clear to me that I didn't have the time to accumulate sufficient experience and flying hours to qualify as a helicopter captain. On the other hand, I considered it my obligation to pilot every type of aircraft in the squadrons under my command at the base. This was a laudable and worthy custom that had always been observed by all the Air Force's wing and airbase commanders. From experience, I knew there was no better way to get to know the true character of a squadron, with its pilots, mechanics and commanders, than to fly its planes and rub shoulders with its people at all levels, without intermediaries. Being a seasoned fighter pilot, I had no difficulty learning to fly new types of jet fighters after a short acclimation course. The situation was different regarding the helicopter squadrons.

There are some essential differences between flying helicopters and flying fixed-wing aircraft. Prolonged experience is required to advance from 'simple' helicopter pilot to the status of captain and helicopter commander, with all the responsibility it entails. Luckily, I was able to pilot a helicopter from the left seat, with a qualified captain sitting to my right, ready to take control if necessary.

Two days after arriving at the base I began a hasty acclimation course on the simpler and lighter Bell 212. Naturally, I determined to begin acclimation to the much heavier and more complex CH-53 in a month's time, only then going on to the Cobras.

Within a few weeks I'd mastered all the types of aircraft at the airbase at the minimal required level of proficiency. I was therefore able to pass through one of my squadrons almost every day and take part in their routine training flights.

One of the squadrons at the base was that selfsame Phantom squadron established under my command seven years earlier. Naturally I felt at home in this squadron whenever I came to fly with it. The squadron's current senior commanders were the youngest of the pilots and navigators from the period of my command. In every part of the squadron I ran into items, terms, methods and exercises with which I was at least partly familiar. It took a special effort on my part to avoid following my heart's desire, which was to fly there rather than in other aircraft with the other squadrons, as I'd determined I should, in order to probe deep into their special problems, which were new to me.

The CH-53 landed in an open area near a low hill in the Beersheba basin. A heavy cloud of dust covered the landing area, beginning to settle down again when the captain lowered the long handle of the collective (a helicopter's primary altitude and power control) and the fierce blast of wind generated by the huge rotor died down. Six pilots wearing grey overalls, myself among them, disembarked from the helicopter, climbed the low hill, and sat down on the slope. The helicopter took off again, leaving behind a fresh cloud of dust. The six of us stretched our limbs. Somebody opened a small carton of battle rations and passed it around.

From afar the noise of the Hercules' four engines could be heard. We saw the plane pass not far from us at an altitude of 5000 feet (1524 metres), heading east. Behind the Hercules dragged a short pipe with a sort of basket at the end of it, its open side facing the rear. This was the apparatus for refuelling a jet fighter or helicopter in the air. The Hercules continued on its way, its noise growing fainter until it disappeared altogether. Those who were watching it could discern it approaching the CH-53, which now looked like a dark dot against the background of the azure sky in the east.

A silence descended on our surroundings, punctuated only occasionally by the echoes from afar of the roar of jet fighters, for whom this was their central training ground. Once or twice the tranquility was disturbed by a double explosive clap, the ultra-sonic boom 'shot' into the sky when one of the planes out there somewhere passed the speed of sound. Among those seated on the hill a lively conversation sprang up, at first of an entirely general character, but going on to deal with the problems of present concern to the helicopter pilots. I listened with great interest to what was being said and offered my own opinions as well. It was a wonderful opportunity for the men to speak their minds directly to the base commander, without any restriction of distance to impede true dialogue. At the same time I, for my part, was afforded a chance to plumb the depths of my pilots' views, and especially their feelings. The time passed quickly.

With a loud roar the CH-53 came out of nowhere and landed at the foot of the hill. After the cloud of dust settled, three pilots leapt nimbly from the helicopter with their helmets in their hands. It was my turn, along with two other pilots to perform the exercise. We put on our helmets and boarded the helicopter. I entered the pilots' cockpit and took the seat on the right, usually reserved for the captain, while the captain-trainer, deputy squadron commander Ran M, sat on my left. Nahum and Ami sat down in back and hooked up to the helicopter's communications system. The noise of the rotor swelled; the helicopter rose to a hovering position, emerged out of the thick cloud of dust, dipped its nose and began moving forwards at growing speed, until it went into flying position and turned east again. It was only my sixth flight on the CH-53, but I'd managed to assimilate the special rules pertaining to this heavy and powerful helicopter with relative rapidity. With the consent of Benny, the squadron commander, and of Ran my 'personal' trainer, it had been decided I could participate in a refuelling exercise.

The protocol for checking communications with the refuelling plane (the Hercules) and with the controller was performed and completed. The helicopter stabilised itself at a point about 150 metres (164 yards) behind the refueller, a little to its left and beneath it.

'Amos, I'll demonstrate linking up once, and afterwards I'll pass control over to you,' Ran said to me. I confirmed.

'Oil from Orange, permission to enter,' Ran requested the captain of the Hercules.

'Orange, permission granted.'

With the lightest touch I accompanied Ran's movements on the controls, without allowing this to disturb his actions in any way. I felt with my left hand how the collective rose a little, adding power to the rotor above us. At the same time I felt with my right hand how the stick was thrust slightly forwards to maintain our precise altitude. The helicopter moved towards the Hercules, and the refuelling nozzle in its nose approached the refuelling basket. The nozzle missed its target by a couple of dozen centimetres, forcing Ran to retreat three or four metres and try again. On the second try the nozzle struck the side of the basket, slipped inside and locked into place. The link-up process was complete.

'Oil, ready to receive fuel, dummy exercise,' Ran reported.

'Roger, Orange, I read you. Permission to disconnect,' announced the captain of the Hercules, without really having piped any fuel into the CH-53's tanks. The helicopter slipped back, disconnected the refuelling nozzle, and retreated to its initial staging position.

'You take her,' said Ran, passing control over to me. Now it was Ran's turn to accompany my motions on the helicopter's steering controls without interfering, but on standby to intervene instantly if necessary.

'I'm taking her,' I confirmed over the intercom, completing the requisite process whenever the controls of an aircraft change hands from one crewman to another.

I was quite familiar with the process of refuelling in the air itself. As a former commander of a Phantom squadron, I'd performed it dozens of times, sometimes during actual operational activity. I now discovered that the refuelling nozzle of the CH-53 was in a much more convenient location than the Phantom's. Whereas in the Phantom it was high on the right, making it difficult for the pilot to see the nozzle's situation *vis-à-vis* the basket and the re-fuelling plane at a single glance, in the CH-53 the nozzle was lower and farther ahead, so that linking up seemed easier to me.

I stabilised the helicopter on a course that looked accurate to me. I pulled the collective, thrust forward the steering stick on my right a little, and was rewarded by the helicopter's immediate response. The distance between the refuelling nozzle and the basket began to close. At a certain stage it seemed to me that the rate of advance towards the basket was higher than it should be, and I gently slowed our progress. The refuelling nozzle was now moving forwards at what seemed the optimal speed to me. To my left, Ran didn't say a word. With almost mathematical precision the nozzle slipped into the centre of the basket in a single, smooth motion and locked into place.

'Oil, ready to receive fuel, dummy exercise,' I notified the Hercules over the radio.

'Roger, Orange. Permission to disconnect.' My execution of the manoeuvre had been picture perfect.

A broad smile spread across Ran's face. 'A father need not envy his son, nor a teacher his pupil,' he spoke quietly, but loud enough so that everyone in the cockpit and in the back could hear.

We repeated the exercise a second time, again with the same degree of success. Then I relinquished my seat to the next pilot whose turn it was to perform the exercise and passed to the rear, relaxed and content. About an hour later the helicopter landed next to the hill, collected the handful of pilots, and returned to land at Tel Nof Airbase.

Presumably the story would spread around the squadron. I ascribed great importance to having my high level of proficiency as a pilot recognised by the community of helicopter pilots, to whom I'd been such a stranger until now.

Only a month after assuming my post, the worst aviatic accident in the history of the IDF struck the airbase: a platoon of para-troopers and the entire crew of a CH-53 were killed when their helicopter crashed into the slope of a barren hill in Judaea in the course of a large IDF training exercise. Fifty-four soldiers and officers died. There were no survivors.

In my twenty years of flying and commanding, I'd never had any real, close-up exposure to the helicopter squadrons and their men. In my previous post as head of operations at Air Force staff headquarters I'd dealt with the deployment of the helicopters on their different missions, and learned to appreciate their various capabilities. However, even then I paid greater heed to the jet fighter squadrons, which had always been considered the 'back-bone' of the service. Not even for one second had I ever contemplated that the process of my getting to know the com-munity of helicopter crewmen would transpire against such a bitter and painful background.

I went through many sleepless nights in the period following the accident. The country was in an uproar, and a thorough investigation was unavoidable. The fact that human error had caused the accident weighed upon my mind and heart all the more.

As regards myself, two weighty questions appeared rele-vant to me. The first was whether different behaviour on my part, in any realistic fashion, could have reduced the probability the accident would take place or prevented it alto-gether. I asked myself this question dozens and hundreds of times, and each time I came to exactly the same conclusion: no, I couldn't have changed what happened by behaving or exercising my command in any other way. The second ques-tion was whether, regardless of the answer to the first question, I had to accept personal overall responsibility and unilaterally tender my resignation and leave my post.

When I considered this problem, I came to the conclusion that if I'd served in my post as base commander for a longer period of time, I would indeed have had to resign. But as a commander who'd just begun his term of duty, I didn't think my resignation was called for. Nevertheless, I decided to leave this matter up to the higher echelons, the Air Force commander and the Chief of Staff.

'Sir,' I wrote to the Air Force commander several days later. 'As the officer serving in command of the base at which the grave accident occurred, and as the person responsible for everything which goes on at the base, I must ask you to consider accepting my resignation from this post, effective immediately.'

General Benny Peled, the Air Force commander, gave a nega-tive answer to my letter and refused my offer to resign.

Immediately after sending it to my commander, I read out the letter to the group of helicopter squadron commanders under my command at the base. I was especially interested in testing their responses – to look the helicopter commanders in the eye, and ascertain what they were thinking. I felt great relief when I heard my subordinates, the helicopter crewmen, voice their strong opinion that I should remain at my post. Chief of Staff Motta Gur arrived at the base with Air Force commander Peled; at a long and wrenching meeting with me and all my squadron comman-ders, the two of them expressed their confidence in the commanders on the spot.

A prolonged and thorny investigation was conducted in the wake of the accident, as a result of which the squadron commander was relieved of his command and a few other offi-cers disciplined in one way or another.

* * *

Only a week had gone by since that terrible accident when another CH-53 and its crew went down over the sea because of a technical malfunction, which was positively identified after the helicopter, with immense effort, was salvaged from the water. The CH-53 squadrons were hit with a grave crisis. Several weeks later another CH-53, the third under my command, crashed in the fields of Kibbutz Gat, again due to a technical malfunction. By now the grave crisis was rapidly turning into an overall collapse.

The situation was so grave that serious doubts were cast over the Force's continued employment of the CH-53. Morale inside the two squadrons was in a state of disintegration. Numerous malfunctions and low serviceability kept down the quantity and quality of training exercises; pilots were afraid to fly, and harsh words were voiced by the squadron personnel, both senior and junior, both regular army and reserves. Bitter accusations were made of a longtime, historic discrimination against the helicopter squadrons, to the benefit of the fighter squadrons, and its prolonged relegation to lower levels of priority. Those levelling these charges accused Air Force staff headquarters of filling the helicopter squadrons with manpower of inferior quality, ignoring their budgetary requirements, and generally treating them with contempt in almost every matter.

I stepped into the office of Lieutenant-General Rafi, deputy commander of the Air Force, at Hakirya, the Defence Ministry compound in Tel Aviv.

'Rafi, the continued existence and operational use of the CH-53 helicopter by the Force is in doubt. The severity of the crisis cannot be overstated. It is clear to both of us what ramifications the decision to disband these squadrons and eliminate the CH-53 from the Air Force might have. The army's entire assault transport network would be in danger of collapse, and the execution of critically important missions behind the lines would in effect be scratched. It would be an intolerable blow to the army. Under my command, Tel Nof Airbase will do everything possible to fight the decision to disband. But in order to rehabilitate these squadrons, we have to redress the balance. For years the helicopter array has been frozen in its tracks without any progress, while all priority has gone to the fighter squadrons. I won't succeed at this task unless I receive overwhelming support from headquarters staff. Commanders, technical officers, pilots, technicians, budgets, construction and facilities, training and exercises – in all these fields I intend to place the helicopter squadrons, and especially the CH-53, at the top of my list of priorities. I demand that you make a similar decision, at the headquarters staff level, and support me all the way down the line.'

'Amos, I fully understand and accept your position. You'll receive all the support for your plans from headquarters. Let's see the details of your plan and go over them in an orderly fashion,' he responded to my appeal.

I opened a file, drew out a document that I'd prepared in advance, and we both rolled up our shirtsleeves. After about an hour the head of equipment department, the service's senior maintenance officer and the head of the manpower department also joined our discussion, which was extended to the fields under their supervision.

At 7.30 am the next day, the basic group of officers who would be implementing my plans – which included myself, my deputy, and all the base's squadron commanders – assembled for a special conference in my office.

'Gentlemen! As you are all aware, to a greater or lesser extent, the situation in the CH-53 squadrons is very bad. The latest helicopter to fall has brought both squadrons to the verge of a calamitous crisis. I am resolved not to allow these squadrons to fall!' I stated emphatically. 'I would like to make it clear to you here and now that in the framework of the base, from now until further notice, these two squadrons are to be given priority wherever the question of priority arises. I'm addressing this especially to the commanders of the staff squadrons, aviation, maintenance and administration squadrons, headquarters itself, and the construction unit. From the other flight squadron commanders I demand understanding and cooperation. It's a grave topic, the situation is critical, and we all bear a heavy responsibility!'

When the group dispersed, I asked Yoram, administration squadron commander, and Aharoni, maintenance squadron commander, to stay behind. Both men were especially able commanders and held key positions in this effort to grant priority to the CH-53 squadrons such as would be felt and seen by all. I needed them unconditionally behind me. When the two of them left my office, they knew exactly what I expected of them.

A long series of actions was undertaken in the weeks and months following the third accident. With great diligence new squadron commanders were promoted, and other personnel changes were made in the squadrons' chains of command. Fine technical officers and a handful of senior NCOs, among the best in the most advanced and prestigious fighter squadrons, were brought to the base and received command of the technical departments. From the technical schools and technical courses only the best soldiers were posted to the CH-53 squadrons. The commander of the maintenance squadron at the base detailed his best men to the helicopters, and those who weren't up to the required standards were replaced. The administrative priorities granted to the CH-53 squadrons began to make their mark in almost every field of ongoing activity.

I roamed the base like a man possessed. Early in the morning, every single day, before anything else, I'd conduct a tour of the two squadrons and of the base's maintenance centre to see exactly what progress was being made and what required my intervention. I made every effort to convey in any possible way, especially through personal example, how critical and important the subject was. Before long there wasn't a commander at the base who didn't know that resolving the CH-53 crisis was the most important issue on the agenda. The obsession began to rub off and spread in every direction.

One of the prominent criteria that I held to and dealt with was the level of serviceability of the CH-53 helicopters. Since I'd arrived at the base, during the period of the accidents and afterwards, there were many days when no more than two or three serviceable CH-53s could be found in the aircraft parking lots. Such low seviceability greatly disrupted the aircrews' training programme, reduced their personal levels of proficiency, and struck their morale a mortal blow as well. Many times, when I'd come to visit the squadrons and passed through the rooms with their commanders, I'd run into groups of pilots sitting unemployed in the pilots' clubs, waiting in vain for a serviceable helicopter to be placed at their disposal. It didn't take much imagination to guess what the hottest topics of conversation were at these confabulations. I knew for a fact that only vigorous aviatic activity, both in training and operational, could break this vicious, poisonous cycle and open a way out of it.

The recovery from this gravest of crises was agonisingly slow. It took months until signs of a resolution began to show. The stores of replacement parts gradually filled as a result of the priority accorded to the helicopters in the service's logistical array. The parking lots were renovated, and new fuelling facilities were installed in them. Advanced working methods used by the Phantom and F-15 squadrons were adopted by the CH-53 squadrons. Most important of all, the officers and servicemen in the helicopter squadrons began to feel that their actions, and mistakes, were receiving immediate notice; that the high command cared for them, and they were no longer being treated like an insignificant element of secondary importance.

From 10 per cent daily serviceability the squadrons went up to 20 per cent, then 40 per cent, even 70 per cent. After more than a year of persistent hard work, the CH-53 squadrons were fast becoming the equals – in terms of levels of serviceability and training programme execution, in their scores in service spot checks and in their general level of morale – of the best fighter squadrons. However, I was still determined to allow no release of the pressure I'd generated. I began to support and promote, on every occasion that came my way, a much-increased operational employment of the CH-53s.

About two years after that terrible accident in which fifty-four perished, I left my house at dawn for my daily early tour of the base. I parked the car on the fringe of take-off runway 'one eight' and walked to the lot in which, scant years previously, the interceptors of my Mirage squadron used to park.

A freezing wind blew into my face from the east. As I was checking the state of the rocky ground beyond the end of the runway, from the radio set in the car I overheard a conversation between the flight-control officer in the tower and a formation in the air. I drew near the car and listened.

'Carpet, this is Screw. Two minutes to landing.' I easily recognised it as the voice of Yisrael, commander of one of the CH-53 squadrons.

I turned up the volume of the radio set and sat on the bonnet of the car. The bitter cold and wind didn't bother me. To the contrary, I avidly breathed in the frigid air and felt it fill my lungs and sharpen my senses. I turned up the furry collar of my flight jacket to keep my ears warm.

Three dark dots that were approaching the base from the north rapidly grew bigger. My ears began to pick up the characteristic, husky roar of the CH-53 engines. I stared bewitched at the heavy steel machines flying towards me. I was entranced by the sight and the noise. At zero altitude the three CH-53s passed in front of my eyes. All three, in perfect coordination, raised their noses and stopped almost on a coin, passing from flying to hovering position above the black asphalt of the runway. Slowly moving forwards, their wheels touched down on the runway and the helicopters continued taxiing to their parking slots in the lot next to the squadron building.

For the first time, after two full years in command, the sweet feeling of success trickled into my heart. There in front of my eyes, the three CH-53s had just returned from another daring clandestine operation. The fate of the CH-53 squadrons had been decided in their favour. I was pleased to have had a crucual part in preserving this force and returning it to vitality.

I got into my car and drove towards the helicopter lot. I approached the spot and went over to the door of the lead helicopter. From the helicopter's rear platform, which was lowered to the runway, the infantry's finest fighters began to spill out with their equipment. Yisrael, the lead captain and commander of the squadron, got down heavily, limping slightly as usual, and came over to me with a smile. His round baby face was glowing with satisfaction. We spoke awhile and took leave of each other with mutual claps on the shoulder.

In another hour the entire base would be waking up to the routine of a new day of flying. Only a very few would be aware of what had taken place that night. Few indeed, to be sure, were able to understand the immensity of the achievement won at Tel Nof Airbase in that period.

I returned to my car and drove to the western side of the base. One after another, two Hercules transport planes landed on runway one-eight and turned right in the direction of the large boarding area, the south-eastern corner of which lay in the shadow of a stand of venerable eucalyptus trees. I turned my car in the same direction.

Lying in rows on the asphalt surface were the young soldiers of two paratrooper platoons, who were on the way to one of their first jumps.

I parked my car at the side of the boarding area and walked across to the paratroopers. The roar of the Hercules filled the air, and the paratroopers all looked alike. They were all wearing their parachute harnesses and had helmets on their heads. I approached them and began walking between the rows. Literally beneath my feet a familiar face popped up. Now I could make out his features.

'Hi, Dad. I'm here!' it was the hoarse voise of Noam, my eldest son.

'Hi, son. How does it feel?' I asked, no less excited by the meeting than him.

'Everything's all-right. We're waiting to board the plane, as you can see,' said Noam.

When he was only twelve, as soon as he knew his own mind, Noam informed the family that he wasn't going to be a pilot. He wanted to be a simple foot soldier, to perform his three years of military service and go about his life. Nobody at home tried to make him change his mind. When he enrolled in the 890 Paratrooper Regiment, it was very strange for the family, during his period of training at the parachuting school, to see Noam lying in a tent only a few metres away from the house. Or, Noam's younger sister, used to run and bring candies and drinks from the adjacent canteen to Noam and his mates in the tent. I bent over Noam and clapped him on the shoulder and on his helmet. I felt a thrill of both excitement and pride.

As I drove away from the spot, I followed the two heavy Hercules planes that were taxiing toward the take-off runway with a father's gaze. Alone in the car, I allowed myself to wipe away a couple of tears from the corners of my eyes. I couldn't do the same with the choking feeling in my throat . . . I'd never imagined that such a simple matter could cause such an outburst of emotion in me. I stopped the car again at the edge of the runway, and let two or three minutes go by.

Now I was on my way to the F-15 squadron, where I was listed for a routine training flight this morning. Eitan Ben Eliyahu, the squadron commander, welcomed me in an atmosphere of business as usual. An hour later I set out with my leader on a complex navigation and assault exercise in what was then the most sophisticated plane in the world.

On the evening of Israel's Memorial Day in 1978, at the annual get-together with the families of servicemen from the base who'd fallen in battle and in training, I stood in front of the bereaved, and the servicemen and officers from the base, and read out what I'd written a few hours earlier:

My light-winged comrades

Tears dry and turn to lumps of salt
Figures and memories in black-and-white, sharp-edged,
Turn to pictures in hazy grey.
Rhythmic voices and sentences turn to background tunes
Fusing with the hum of the wind and the roar of the plane engines.

And here we are again, together,
With a sense of slightly muted sadness,
Knowing there will always be a blight upon our joy,
Searingly aware that we can no longer delight
Like little children whose account has just opened.

The paths down which we travelled a long way
Are stained with the blood of the best of comrades.
To some of us the fallen are a legend,
To others, friends whom we shall never meet again.
Numbers one, and two, a soldier, fighter, subordinate or commander.

And what did they not have in them?
There was joy and a smile and a song,
There was power and confidence and resourcefulness,
And a little fear – as in all of us,
And persistence and ambitions and a dream.
Everything, they had everything.
The acute of ear may yet hear the rolling echoes of their thundering engines,
But the marks where they struck the ground have been robed in green
Or covered by the sea
To be recognised no more.

To the families they are the essence of life itself
Hopes cut down, cracks in the hearts,
Glittering flowers – which have withered.
To us they are a source of faith and strength.

And their memory is in our hearts.

As I was trying with all my might to hide the tremor in my voice, a single, stubborn salty tear fell and made a round, wet stain on the paper in my hand. It continued to spread slowly until it overlay the words, 'Covered by the sea'.

CHAPTER THIRTY-THREE

Lebanon, June 1982

The telephone in our home rang at about eleven pm. Air Force commander David Ivri was on the other end of the line.

'Amos, I want to place you on call with Raful [Chief of Staff Rafael Eytan] as aerial adviser to the Chief of Staff, for an operation which is due to begin tomorrow morning. Be at Sde Dov Airfield at 4 am, ready to join Raful's entourage and fly north with him by helicopter.'

'Alright, David. I'll be there as required,' I replied.

Having served as Air Force deputy commander until only three months previously, I knew exactly what he was talking about. During my term of duty as deputy commander, I'd taken part in dozens of conferences and briefings at Air Force headquarters and at General Staff headquarters that dealt with the targets, methods and other elements of a large operation in Lebanon. The operation appeared to be inevitable against the background of clashes with El-Fatah forces in southern Lebanon, many of which ended in barrages of Katyusha rockets on communities in northern Israel.

The attempts to respond to the attacks in the north by means of fighter aircraft alone appeared to be of no use. In most cases the targets relayed to the pilots lacked any real military value, or it was impractical for swift planes efficiently to identify and strike them from an altitude of 10,000 feet (3048 metres) and above, using inaccurate bombs. Consequently, hundreds of assault sorties were performed, although their results were negligible and had no real influence on terrorist activity in the field.

Of greater efficacy was the Air Force activity conducted by its helicopters. They played an important role in flying special forces to and from their targets deep behind the lines, and in rescue operations, some of them hair-raising, of units and individuals who were in trouble or had been hit in the field. From an overall perspective, however, these operations also couldn't resolve the complex situation in Lebanon.

Twice in the past year, our forces had already been deployed to set out on an extensive assault in Lebanon, in the framework of a sweeping ground campaign, with the full integration of aerial and naval forces. The defined objective had been to destroy the terrorist organisation infrastructure in Lebanon. In the more senior and select forums of conversation, there was explicit talk of the possibility of broadening the campaign and extending its strategic objective to replacing the political regime in Lebanon, in the course of linking up with Christian elements friendly to Israel.

The depth and intensity of Syrian involvement in Lebanon were known to all. Clearly there was a close link between the operation's defined objectives and the chances of direct conflict between IDF forces and the Syrian army. It was clear to any military man with a brain in his head that the adoption of the broader objectives would undoubtedly lead to such a conflict.

The Syrian army battalions and military camps facing the Golan Heights in the south and the Vale of Lebanon north of there were defended by one of the densest and most sophisticated surface-to-air missile arrays in the world. Since the end of the Yom Kippur War, in view of the lessons they'd drawn from that war, the Syrians had spared no effort or expense in strengthening and extending this array. Closely advised by the Soviets, they'd installed batteries of different types of missiles, in a transparent attempt to compensate for the disadvantages of some types with the advantages of other types.

The Syrians recognised the inferiority of their air force in contending with the Israeli Air Force for control of the skies. In view of their bitter experience conducting ground operations without benefit of an aerial umbrella of protection, exposed to the mercy of the Israeli Air Force, the Syrians were always careful to move their forces together with the missile array.

Over the years, I'd experienced this bitter contest between the jet fighter and the anti-aircraft missile. Seated inside the pilot's cockpit, I'd fought against these missiles in the Six-Day-War and the War of Attrition. With bitter frustration, I'd engaged in battle with them sitting at the planning tables, as a senior staff officer at Air Force headquarters, and as staff head of operations during the Yom Kippur War and afterwards.

That night, before setting out to join the Chief of Staff's command group, I estimated that it wouldn't be too many hours before the issue of the Syrian missile array and its influence on the Lebanese battlefield would come up on the army's agenda, and mine as well.

On the third day of fighting, nobody was talking about an 'operation' any longer. It was a war in everything but name. Our armoured forces advanced northwards into Lebanon along three routes – western, central and eastern. Their progress was accompanied by all the familiar auxiliary forces, the Air Force foremost among them. Several times a day I'd talk with David, Air Force commander, or with his deputy back at staff headquarters in Tel Aviv. I relayed reports from the field to them and received information and instructions. I took advantage of my standing and familiarity with senior officers in the service's staff headquarters to relay detailed, 'point' information, which I'd obtained firsthand in the field itself. I requested the dispatch of plane formations to provide assistance in attacking problematic targets that were posing a hindrance to our ground forces.

The clearly unavoidable clash with the lead Syrian forces on the eastern axis took place on the second day of fighting. It was obvious to me that the descent of Syrian armoured divisions from the northern Syrian plateau into the Vale of Lebanon, if such were to occur, would necessarily ensue in an extensive, pitched battle between Yanosh Ben-Gal's northern corps and these Syrian forces. Control of this arena's skies, I knew, would be key to gaining the victory. From the Air Force's point of view, wresting such control required the destruction of the entire Syrian missile array – over twenty missile batteries. I tried to draw out the commander regarding his position on this matter. One had not been formulated; the lack of it seemed odd to me, but not yet critical.

In the afternoon of the third day of fighting, intelligence reports of the movement of two Syrian armoured divisions into the Vale of Lebanon began to arrive. There was no longer room for theoretical musings. Now the need had arisen to take a decisive position on the question of destroying the missiles.

I was spending most of my time with the Chief of Staff and moving with him from place to place by helicopter or by car. I arrived with the Chief of Staff's entire entourage at the northern command outpost towards the evening. I left the group and went over to the rooms of the Air Force delegation. From there I telephoned the head of operations at Air Force staff headquarters and updated him. I also shared with him my assessment that the assault on the missile array was impending, and told him he'd do well to complete all the preparations for such an operation. I also discussed this matter with General Amos Lapidot, the Air Force delegate to northern command. Then I asked to be connected to David, the Air Force commander.

The requested connection was established; David was at the other end of the line. I delivered a summary report on the situation and asked him his position regarding an assault on the missile array. His responses were something in the nature of 'Let's wait and see'; 'We'll place the squadrons in readiness for an operation'; 'The situation is unclear' and the like. For the second time, I couldn't help but notice that the Air Force commander was trying to avoid – and not by accident, apparently – taking an unequivocal position regarding this crucial question.

The discussions inside the northern command group outpost went on long into the night. The first round of discussion was led by the head of northern command. It was followed by another discussion, this time led by the Chief of Staff. The assault on the missile array by the Air Force the next day stood out as the most crucial issue to be decided. When it was my turn to speak, I clearly voiced my opinion that the Air Force should be ordered to attack and destroy the entire missile array. I expressed strong opposition to a more lukewarm proposal by the Chief of Staff, who wanted to attack 'one or two batteries' in a sort of warning strike and suffice with that, at least 'for the time being'. Everyone was waiting for Defence Minister Ariel (Arik) Sharon to join the important night-time conference.

Before the Defence Minister came into the conference room, I conducted another conversation by telephone with the Air Force commander. It was a brief one; no new decisive facts had come in. This time too I was unable to get a simple and unequivocal answer. When I laid down the receiver, I understood that nobody was going to do the job for me. I decided that I would express my position clearly, explain my reasons for it, and stand behind it without flinching. But my heart was heavy within me at the attitude displayed by my commander.

In my humble opinion, in all the Air Force there wasn't another officer as competent as myself to understand the complexity of the operation facing us. There was nobody better suited to assess the balance of risks and probabilities in the arduous, innovative battle that would begin the next day. I felt it was my duty, to speak in a clear and pellucid voice. When I'd finished speaking in my turn at the conference, there was no room for doubt regarding my position: 'Freedom of action in the skies of the combat theatre is a vital need for the Air Force. The entire anti-aircraft missile array can and should be destroyed!'

At 4 am, Defence Minister Sharon summarised the deliberations. He gave his unequivocal support to the plan for an assault on the entire Syrian missile array in the north. He made reference to all the other proposals and plans, and rejected them. He then went on to summarise all the questions concerning the ground campaign. At the conclusion of the conference, he announced that he was leaving by helicopter for Jerusalem to attend the daily cabinet meeting and request its approval for the missile assault. 'Yes,' he added, 'I'd like Amos to join me for the cabinet meeting.' It might have sounded like a request, but it was an order, and quite an unusual one. After all, Sharon hadn't asked the Chief of Staff to join him, or the Air Force commander . . .

'Mr Minister,' I said, 'I'm here in my grey pilot's overalls, and I haven't got any other clothes to make an appearance in Jerusalem.'

'Come as you are, just pull up your zipper a little . . .' Sharon deftly closed the debate. My attempt to wriggle my way out of this mission foundered. The few people around us chuckled; Arik Sharon was not somebody who could be easily swayed to change his mind on any issue, large or small.

I asked Lapidot that the fact of my attendance at the cabinet meeting be brought to the attention of the Air Force commander. I was well aware that according to protocol it was he who was supposed to be there, not any other officer from the service. I really didn't want this move to be perceived as a circumvention of authority within the Air Force chain of command.

At about 7.30 am, I accompanied the Defence Minister into the office of Prime Minister Menachem Begin. Cabinet secretary Aryeh Naor was sitting beside him. Begin peered at us through his thick glasses and invited us to sit around a low table in the corner. The Defence Minister introduced me, blushing furiously in shame at my plainly inappropriate attire, and we sat down. A very lively conversation ensued between the two men, Sharon explaining the situation to Begin and emphasising the vital importance of the assault on the missiles. The conversation also strayed to more political channels, and an attempt was even made to establish contact with American special ambassador Phillip Habib, until it transpired that he was in the air on his way to Damascus. The Prime Minister appeared to have been convinced by the Defence Minister's arguments. He said he would bring up the topic for debate and approval by the plenary session of the cabinet, forthwith.

The cabinet session took two-and-a-half hours. Defence Minister Sharon was active throughout it. He responded and intervened in the debate almost all the time, with almost every speaker. An attentive silence fell on the room when Dr Yosef Burg assumed the speaker's mantle. He fluently expressed his opinions and finally summarised his position in support of the assault. I saw Sharon lean forward, write a small note, fold it over and send it along to me. I opened the note and read: 'Amos, I've been raising horses a long time, so it's the highest hurdle that's important to me. Dr Burg is the highest hurdle! We've passed it! Go and make sure that everything's progressing as it should. Arik.' I smiled briefly, and left the room for a few minutes to get in touch with the head of operations at Air Force staff headquarters.

'In my estimation,' I told him, 'we should be getting cabinet approval for the operation within half an hour. How are things at your end?'

'There was bad weather in the morning, but now it appears to be clearing up. We'll start to send out the men to the planes, and wait for final confirmation through you,' was the reply I got.

The Prime Minister began to summarise the debate. There appeared to be a majority in favour of approving the operation around the table. The Prime Minister prefaced his remarks by turning to me and asking for my estimation of the expected casualties to the Air Force in such an operation.

'In every operation of this kind we're liable to suffer casualties. In my estimation, however, if we do suffer any, they'll be extremely few,' I replied in a confident tone of voice.

Approval was granted. The Defence Minister told me to go out and pass the order on to the Air Force. I leapt to the telephone and gave the green light to staff headquarters in Tel Aviv.

The tense spring uncoiled, and the operation commenced!

In the late afternoon hours, the assault on the missile array began. The 'roof' of clouds that had covered Lebanon during most of the day moved eastwards right at the critical moment, and the entire theatre of war came into the view of the attackers' eyes.

Three hours later, when the last of the assault aircraft turned south to return to their airbases, they left smoking ruins behind them where the missile batteries had been. The missile array was obliterated. Out of nineteen batteries attacked, fifteen were completely destroyed, and three were heavily damaged. Control of the battlefield skies passed in full into the hands of the Israeli Air Force. All the planes and their crews returned home safely. All the forces, including the Arab and Soviet armies, that had placed their trust in anti-aircraft defences, were left flabbergasted by the crushing defeat of the Syrian array.

In the days following the operation, fully exploiting their control of the skies, our Air Force pilots shot down about eighty Syrian fighters, without a single loss to our forces.

I wasn't a politician. I was a senior military officer, and an aviator, and that was how I looked at the battlefield. In war, I knew, it was the army's job to win! During the long years between wars, military commanders prepare the men and the means, so that during the crucial minutes and hours they should make the right decisions and employ their ability and skill to the fullest in order to achieve their objectives and win. I felt that this was how I'd always conducted myself, the present instance being no exception, and it was good that I had.

The bloody score had begun in the summer of 1970, when six Israeli Phantoms attempting to destroy the missiles at the Suez Canal were shot down, and their crews killed or taken prisoner. It had continued with greater fury during the Yom Kippur War, when Syrian and Egyptian missiles brought down dozens of our Air Force planes. The score was finally settled on 9 June 1982. The plane reclaimed its hegemony from the missile in the aerial theatre of combat.

The Syrians, who'd placed their trust in their sophisticated and expensive missile array, were left confounded and exposed in this new state of affairs.

In my heart I had no doubt that the operation of 9 June 1982 would have far-reaching ramifications for the Syrian leadership, as well as for many other countries in the world that had similar doctrines of warfare. Those who'd been nursing plans for a massive ground assault on Israel, trusting in the protective wall of missiles, would now have to revamp their thinking. Any Arab hopes of denying the State of Israel its deterrent capability in the form of its powerful Air Force, under the cover of the missile arrays, were dashed for many years to come.

I had a profound feeling of pride at my central role in this great achievement, which smashed the Syrian military option and may have opened a small window for peace. Despite this magnificent aerial success, however, my feelings soured as the war went on and I was forced to look on as almost all the army's achievements bogged down and disappeared in the mud of Lebanon.

CHAPTER THIRTY-FOUR

Hakirya (Defence Ministry Compound), 1982

I took leave of Rachel with a wave and stepped out of our elegant house to my car. I tried to the best of my ability, but with only partial success, to conceal my tremendous excitement on this crucial day.

I shut the heavy door behind me.

Noam, my eldest, was nearing the end of his service with the paratroopers and would soon be discharged. Ram had decided to try to follow in my footsteps and had volunteered for pilot training, but he wasn't yet enlisted. Or, our daughter and the light of my life, was about to enter high school. What a wonderful bunch. Rachel was always there. I appreciated and respected her, and her presence was a comfort to me. But there were cracks in the foundation of our relationship of whose existence both of us were aware; nevertheless we couldn't find a way to mend them.

Would we ever succeed? I didn't know the answer.

The summons to meet with the Air Force commander had come at noon on the previous day. I wasn't in need of any explanations. I knew that at this meeting the commander would be informing me of the decision concerning the appointment of his successor, the next Air Force commander.

Twenty-seven years of dreaming dreams that had become more realistic from day to day; thousands of flying hours; over

300 operational sorties behind the lines; and an impressive record of command by any account were all about to culminate in a single, unequivocal and ostensibly simple decision. I would either receive command of the army's most sophisticated service, or I would not.

I drove to my office at the military college camp. I spent the three hours that remained dealing with ongoing affairs and managed on the whole to lose myself in them.

At eleven am I left the camp and drove straight to Air Force staff headquarters at Hakirya in Tel Aviv. I returned a salute to the servicewoman at the gate and, passing her, took the path I'd walked for many a year when I was serving at staff headquarters. I climbed the stairs with which I was so familiar and arrived at the commander's office exactly two minutes before the scheduled hour.

On the way there I'd tried to picture what was about to happen. I knew there was no guarantee the appointment was in the bag, but I couldn't help imagining what I'd do if and when I were to receive the hoped-for appointment. Who would I call? What would I say? Who would I thank? And what would my initial steps be? On the other hand, what would I do if I received a negative answer – how would I respond? Would I ask for anything, and what? What would my following steps be?

As usual, I was welcomed warmly at the commander's office. The officers and clerks there knew me well and offered me coffee and a newspaper. David, the commander, was sat at his broad desk.

'We've come to a decision regarding the appointment,' he said. 'You, Amos, are blessed with excellent leadership and decision-making qualities, and that's good. But,' he went on to add with a serious face, 'other qualities have made me decide in favour of Lapidot.' He said two or three more sentences, which echoed hollowly in the room, without actually penetrating my consciousness. I wasn't really listening anymore.

A silence fell on the room. I felt no desire to waste words. There seemed no point. I didn't want to stay in the office another minute.

'Thank you! Goodbye!' I said in a dry, clear voice. I stood up, saluted and left the room.

A searing sensation of anger and humiliation spread through my limbs. A fire was blazing in my soul. Here this day, in this battle, I'd been defeated. I, for my part, was wholly convinced that I could have performed the job better than any of my competitors.

I knew this feeling of defeat was personal and subjective, that it couldn't be shared with anyone and might even be unjustified. All of this didn't subtract one iota from its intensity.

I left the commander's office with long strides, as always. I said goodbye to the secretaries, went downstairs and got into my car. I started the engine and drove through the gate of the camp, again returning a friendly salute to the servicewoman on duty.

I turned the car in the direction of the Tel Aviv beaches near the end of the cliff, and I stopped there. I recalled my father and the pageant of British Hurricane fighters that we saw together not far from here, from the Tel Aviv promenade, forty years earlier. That may, perhaps, have been the pivotal event of my life.

With my face to the sea, quietly looking out at the watery expanse, I switched off the engine and remained sitting there for quite some time.

At about ten pm knocks were heard upon the door of our house. I opened it. Two 'young' lieutenant-colonels were standing in the entrance: Giora Epstein, the Air Force's ace fighter pilot, and Eitan Ben-Eliyahu, one of the most gifted commanders ever to emerge from its ranks.

The two of them had 'dropped over for a cup of coffee' – it was a gesture of friendship I will never forget.

Postscript:
A Storm Subsides

'**D**ad, go up and sit in the cockpit until I sign the books and do the external check. When I've finished I'll come up to you,' requested Ram.

'Alright, my young commander,' I answered with a broad smile.

The F-16 was even more elegant and beautiful than the French Mirage. Even I had to admit it. Something had happened to these Americans since they abandoned the Phantoms and Skyhawks and went on to the next generation of jet fighters. The F-16 and F-15 were as pretty as their performance was impressive.

I did a turn around the plane, more to enjoy its form, structure and equipment than to perform a regular check. After all, it had been many years since I'd piloted any jet fighter, and I'd never undergone a proper acclimatisation course to the F-16.

Ram, a major in the F-16 squadron, finished putting his signature in the books and checking the plane and joined me, now a lieutenant-general in the reserves and a former deputy commander of the Air Force, at the foot of the ladder to the cockpit. He took my flight helmet from me and invited me to climb the ladder with a gesture of his hand. Ram clambered up after me and bent over me at the side of the plane's rear seat. Patiently, in the clear, fluent and practical language of pilots, he explained everything inside the cockpit to me. He placed special emphasis on everything concerned with flight safety procedures, proper behaviour during an emergency, possible ejection, and operating the communication system.

*   *   *

The two F-16s came to a stop, one beside the other, on the take-off runway. In the forward mirror I could see the eyes, so very familiar to me, of my son Ram. I listened to the voices spilling out of the communication network. The sentences were brief, the confirmations in clicks without even a single word, the breathing calm. It was all so familiar, so close, and yet impressive and remote just the same.

'Dad, is everything all-right?' Ram asked me over the intercom.

'I'm 100 per cent, Ram!' I answered immediately.

When the brakes were released and the engine reached to full power, I recalled the take-off I'd experienced from the American aircraft carrier off the shores of California. A tremendous force glued me to the seat when the plane leapt forward in wild acceleration. When Ram lifted the plane's nose almost vertically immediately after take-off, I realised just how far aerial performance had progressed since my own time.

'Red, outside turn!' announced the leader.

Ram banked to the right and quickly drew away from his 'adversary', his leader, in order to perform the exercise.

'Red, inside turn!'

The two planes turned in each other's direction. I knew what was waiting for me when they passed each other, but the speed and intensity still caught me by surprise. The pilots began manoeuvring very sharply with the objective of arriving at a convenient missile launch position and 'shooting down' their 'adversary'. Several times my eyes went black from the G-force generated by the plane's acceleration. The acceleration rates weren't much higher than what I'd experienced in my Phantoms and Mirages in the past. However, the length of time the F-16 could fly at such rates of acceleration was, to me at least, virtually interminable.

Here and there I managed to steal in a word or two in Ram's direction. He was wholly engrossed in manoeuvring his plane against his 'adversary'. I hoped I'd be able to contribute something to my son's 'war effort', but I had few illusions regarding the matter.

*   *   *

On the way home, when the 'G-force attack' had passed and the blood in my body returned to the places naturally intended for it, I asked Ram to hand over the controls to me.

'You take her,' said Ram.

'I'm taking her,' I replied, taking the steering controls under my hand. My heart swelled with joy and pride.

Nearing the runway on which I'd first learned the fundamentals of aerial combat, in the airfield that I'd commanded, at the base where my daughter and sons were born – I straightened the F-16's wings on the final approach for landing.

The wheels of the elegant plane touched down on the black asphalt. With the skill of a practised veteran, I lowered the plane's nose until the nose-wheel touched down on the runway too. From the mirror in front I saw Ram's eyes peeking at me. I pressed on the brakes with feeling. We began to slow.

Like a blaze in the sky, the setting sun reddened the western reaches with its scorching touch. The hemisphere of the sky above was pierced from pole to pole by a glowing white vapour trail, left behind by a large jet fighter flown by a small man.

Index